THE GLOVES

THE GLOVES

ROBERT ANASI

A BOXING CHRONICLE

NORTH POINT PRESS

A DIVISION OF FARRAR, STRAUS AND GIROUX / NEW YORK

North Point Press
A division of Farrar, Straus and Giroux
19 Union Square West, New York 10003

Copyright © 2002 by Robert Anasi
All rights reserved
Distributed in Canada by Douglas & McIntyre Ltd.
Printed in the United States of America
First edition, 2002

Library of Congress Cataloging-in-Publication Data
Anasi, Robert, 1966–
   The gloves: a boxing chronicle / Robert Anasi— 1st ed.
      p.   cm.
   ISBN 0-86547-599-7 (hc.: alk. paper)
   1. Boxing—United States.   2. Golden Gloves Tournament.   3. Anasi, Robert,
   1966–   I. Title.

GV1125 .A56 2002
796.83—dc21   2001044111

Designed by Jonathan D. Lippincott

www.fsgbooks.com

1 3 5 7 9 10 8 6 4 2

CONTENTS

The male cannot bear very much humiliation; and he really *cannot* bear it, it obliterates him. All men know this about each other, which is one of the reasons that men can treat each other with such a vile, relentless, and endlessly inventive cruelty. Also, however, it must be added, with such depthless respect and love, conveyed, mainly, by grunts and blows.
—James Baldwin, *The Evidence of Things Not Seen*

THE GLOVES

· 1 ·

A WAY OF LIFE

The gym becomes a way of life. Arrive on 14th Street at 5:30 P.M., and there might be a few fighters left from the first wave, the ones too young for day jobs, the ones who work odd hours or who don't work at all. You shake hands with your teammates (boxing culture requiring a certain formality) and take your gear into the bathroom. Off with the shirt, shoes, pants and, after a quick glance in the mirror to see how you're cutting up, on with the T-shirt, shorts and high-lace boxing shoes. Back in the gym, if no one else is around, Milton may be dozing. He lies on the upholstered bench, long legs bent off the end and touching the floor. A padded trainer's mitt is set over his eyes. He is only half asleep and will make lazy comments or stir to answer his cell phone. His energy ebbs and flows with the activity in the gym. If fully awake, he might have a hand in a packet of cheese curls or wrapped around a candy bar, interchangeable components of the toxic flow of junk food that sustains him.

You sit on the varnished planks of the wood floor and begin your workout, lengthening hamstrings, flexors, adductors, gluts and lats, the rubbery sheath of your skeleton. Stretching is somewhat abstract to Milton's fighters; some of the best seem to do without it altogether. Milton certainly doesn't emphasize it. Stretching isn't very street, isn't very . . . *tough*. Stretching seems abstract, seems abstract until the day you step forward in the ring and have your quadriceps seize or you wrench your back and can't train for weeks. Perhaps Milton's best fighters know the limits of their bodies better than you (certainly they move with a loping looseness that you envy), or perhaps they don't and are putting bodies and dream careers to risk.

After ten minutes of floor stretches, you rise and begin to loosen your arms and back. A boxer needs flexibility in his waist, is always ducking, bending, rotating on the axis of his hips. The wall mirrors watch you as you twist, a presence doubling the scene so that you can follow whatever happens through the length and depth of the room. The mirrors knit the gym together; always scanning with some part of your attention, you are immediately aware when anyone enters. As you stretch, your body quickens to the rhythm of the music—hip-hop, generally, on the radio, old tapes or new CDs. Along with old school stuff like Wu-Tang and Biggie, this year's big sellers are DMX, Jay-Z and Nas, the harder the better for the young toughs, murder, robbery, shooting and looting while you bounce. The music is loud enough to make conversation difficult, loud enough to make Milton scream, "Turn this shit down!" The boom box bass dictates the boxers' rhythm. Those times a white person tries to slip on a rock CD the other fighters shake their heads and ask, "How can you people train to this shit?"

Next comes the rope, slip-slap cadence of which takes at least a few months to negotiate (awkward leaps of novices as the rope tangles feet and limbs, as the plastic band scalds bare skin). The rope for balance, for coordination and to raise energy for the workout to come. All sorts of pretty tricks come with dexterity on the rope: running in place, double passes under each jump, and perhaps most impressive, the crossover, in which the wrists cross as the rope goes beneath you, very smooth. Milton has his own warm-up drills as well, custom-designed to make the leadfoot fleet, for the good boxer dances as well as hits. You hop back and forth across a tapeline on one foot, back and forth along the hallway forward and back, then run crisscross up the tapeline and return backpedaling. After a few minutes of this, you step into the ring with a pair of dumbbells. You circle the ring in a fighter's shuffle while punching the dumbbells straight into the air, then circle rotating the weights before you, elbows bent, all toward a further dexterity in moving the hands and feet together. Next is Milton's patented "dunh, dunh-duh," his own waltz, two steps sideways and then a pivot off the leading foot to bring you back into stance and facing your opponent. "Dunh, dunh-duh," to get out of trouble and pivot on an opponent who may be following too close, to pivot and *counter* with a hook or cross. You move and circle, breath coming faster, the faintest dappling of sweat on your forehead and staining your shirt. The day grind, the coffee and greasy lunch burn out of you as you move. This evening, like so many others, you barely dragged yourself to the gym. A thousand obstacles, a million rationalizations presented themselves. You were up late last night. You had a headache. You wanted to go out for dinner instead, see a movie, you have a deadline at your day job. . . . As you climbed the stairs and dressed, those obstacles evaporated, and as you move now, their last traces break and fade in the air. The obstacles seem so insignificant, in fact, that if you even think of them, you can't understand why they so hindered you. You are alive in your body, now. Your eyes open wide. Looking around, you see the gym has filled, people in conversation clusters, in various states of dress. You leave the ring and shake more hands. With an audience present, Milton no longer dozes but is up and talking. Not just talking but expressing, directing, edifying, illuminating, the impresario of this shadowed room.

"Hey, Gumby! What is that? You're punching handicapped."

"So when I was in camp with Shannon Briggs, I told him, 'They have you standing straight up, fighting like a white guy. That's not what got you here. You have to start moving your head again and breaking at the waist.'"

"Hey, somebody get my phone. Hello, Supreme. Yeah, I'm here every day starting at eight in the morning, and we close at ten at night. So come on down and be our next contestant."

"Julian! Are you working out, or cutting out?"

The bell (bell in name only—not a bell but a buzzing electric clock) marks rounds, the base unit measure of gym time. Rounds last three minutes with a warning buzz at two minutes thirty and another buzz at round's end for a rest of a minute, work/rest, work/rest, work/rest. "I did five rounds on the heavy bag, five on the rope." "How many rounds have we been sparring?" "One more round!" From your gym bag you draw the length of cloth that will protect those most delicate of weapons, the hands. Scrupulous fighters always draw perfectly rolled wraps from their bags, wraps rewrapped after drying from their last use so that they will roll on smooth and unwrinkled, but you, maybe you threw yours in the bag after pulling them off and forgot about them until now. They come to daylight, crumpled cotton lengths white, yellow or faded red, a little stiff with dried sweat, smelling of the same. A not unpleasant smell, you think, the salty must that permeates boxing, a combination of sweat with the glove leather it soaks. Boxers cultivate sweat, for sweat reduces them, makes them lean, symbolizes necessary exertion. All serious athletes sweat heavily, but in boxing sweat is the essential element, the sea in which the boxer is born and through which he swims.

After the rope and the warm-ups comes shadowboxing, the heavy bags, exercises and more shadowboxing. Milton may have you work pads with him as well, directing you to strike the oversize gloves on his hands while he shouts instructions and corrects your movement, using such choice idioms as "retarded," "robotic," "paraplegic," "idiot" and "bullshit," among others, punctuated with little smacks to your head. All this training, however, diminishes beside sparring. Sparring is the psychic center of the gym, as the ring is its actual material center. Milton's gym is a fighters' gym, not a health club or "fitness center." Fighters fight. To prepare to fight, fighters must spar. "We'll go with anybody," Milton states as a point of pride, that's how tough he believes his "Supreme Team" to be, and in point of proof, boxers, professional and amateur, come from all over the city to match up against his team. So sparring remains the center, and the other life in the gym revolves around it. People halt their workouts to watch. Milton insists that you watch ("That's how you learn," he says, "by imitation"). People come in just *to* watch. In the old days, tickets were sold for sparring sessions at the big gyms near Times Square or at the camps of champions as they prepared for title fights. Milton dreams of opening a streetfront gym to attract clientele.

"That would be the way to do it," he says. "Have it behind big windows right on Fourteenth Street. There'd be a crowd watching us twenty-four/seven. Once they saw how you guys spar, we'd be getting new people walking in all the time, begging us to teach them."

Your regular sparring partners have arrived and ask you if you want to work, or you ask them. "We'll go light," they say, or, "Just a couple of rounds," or, "I'm sore today, so we'll take it slow." Whatever they say, it's a decision of moment. A whole new set of excuses and escapes present themselves: You're tired; you want to avoid a headache; you have a date; you've sparred too much this week already. . . .

Milton presses the issue. "Hey, you want to go in with . . . ?" A zeal for contact drives him. He wants more! Now! And will throw all willing or semiwilling bodies together, heavyweight and featherweight, man and woman. Milton seems to love his gym work best when it comes to the threshold of real combat, when he can stand with his arms on the ropes shouting instructions. "Two-three! Slip, then pull back! Throw more jabs. Sit down in your punches!" Or he jumps up and down with a hand in the air, his fingers semaphoring the number of the punch he wants thrown (to conceal it from the boxer whose back is turned).

Sparring alters the normal routine on the floor. Milton will advise you to stop hitting the heavy bag or to go easy with the dumbbells. You do not want to get arm-weary. To agree to spar is a momentous decision and is nothing at all. Simply life in the gym. After nodding agreement, you shadowbox a few rounds in the mirror, skip rope, shake out your shoulders. Milton wants the show to begin. "Are you ready yet? Come on. Today. Hurry up and get the gear on." Finally, you accept that you are ready. Slip in your mouthpiece, the molded plastic to prevent your teeth from slicing your lips. You pull up the groin protector, draw the headgear over your ears, slather Vaseline around your eyes, across your nose, cheeks, lips (not too good for the skin, that, but it keeps the glove leather from chafing). Someone girds you with the fourteen- or sixteen-ounce sparring gloves and you step through the ropes. The preparation has a ritual air; though it's possible to pull on your gloves and fasten your chin strap yourself, it's better to have someone else do it for you. The care sanctifies you, helps separate this activity from all others. You dance about in the ring, throw a few flurries, jaw with your partner until Milton commands, "BOX!"

Two opposed philosophies dominate sparring. One states that sparring should always be light, not combat simulation but a venue for excising flaws and polishing technique. The famous Irish trainer Brendan Ingle (whose pupils include such champions as Johnny Nelson, Herol Graham and, of course, "Prince" Naseem Hamed) will allow his students to throw only body punches, thereby protecting the tender, skull-cased brain. Signs posted on his gym walls read: BOXING CAN DAMAGE YOUR HEALTH. IMPORTANT, NO SPARRING WITH-OUT SUPERVISION. FOR YOUR OWN SAFETY, GUMSHIELDS AND HEADGUARDS MUST BE WORN. This Ingle approach emphasizes such terms as "light" and "easy" and "work." The other philosophy states that the sparring should be hard (hard but not wild). Most trainers will claim to belong to the first school. Most trainers actually belong to the second. The reason for this duplicity, conscious or not, is the doubling that serves to cloak the realities of pugilism. Boxing is a combat sport, and fighters are directed to inflict, within the rules, a maximum amount of damage. This truth must be concealed to some extent. Few trainers will say to each other before their fighters spar, "I hope my guy kills your guy." Although they want exactly that: a demonstration of their students' prowess in the clearest manner possible. The trainers cannot make such a statement; the challenge would raise the stakes from sparring to a gym war. Instead they mention "good rounds," "going easy," "working with" someone. As in the romance around sex, the stereotyped, delicate language serves to cloak a more brutal reality.

As a trainer Milton stands completely in the second school. He will overmatch his fighters and watch as they sustain real beatings (one of his tricks is to turn off the bell near the end of the round so that the fighters' endurance will be tested). The result for you, in the first months, is headaches, bruises, pain. This sparring serves a purpose. Endure those first months and you will have little to fear.

When the bell buzzes, you smack leather with your partner by way of salute and then begin to circle. You are boxing. A thousand times you've done this and still the tension, pressing and binding. Moments ago you were talking to a friend about work and telling jokes. Now . . . In the distortions of mouthpiece and headgear, your partner loses his human characteristics and becomes half monster. The first round moves slowly as you warm to the action, building up until, bang! A shot stings your face, ricochets from your headgear, crushes your lips. It's a good-morning cup of coffee; you begin to accelerate, clear and rising. Now you will hit back. This is not your friend. The person facing you has become a series of problems to solve, a greater or lesser degree of intimidation. Things you try work or don't work. Depending on his mood, gym occupancy, activity on his cell, Milton becomes more or less involved. "Feint two-three!" "One to the body, one to the body, then something else." "Think out there! You've got to think!" "Use your defense!" You try to act on his commands and keep your eyes focused on the man trying to kill you.

When the buzzer ends the round, you take water, listen to Milton's promptings and circle the ring, shaking out your arms. This continues for three rounds, or six, or ten. Sweat runs; sweat streams, flows, pools. You are an aquatic animal. Sweat drenches your brow, burns your eyes, renders your white T-shirt translucent and drowns your socks.* All your training does not prepare you for the ocean. You gasp but there is never enough air; your gloves become anchors dragging you to the bottom. As the rounds progress, you may gain confidence, put together combinations, slip and pivot like a pro, drive your partner back. Or your confidence may flag; you may retreat, thrash the air with wild punches as thunderbolts split your head. The two of you may forget that this is "work" and tend toward murder. There is no fellowship then. Your partner is a thing to be broken. "Good hook," Milton shouts, leaping from his bench as the action boils. The tension slows time. You must stay focused. Break concentration for an instant, and the result is not embarrassment (the other team scores, you lose the beat in music or dance) but pain. The tension frets your energy, erodes it. "Relax your shoulders," Milton shouts. "Think!" The water rises over your thighs, your neck, your mouth.

Suddenly it ends. Either you quit or your partner quits, or Milton wants the ring for somebody else. The alien landscape that you sped through vanishes. You gear down and step through the ropes back to a gym different from the one you left. A fog obscures the room, even if you haven't taken any shots to the head. You return to a lesser place, less vivid, less encompassing. Someone has to unlace your gloves for you. The boxer with gloves on is helpless for anything except striking. He must be fed water. He cannot scratch an itch on his shoulder and asks his trainer to do it. Your hands emerge, small and swaddled. You wander around the floor for a minute, acclimating. You wipe the traces of Vaseline from your face with a shirtsleeve, look in the mirror to see if you are scraped or bruised. You drop gear here and there across the room. Sometimes it's not until days later that you realize your helmet and cup have gone missing and you return to the gym to find them hanging from pegs on the wall.

After another few hits of water, you pull on bag gloves and go to work on the heavy bags. You've thrown thousands of punches in your

---

*Boxers generally wear shirts when sparring, to protect their skin. Amateurs wear them when fighting as well.

months at the gym but they never seem good enough for Milton. "You're still punching retarded," he says. Punching too high ("Who are you trying to hit, the Green Giant?") or too low ("Stop hitting those midgets"). "You're punching handicapped. Let your hands go. Let them be free." Milton might not notice you for a week or more, but just when you think he has forgotten you, you're laved by such words of love. Through the circuit you go: heavy bags and hook bags and the jumpy little double-end bag that snaps back after being struck. Then shadow-boxing, the rope again and exercises: sit-ups, crunches, push-ups, dips and the little weight lifting fighters allow themselves. The muscle that comes from weights tightens the body, reducing range and speed. Boxers need to stay loose and quick; a good punch snaps at the maximum arm extension. "Power thrills but speed kills" is a boxing maxim; the faster man will beat the stronger man. Boxers also don't want to add bulk because bulk is weight and changes one's class. As you cool down, you say goodbye and arrange your next sparring session. You've been in the gym for nearly three hours. On the way home, your body crashes, even after Gatorade and energy bars. Sluggish, sullen and starving, you're good for little more than television for the next hour or two.

· 2 ·

DECEMBER

The first day I walked into Milton's gym I was afraid. Not because I didn't know what to expect, but because I did. I was the new boy. It would be like changing high schools at fifteen. Everyone already knew everyone else and New Boy would have to prove himself before a disdainful audience. To make matters worse, I had trained with a man who despised Milton and whom Milton despised in turn. New Boy had transferred from the crosstown rival and been caught the week before tagging the façade of his new school with obscenities. For a final demerit, I was old (thirty-two) and white (city indoor pallid) in a world dominated by the young and ethnic, the brown and tan. What else I knew of Milton brought no comfort. He was a sarcastic, hot-tempered man who had feuded with almost everyone in amateur boxing in New York. Milton knew me by sight. He had seen me at another gym and spoken to me a few times at a bar on the Lower East Side where he served as a maître d'/bouncer. Some four years earlier he had tried, in desultory fashion, to lure me away from my trainer. Recently I had told him that I was considering a run at the Golden Gloves. Perhaps I'd been a little drunk at the time. Those unpleasant thoughts circled in my mind as I made my way from the elevator down the hallway to the gym.

I pushed open the door and stepped into the smallest gym I had ever seen. A puny ring swallowed two-thirds of the room. In the ring, a woman heaved punches at a crouching, weaving man.

My friend David, an actor who trained there, had arrived before me. He introduced me to Milton and we shook hands.

I know this guy already, Milton said, studying me, from down at the bar. And from Julio's too.

I agreed.

You never fought in the Gloves before, he said.

I shook my head no.

Milton and a half dozen boxers crowded what little space was not ring. In that strip of floor they attempted to train, hitting the one heavy bag and shadowboxing in the wall mirror. One or two of the fighters I recognized from other gyms in town. They too had left their trainers and come to Milton.

Milton LaCroix, the tall Puerto Rican with the French last name, was something of a mystery to me. I knew that he had once run the boxing program at the Pitt Street Boys' Club on the Lower East Side. Later, in 1996, six fighters from his Supreme Team had reached the Golden Gloves finals, and five won, an accomplishment for a trainer on the level of, say, winning the Kentucky Derby astride a Shetland pony. The style Milton taught defied every boxing truism. He turned his right-handed fighters southpaw and had them fight with their hands down around their waists. People mocked this style, even as his team won trophies and titles. I knew that Milton had been barred from working corners at one point, a ban only recently relaxed. He had also been ejected from half the gyms in the city. (I imagined his disdainful manner played a role in this.) Now he had his own private gym on East 14th Street in Manhattan. I anticipated difficulties. Still, Milton specialized in southpaws, and I was naturally left-handed. And his fighters won, which was all that really mattered.

You trained with Julio? Milton asked.

No, Darryl, I said.

Darryl? Christ, even worse. How old are you?

Thirty-three.

And you want me to have you ready for the Gloves in two months? Milton shook his head. Well, go and get changed, and we'll see if you have anything left.

I left the little room and crossed the hall to the bathroom. As I changed, I examined my upper body in the mirror over the sink. At thirty-three, I had not let myself fall apart. I weighed approximately the same as I had in college and I wasn't soft; daily workouts, running and soccer kept me toned. My confidence rose as I put on my trunks and tied my shoes. Even though I hadn't been inside a gym for almost two years, I was far from green. I had boxed on and off since age twenty-five and had won fights. I still shadowboxed for hours every week to polish my form. The previous spring I had twice brawled larger men on the street, with encouraging results. Milton might even be impressed by what I had left.

Back in the pygmy gym, I stretched and then started to shadowbox. Warming up, I moved stiffly, and I knew the other fighters could see it. Milton didn't look at me directly, but I felt the pressure of his sidelong gaze as he spoke into his cell phone, directed students, commanded assistants—a combination MC/air traffic controller. As I shuffled around, my arms began to loosen. I snapped out my jab—pop pop pop— following it with hooks and straight lefts. I was proud of that jab; I'd been cultivating it for years. I shuffled and jabbed, double-jabbed and threw a left, kept moving, threw a left-hand lead. I was fast; I was slick; I was good. I slipped inside an imaginary opponent and threw combinations at his body. They had to see how good I was.

Then I heard David say, Come on, you guys. Stop giving him a hard time.

It wasn't me laughing, Milton laughed. It was him.

He pointed to one of his lieutenants, a black fighter I recognized from my last gym. I saw the smile on his face. They were laughing at me.

Come over here, Milton sighed. I'm gonna show you something your old trainer, Stupid, never did.

As I stepped through the ropes in a rage of shame, I already regretted coming to Milton. While I had anticipated his attempt to break me, it felt worse than I had imagined. I asked myself why I had returned. I was too old to stand being humiliated in that way. Thirty-three years old in a sport where the average professional's career is over in a few years. Old age was the reason I had told myself I was leaving the sport two years earlier. At twenty-nine I had planned to enter the Golden Gloves, the foremost amateur tournament, amateur boxing's glory and grail. As I trained then, I discovered that I couldn't plane away the pounds. No matter how much I sweat, or how many miles I ran, I could not reduce to my fighting weight of 132. Someone had told me that you put on weight as you grow older, ten pounds a decade, they said; I imagined this was happening to me. Everywhere I looked, there it was, my peers rounding (and balding) on the road to thirty. And I never had enough time for the gym. To train seriously took time, and I wasn't a schoolboy with student leisure. I had to work. I had to plan for my future. I was educated and ambitious; my future certainly wasn't boxing. The beatings had caught up with me as well. It took days to recover from four or five rounds of hard sparring, my back and neck braided with pain. At twenty-five, I hadn't felt anything the day after, no matter how many right hands I took.

On the floor, Milton instructed me with a pleasant blend of insults and commands as I stood sullen before him.

All right, get into your stance. More sideways. Sideways! Step up to the mitts. I said step! Don't skip. Who do you think you are, Peter Pan? All right, hit the mitt with a jab. You call that a jab? Stop standing like that. Relax, goddammit, relax! Let your jab snap out. No. Let it *go*. Like you were snatching money out of my hand. Reach out and grab. Okay, watch this. Milton reached into his pocket and extracted a five-dollar bill. Now I want you to grab this handsome fellow out of my hand.

I reached out for it.

No, don't reach. Grab it like you fucking want it. Snatch it.

I snatched.

All right. That's how I want you to throw your jab. Like you're stealing my fucking money. Do you understand?

I did not but nodded that I did. My humiliation continued.

Grab. No, lamebrain, *grab*. Like you . . . like you want to tear my fucking face off! Stop cringing. What the hell is that? Throw your left. No, your *other* left. Jesus Christ. Did you ever fight before? You did? You fought? And you won? Oh. Who did you fight, Stevie Wonder and Ray Charles? Show me your three. That's not your fucking three. Your hook! You call that a hook? Throw it like you're stirring a bowl of soup, moron. Faster. Wrong. Nope. Wrong. Like you're stirring a bowl of soup. No. You expect to go in the Gloves in January? You should be here six months ago already. Give me the three. Will you just do it? Relax, for Christ's sake.

And on it went, a torment in which I could do nothing right. It was the first week of December, but the little room was not ventilated and soon my clothes were sodden. In his frustration, Milton sometimes cuffed me with a pad. The Gloves would begin in January. I had intended to pop into the gym for a few months, scrape away some "ring rust" and be reasonably prepared for the tournament. Here Milton was going back to the beginning, treating me like a novice who had never worn a pair of gloves in his life.

All right, stop, he said in disgust, just stop. You want to learn something? Okay. Look at her.

He indicated the woman still chasing the man in the ring. The woman threw hooks and rights; the fighter blocked and dodged.

Do you see that? Milton asked. Look at how she lets her punches go. She throws harder than you do.

I disagreed but said nothing. Speech would only ensure further abasement. I looked at the way the woman swung her hook. She wasn't a boxer, but she did have power. Her punches boomed against the man's raised gloves.

Milton put me to work stepping along a tapeline in stance. I marched back and forth, back and forth, poking out my jab, clumsy from his attentions. I did this hundreds of times, with Milton glancing over to proclaim my flaws ("Will you stop skipping, for Christ's sake?").

If I felt Milton was being hard on me, however, I soon received a preview of much worse to come. While I stumbled and lunged, a white kid, seventeen perhaps, walked in. Milton greeted him and asked him if he was there to spar. The kid said yes.

Victor, get ready, Milton said to the fighter who had laughed at me but had since sat off by himself with a scowl on his dark face. His name was Victor Paz. Since I'd last seen him at Kingsway he had put on a great deal of muscle around his shoulders and chest. The two donned the requisite gear and stepped into the ring. Milton grabbed my shoulder to stop me.

Watch this, he said, and learn something.

In the first minute the white kid rushed straight at Victor and threw wild overhand rights. Although Victor dodged most of the blows or caught them on his gloves, a few heavy buffets dropped flush upon Victor's head and drove him backward. The white kid had power.

Be careful, Victor, Milton said. This guy hits pretty hard.

Into the third minute of the round the dynamic shifted as Victor began to evade the assault. Every wild miss slewed the kid off-balance, and Victor would step in before he recovered with a two-punch counter, *cross-hook* or *hook-uppercut*, a deep thump-thump of solid contact. By the second round, steady punishment had taught the kid caution and he no longer flung himself forward. Victor then began to pursue, freezing the kid with feints and hitting him as he stood frozen. I knew how the kid felt, faltering between anger and fear. Whenever Victor scored, anger won out and the kid lurched forward again. Victor had timed his predictable attack, however. Now when the kid swung, he almost never connected or would receive three blows to his one. His face reddened and his mouthpiece bulged from his panting mouth. A hook to the rib cage dropped him to one knee. He stayed that way for a few seconds, gasping. Milton asked him if he wanted to continue. The kid mumbled something, rose and chased Victor until the bell.

One more round? Milton asked. Both boxers nodded.

At the beginning of the third round, the kid lunged after Victor with his head down. I had been in the same position many times, enraged at the punishment, wanting to hurt back, frustrated that I could find nothing to hit. Hours seemed to have passed; I wished they would stop. It finally ended when the kid, stumbling forward, caught an uppercut on the chin and slumped to the canvas. He stayed there on all fours.

All right, Vic, Milton said. That's it.

Victor removed his gloves and spit his guard into his hand. You ducked right into it, he said to the kid by way of excusing himself. Victor then removed his headgear and returned to his seat and scowling silence.

I did pretty good, right? the kid asked, intoxicated from his beating, a double dose of epinephrine and enkephalins.

Well, Milton said, unlacing his gloves, you got plenty of heart, but you're getting hit with everything. We have to get you to start coming down here and doing the drills.

In the following days, bad did become worse for me. While aware that Milton taught an unorthodox, even bizarre, style, I had no interest in learning it. My previous trainer had mocked it sotto voce as we had watched Milton's fighters spar.

You ever seen that before, Bob? Darryl asked. Every fighter is a southpaw, and they all keep their hands down. And look at those hooks they throw. It's crazy.

He was right. Milton's style violated the rules of conventional boxing, and I planned to ignore it. I thought so little of his style, in fact, that I had prepared a speech to set him straight on where we stood. "Now, Milton," I would say, "I know you have your way of doing things, and of course I respect it. I'm sure it works just fine for your guys. However, there just isn't enough time for me to learn your way, so if you could concentrate on improving my style—you know, sharpen my defense, get me some sparring—I'd appreciate it."

Although I had boxed through my late twenties and even won matches (against opponents who were not blind musicians), I still hadn't entered the Golden Gloves. One year, I was out of the country; another year, I missed the physical; another, I was injured. Behind those reasons loomed the suspicion that I wasn't a real fighter, that the Gloves for me would issue in a dreadful thrashing. This year, though, I was resolved. There were other tournaments but none as essential as the Gloves. To fight amateur and not do the Gloves would be like going to Cairo and not seeing the pyramids, not even leaving the airport hotel. "And you went there . . . why?" Adding pressure was the fact that the year marked the end of my amateur eligibility. Miss this Gloves, and that would be all. For the rest of my life I would look back and know I had blinked. I had trouble explaining why this mattered so much to me. In fact, I found it somewhat ridiculous. Yet there it was.

I first encountered Milton at Julio's Boxing Gym on East 12th Street. Milton had appeared with a group of fighters he had developed at the local Boys' Club. Friction between Milton and Julio, a monosyllabic Puerto Rican, led to Milton's ejection. Julio, ostensibly the owner of the space (located in the subbasement of a senior center), had then circulated a petition among the boxers to ensure that Milton never returned. Although Julio's English vocabulary contained about forty words, his petition began, with florid gravity, "We the athletes of Julio's 12th Street Gym, wish to debar the continued presence of Milton LaCroix from our environs, for the sake of our current peace and continued future happiness." A few weeks following his ejection, I found Milton standing outside Julio's.

Hey, he called, come over here.

I walked toward him.

Do you know how to read? he asked.

I allowed that I did.

Oh, you do? he said. Good. Well, then, I want you to go out and get this week's *Village Voice*. There's an article about what a rip-off artist Julio is. He shouldn't even be able to charge people to use that gym. This week's *Village Voice*. Can you remember that?

I nodded my head and walked away, smiling.

The *Voice* article questioned Julio's title to the subbasement and noted that the space had originally been established as a recreation center for local youth. Julio, it seemed, was no more the owner of the gym than I was, and the minimal maintenance he did gave him little domain. Years later, after I joined his team, Milton told me that he had instigated the article by calling everyone he knew who might have had political influence (he received the best response from a letter written to the mayor's wife). According to Milton, Julio had established himself in the space by paying kickbacks to the manager of the senior center upstairs, a practice that repercussions from the article brought to an end; the repercussions brought an end to the gym as well.

I had anticipated Milton's assault, but that didn't make it easier to bear. How do you prepare yourself for the firing squad? By day three I had discovered that according to Milton, I didn't throw any of my punches correctly, didn't have any defense and moved like an Erector set robot.

Let the hands go! he said. You're punching to yourself. Stop cringing. What the fuck is that? Four! I said. Four! Turn the wrist over! Stop punching up. Who the hell are you trying to hit, the Jolly Green Giant?

After having me hit the focus pads (oversize gloves that resemble a baseball catcher's mitt with a bull's-eye in the center), cursing my technique and giving me the occasional disgusted shove or caricaturing my movement, Milton had an idea.

Let's try something, he said. I want you to turn around like you're right-handed.

He had me punch from the "orthodox" stance—that is to say, leading with the left—rather than my usual "southpaw" stance. Suddenly he liked what he saw. He liked the extension of my jab and the power in my left hook.

That's it! he shouted as my left smacked the mitt. Do you hear that? Do you feel the difference? That's a punch. That could do some damage.

Then and there, Milton decided he was going to "turn me around," although I was a natural southpaw and had trained left-handed since I'd started boxing. My prepared speech remained unspoken.

I left the gym in pieces. I had been dismantled as a boxer and, thereby, as a man. Milton's decision to turn me around said he considered me so tainted with bad habits that it was hopeless to train me as a southpaw, that it would be better to start from day one, wipe the slate, return to go.* I had been boxing for years. I had won fights. I couldn't believe that none of it mattered. Milton's criticisms fed upon my deepest insecurities as a boxer, the fears that lie within every boxer's frangible, adamant ego, fattening upon the smallest disappointments. I had always questioned my ability. For one thing, I was hit too often. I couldn't understand why: Was I too slow, too old or just too stupid? The punches erupted in my face and I slogged witless through the carnage. There was always something missing for me, always the fear that I played at being a boxer.

At home that night I decided to quit Milton. I hated his profane tirades and sarcasm. I was tired of being called Peter Pan while the young fighters snickered. I couldn't raise my right arm or move my neck from the pain. And now he wanted to turn me around, two months before the Gloves. I would find another gym. I would leave after the first month (I'd already paid, after all. After some haggling, Milton and I had agreed on the lavish sum of a hundred dollars a month). Then I would enter the Gloves as an unattached fighter. I'd have a friend work my corner.

---

*I later discovered that Milton turned everybody around. It suited his solipsistic grandeur to believe he could do better with nothing than with something that came through someone else.

The relationship between trainer and boxer is perilous: Boxers' egos are large and tender, and ego abrades ego in the pressure of the gym. Every trainer needs to impress a new fighter and begins by delivering some version of "You're good, kid, really good, but you'd be even better if you did" this, that and this. The trainer needs to be needed, after all, and if the fighter weren't incomplete, he wouldn't have gone to the trainer. Of course, the trainer must be careful not to be wholly negative. As he wins the fighter's trust, he must also build his confidence. "I am showing you what you do wrong," the trainer implies, "so that I may show you what to do right." Trust binds the trainer and fighter: In the minute between rounds, a boxer often needs to adjust his strategy and has only the voice of trainer to help him. After many lost fights, the fighter who lacked trust in his manager will acknowledge that he should have listened. The trainer encourages his fighter as he faces one of the loneliest situations in the world. The phrase "to have someone in your corner" underscores this bond. A good trainer convinces his fighter that if he follows the proper regimen and shows calm, courage and intensity, he can defeat any comparable fighter. This requires the trainer have an ego of a magnitude equal to that of the fighter.

To build confidence, my first New York trainer used psychology. As his fighter hit the bag, Darryl would approach a bystander.

Look at my kid, Darryl would say. Look at how hard he's throwing his hook. Look at that combination. Look at how he's slipping. You remember him a month ago, right? All that in one month.

The observer, of course, would nod and say, Oh, yeah, he's looking better. One hundred percent better. No doubt about it. This dialogue taking place within earshot of Darryl's assassin-in-training.

A few days later Milton paired me with the white kid Victor had demolished. I looked him over. His eyes were clear. Nothing appeared broken. Milton had the two of us stand in the center of the ring and trade three-punch combinations. Three punches: a hook to the head; a straight right to the head; a hook to the body (punches numbered three, two and four). Milton also demonstrated various methods of either diverting the punches with gloves and arms or avoiding (slipping) them. The movements were simple and effective and I wondered why no one had taught them to me years earlier. As we grew comfortable, the kid and I began to punch harder and faster. On the tenth or twelfth combination, I froze at the second block and suffered all of the kid's right hand. I shook off the punch.

Are you okay? Milton asked.

Sure, I smiled.

A few cycles later I made the same mistake with the same result: a hammer to the cheekbone. I cursed and returned to the drill.

Bob, you're pretty tough, Milton said.

You're pretty tough, he repeated, and then qualified himself: For a white boy.

A few passes later it was the kid's turn to balk and eat my right hand. I tried to hide my satisfaction; Milton was less delighted.

Could you guys take a little off your punches? he said. You're both on the same team. This is practice, for Christ's sake.

Fair enough, I thought, but he hadn't cautioned us when the rights were clanging off *my* head.

Milton next had us spar, with the constraint that we punch with our lead hands only (jabs and hooks). After the first exchanges, the kid's body language became hesitant and stiff. It was subtle but enough to encourage me as we circled, a power shift in my direction. After we finished, the kid had to leave for work, and I mentioned his indecision in the ring to Milton.

Well, he was a little rattled by that shot you landed, Milton said in irritation. He's new at this. He's not used to being hit. You're more experienced. I guess you had to learn *something* in all that time you been training. Tomorrow I'll give you some real sparring. Laura's getting ready for the Gloves too, and she's about the same weight as you. Just wait until you see her.

I was tough! Those few words of praise from Milton meant more than anything else he could have told me. If he had said, "You got fast hands," or, "You're hard to hit," it would have mattered, yes, would have stroked me, but it still would have lacked the savor of being called tough. I'd treasured that word since childhood. When an older boy blindsided me in a football game the February I was ten, I soared through the air and bounced headfirst off the frozen ground.

Are you okay? he asked as I jumped to my feet.

I'm fine, I said.

You're pretty tough, he said, and I inflated with pride. Throughout my childhood, when I crashed my bike or sprained my knee or caught a baseball with my face, I shook it off and heard that same murmur of "a pretty tough kid" and felt the same senseless joy. Twenty-five years later it still mattered, more than it should have. If I had to choose between a six-figure salary or being tough, I'd pick tough! Winning a Nobel Peace Prize or? Tough! No question. Any day. Anything. To be tough!

Toughness, or "heart," figures enormously in boxing. I once held a dismal job schlepping furniture and objets d'art for a shipping company in Long Island City. On a slow morning in the warehouse, I started talking with the company carpenter, Anthony. Anthony, just on the good side of forty, wore a graying ponytail. He built the packing crates for the putrefied relics we handled. As we talked, we quickly discovered that we both boxed. There is joy in meeting another fighter (a member of the same cult, with its special handgrip and secret knowledge). "You used to box? Well, so did I." Where, when, how, the flood of detail and anecdote, the discussion of the great historical fights. "Duran had great interior defense." "Didn't he, though?"

A serenity mantled Anthony, the same that surrounds many former fighters. After the fire, calm. He told me he had started boxing twenty-five years earlier, right there in Long Island City because he "always wanted to be like the brothers," and had gone on to have four pro fights. He talked about the fast life he'd led in Los Angeles in the late seventies, a lifestyle that helped terminate his career. Although shorter than I, Anthony fought as a lightweight (130 pounds).

Most guys try to lose weight, he said, but I was always trying to gain weight. I used to eat the heavy stuff to get big. Binding foods. Food that would really stick with you. I was a straight-ahead fighter. One direction: forward. That was it. I never took a step back. Which wasn't always a very good idea. In my last fight it got me beat up pretty bad. But I already knew that I was reaching the end. I didn't train right for that fight. On the day of the fight I came into the weigh-in hungover. See, I'd been running around with this crazy actress and—

The brevity of his four-fight career mattered little beside the words "I never took a step back." What a beautiful phrase, what stupid glory.

Spoken quietly, with laconic bravado. Boxers rely on understatement. "I had a few fights." They'll shrug, meaning ten or two hundred. Or, "They used to think I was pretty tough." All subtlety there in the qualifier.

Three days later I collided with Laura. I had seen her measure me as an opponent in those brief intervals when we shared the gym, as I left and she entered (she worked late). We were roughly the same height and weight. Milton never stopped praising her.

Just wait until you see how she boxes, he said. You won't believe it. She doesn't fight like no woman. When you guys work, you'll get a good idea of our style. You should have seen her win the Gloves last year. I'll show you the tape. She beat this black girl from ringpost to ringpost. It was an execution.

Laura was another refugee from Kingsway, but as with Victor, we had never spoken there. I remembered her, though. She was a striking woman, strong-featured, her blond hair jagged against olive skin. The most remarkable thing about Laura, though, was her physique. She was braced, packed, ripped like a muscle magazine model, veins a blue tracery over solid muscle. Amazon warrior out of mythology, falcon, cheetah, all long muscle and sinew. Milton boasted of how the officials reacted at her first weigh-in.

You should have seen the look on their faces when she took off her shirt and stepped on the scale. They were like, "What the hell is this?" Their jaws were on the floor.

Certainly Laura was more toned than I was (or anyone else not eating steroids like M&M's). I had never fought a woman champion, and I wondered how Milton expected me to behave in the ring, if I was supposed to go light with her. Laura intimidated me slightly. She had won the Gloves after all, and her arms were thicker than mine. While I had moved with women a few times at Julio's, they hadn't been any good. I had played patty-cake with them and worked my defense.

I shouldn't have worried about ring etiquette. Laura's first jabs shoved me backward, and a straight left whiplashed my neck (Milton had turned Laura around as well). Woman no more, Laura was an enemy to kill. Unfortunately, this proved difficult, as she slid beneath my lunges or stepped smoothly out of range. If I waited, she pushed the fight to me, flicking jabs and throwing lead hooks that always landed. As the round passed, I became angry and awkward. My punches left me off-balance and vulnerable. My hands didn't draw back quickly enough to block her counters. When it was her turn to attack, she confused me with jabs and then smacked me with crisp double hooks. It didn't occur to me that step by step, we were reenacting Victor's demolition of the white kid.

Sweat saturated my clothes and burned my eyes. I ran, backpedaling, dashing left and right, stumbling over my own feet. About halfway through the second round, Laura distracted me with a jab and hit me flush on the temple with a solid left. I suffered a frozen explosion of darkness, great black shock through my brain. Now she had to die. I backed her against the ropes and scored a few times in a flurry of wild punches. When I sprang away in fear of a counter, Milton shouted instructions to Laura on how to handle my rush.

Slip and then come back with something, Kielczewski. He's leaving himself open. Make him miss, then hurt him.

The bell rang and I stood breathless and dazed. Laura remarked on her brief difficulty against the ropes.

Milton glared at me. This isn't a tournament, Bob. Don't go crazy in there. Try to think.

I wanted to whine about how badly she was abusing me but simply nodded. In the next round I tried to control myself. This had always been where I failed as a boxer, in that place between fury and fear. I gasped through a third round, a three-minute thousand years. My lungs burned and my hands drooped; I wanted to quit. Instead I ran, avoiding contact until the bell.

What did you think of her? a smiling Milton asked as I stepped between the ropes.

She hits hard, I said with bravado. Harder than guys in bars.

Did you hear that, Laura? Milton laughed. He said you hit harder than guys in bars.

Well, I work as a bouncer, Laura said.

Now you see what we can do for you in here, Milton said. When I got Laura, she was retarded, just like you.

You remember Kingsway, she said. All they teach you is jab-jab, block-block.

We'll work on your defense in the next few days, Bob, he said. We'll work on everything. Still, for an old man, you can really take a punch. This sparring is good for you.

By the way, Bob, Milton said, looking at my feet, do you have boxing shoes?

No, I said, are these shoes bad for the ring?

The ring requires special shoes, high-laced, flat-soled shoes that will not scuff or tear the canvas. I wore my indoor soccer boots, virgin to soil and street.

No, Milton said, but I have some boxing shoes to sell, and I'm Puerto Rican.

He laughed in self-delight.

After the beating, I soldiered on for another week. In the morning mirror, I looked ten years older, creases like hatchet marks on my drawn face.

You look like shit, my boss said. Have you been on some kind of drinking binge?

No, I said sullenly, not drinking. I've been training.

Three weeks into December, I realized that I wasn't ready to fight. Milton kept trying to match me with Laura again; fortunately our schedules would not converge although once she did rescue me.

Give him a break, Laura said as Milton scourged me. Do you think your screaming at someone like that helps them learn?

Why don't you just pay attention to what you have to do, Kielczewski? Milton said. They bickered for the next ten minutes and I welcomed the respite.

I wasn't ready to fight. I couldn't get comfortable with the new stance and switched back to southpaw whenever Milton wasn't looking. My work schedule intensified, and I was too broke to take days off (my boss was months behind on payroll and I still hadn't paid my full dues to Milton). I was always tired. Up at seven-thirty and in the gym twelve hours later, drudgery, poverty, pain. I shared my concerns with Milton and he agreed.

Why don't you wait until next year, Bob? Go in this year, you'll just
be fighting for a T-shirt [he meant the sleeveless Ts the *Daily News* sup-
plies to all entrants to its tournament].

Next year I'll be too old, I said.

Next year, what did I know about next year? I wasn't certain about
next week.

That's no problem. We can "lose" your book and get a new one with
a different birth certificate.

You can do that?

Leave it to me, Milton said.

I did not want to rely, though, on a vague intimation of shady dealings, and if I got caught, well, that would be the end.

Then escape. As I cut out the entry form for the Gloves from an issue
of the *Daily News* ("It's that time again," read the title caption), I notice
that the age limit is thirty-five. I check it again, disbelieving. Still
thirty-five. A call to the *News* confirms it. For the third time in the last
demidecade, U.S. boxing has raised the age limit for amateur competition. After the math, I realize I have one more year of eligibility. I do
not return to the gym the next day or the day after that, and then it's
Christmas and I'm not thinking about boxing at all. I assure myself that
in a month or two, as soon as my finances stabilize and I have a little
more time, I'll get down to the serious business of training.

· 3 ·

HISTORY

SAN FRANCISCO

A common stereotype about boxing is that it is a relatively simple thing to do if one is simple enough to do it. By this notion, a boxing match is a bar brawl with padded gloves, two proto-humans inflicting pain and injury upon each other. There is often an unvoiced racism in this, a variation on the racism that implies great (black) athletes are "remarkable physical specimens" and not possessed of an equivalent intelligence. With boxing, however, the stigma is even greater than in basketball or football; the fighters are considered animals, a dangerous mixture of instinct and ferocity directed toward harm. Long after the examples of Jack Johnson, Marvin Hagler and *Sports Illustrated*'s "athlete of the century," Muhammad Ali, should have put it to rest forever, the stereotype remains.

My first gym was on the west edge of San Francisco's Tenderloin. San Francisco has changed greatly in the past decade, but in the early nineties the Tenderloin was a sleazy twilight of welfare hotels, junkies, transvestite hookers, strip clubs and bottom-feeder bars—a condensed fragment of Sodom. A black economy suspended at the edge of the big tourist district, the Tenderloin reeked of urine and waste over rainless California months. I remember the devastated, watching faces, the back doors open to Chinese laundries where men labored over presses, the lineup for free meals outside Glide Memorial Church. I remember watching a transvestite argue with his blue-collar lover.

"But she's my wife," the man says, distressed and looking as if he just got out of bed.

"I don't care," says the TV, rouge and lipstick over his stubbled face, "I'll kill the bitch unless you tell her about me!"

The Tenderloin's sordid magic made it the perfect haven for a boxing gym.

The first day I took the bus to the gym, I did nothing more than look through the windows, thick floor-to-ceiling panels of glass giving perfect exposure on the ancient gloom of the interior. I don't remember if anyone was training inside the gym, but I remember its still beauty—beauty of the taped leather bags, the polished wood of the floors, the mirrored wall for fighters to watch themselves shadowbox. I stood at the windows and stared but could not bring myself to cross the threshold. As I walked away down the fragrant sidewalk strewn with bodies (who knew how much unwashed humans smelled of earth?), I resolved to come back another day.

On my return the following week, I managed to push myself through the door. The gym was empty, and I made my way to a small office in the back. An old gnome with an abused face sat behind the desk there, dead or dozing, the office walls around him papered with the usual fight posters and newspaper clippings. The gnome lurched at the sound of my voice and asked what he could do for me.

I want to learn how to box, I told him.

He sighed at my enthusiasm, pushed himself up from his chair and led me back into the gym. After being dispatched down the street to buy a cheap pair of bag gloves, I returned for my first lesson.

Okay, he said, take two steps to the bag, jab, then two steps back.

The old man demonstrated. It seemed easy enough.

No, not like that. Keep your hands up. And don't lunge.

I tried again. Wrong. And again. Wrong, and wrong again, like an elephant trying to knit. Two steps forward, two steps back, two steps forward, two steps back. The gnome seemed satisfied with his work for the day and retreated to his cave. I zealously repeated the movements thousands of times. Sweat dribbled from my pores and leaked into my shoes. I became bored. Back in the office, the old man had returned to his somnolence and blinked at my return.

What can I do for you? he asked, not seeming to recognize me.

I've been doing this jab thing for a long time now. What else can I do?

He wearily pulled himself to his feet and led me back to the bag.

Try and hit the bag with a one-two.

Another demonstration.

Now, you give it a shot.

I stepped forward and hit the bag as hard as I could, thereby injuring my hand. I didn't care. Hitting things: This was what I had come for. I stood there whaling away for a few minutes while the gnome peered at me doubtfully.

How am I doing? I panted after a minute.

You don't have to kill the bag, he said, but it's fine for now. Do it until you get tired.

Once again, he retreated to the office. I stood and punched while sweat dappled the floor around me.

I left the gym that day sore but satisfied. My wrists burned, and my knuckles were bloodied, but I had smashed the bag a thousand times. Hitting things. I liked to hit. I thought I was a natural. The gym had drawn boxers as I punched and now resembled a mental institution, a few men in a squalid room performing lunatic, repetitive actions, one circling endlessly in the confines of the ring, another jumping up and down on a rope, a third punching the air with little gasps.

I was twenty-five: young for a man but old for a boxer. I had come to the gym at my advanced age for a number of reasons, twined and tangled reasons that grew heavy and pressed me to action. A short man in a nation of burger-gobbling giants, I stand shy of five-seven and have never weighed more than 140 pounds. I never wanted to be small. What man does? I wanted to tackle. I wanted to destroy my enemies. My childhood was one big melee with brothers and friends. We tore the knees from our dungarees and kept count of the black eyes and bloody noses we inflicted on each other. But I stayed small. I remember crying at age twelve when my mother refused to let me, her four-foot-eleven-inch son, play Pop Warner football (and thereby probably saved my life). In his book of boxing essays *A Neutral Corner*, A. J. Liebling writes: "Small men are apt to be a bit peppery." Linked to a natural aggression, my stature made me disputatious.

Before boxing, I had studied another martial art, kung fu, studied it for years and obsessively trained the forms. I delivered ten thousand punches and one million chops. I stood on one leg in the crane stance and crawled across the floor in the lizard stance. I could kick over my head. I learned how to jump, how to tumble, how to fall, but not how to fight. The little contact we did have was something of a pas de deux—all twining arms and pimp slaps. After three years of kung fu, my trainer still said I wasn't ready to fight. He said I needed to remain patient and master the forms. Combat would come in time. In time? In three years I could acquire a law degree or learn ancient Greek, yet for all my kicks, all my cranes, horses, tigers and lizards, I still didn't know what I would do if someone bashed me in the face. I might run, fight, fall down, I couldn't say. I wanted to know. I needed to know.

I first went to the Tenderloin gym not long after my girlfriend and I split up. Four years together and she left for Los Angeles (at least I got the better city). Our relationship had disintegrated gradually, a year-long crumbling in frost and flame. I had disappointed her in every way possible, all reducible to the same complaint: I wasn't man enough for her. Not man enough to protect her, provide, impress, elegantly order wine in restaurants, conduct myself calmly among strangers. "The only time I feel like I'm with a man is when we're in bed," she told me. I didn't know that I wasn't supposed to be a man, not quite yet, an American male at twenty-four still half boy. I didn't own a wallet or watch; I wore ripped jeans and sneakers. Still half a boy, and a sensitive one at that. No skin at all, just nerves that clanged at sunlight and the glances of strangers, my brain exposed to the blue expanse of sky. My girlfriend's rejection hacked me off at the knees. I swore that I would prove to her that I was indeed a man. That she was four hundred miles away and no longer my audience didn't matter. I lived in constant rage, always on the verge of a fight in bars and at parties. A friend and I had shared the boxing dream (he also had much to prove). When he found the Tenderloin gym and returned praising his first lesson, I didn't need to hear another word. He never made it back for a second lesson, but within two weeks I was an addict.

Two steps forward, jab, two steps back. Two steps forward, jab, two steps back, two up, jab, two back, then a frenzy of lefts and rights. The old gnome (Bernie) emerged from his office and pointed me out to his cronies as a source of amusement as I flailed. I wasted months there. I didn't know it wasn't a fighters' gym, that the only fighters' gyms in San Francisco were two private Mexican clubs deep in the Mission. Bernie's gym was a boxing mausoleum, sustained by a few aging Filipinos, Irish office workers from the financial district and an assortment of characters peculiar to the boxing twilight. Neighborhood gyms had been dying all across the country for generations. Young Americans no longer boxed. The Filipino veterans talked about the old gym, which had been just up the street, a boxing palace with two floors and three rings. Old Bernie had failed in an attempt to have the old gym given landmark status, and now he mumbled and swept the dark, usually empty room.

So I moved back and forth. I battered the bag and thought I was doing all right. It took weeks for Bernie to inform me that the reason my hands were scraped and bleeding after every workout was that I didn't use cloth hand wraps under my bag gloves. No one had told me; I thought my hands were supposed to look like ground sirloin.

After my first delusory month, one of the Filipinos took pity on me and began to show me the rudiments of his sport. Ray was a short, thick-waisted man with the face of Crazy Horse and black hair pulled back in an ass-length ponytail. He shouted at me to keep my hands up and tried to get me to throw a straight jab. He had me practice footwork. I stepped along the polished floors in waltzlike squares. Something of a ringside philosopher, Ray outlined the fundamentals and offered some of the theory behind them. A boxer points his shoulder toward his opponent, thereby displaying the narrowest target possible. The boxer's legs, however, are held at an approximation of a forty-five-degree angle to provide a stable base. The boxer does not walk directly forward but describes an arc to present a moving target and find an angle where he can hit without being hit. Simple lessons, it seemed, but how long it took my body to learn them! For years I would do what comes naturally after being hit: drop my hands, lower my head and try to kill the person who had hit me. A natural reaction, but boxing is far from natural. It is a highly evolved combat sport, like its East Asian cousins karate and kung fu (which no one considers the domain of the savage). The boxer must learn to continue reasoning when adrenaline and instinct are washing away his mind. Boxing is an extreme sport for the poor, one that doesn't require helicopter trips to unskied slopes or outboard tows to monster surf.

After three months Ray allowed that I might be ready to spar. I had been bothering him daily for weeks, a virgin at the prom. For the first time I put on the headgear, bit down on the mouthpiece and slipped on the cup. Ray himself was going to be my first sparring partner. In philosopher mode, he delivered a brief oration before we stepped through the ropes.

This is the real test of whether you're meant for this, Ray said. You have to be a little bit of a masochist as well as a sadist to enjoy boxing. Most people, when they get hit in the face, they think, "What am I doing here? This is bullshit," and they jump out of the ring. But a real boxer, he almost likes getting hit.

After the bell rang, he lifted a glove in salute, and my oarless boat was shoved into the current. I spent the next three minutes in reverse. To my surprise, however, my runaway jab kept bouncing off his head (he confined himself to long hooks to my torso). I felt brilliant. Here I was hitting a man with over twenty years of boxing experience. We went for a second round with the same result and Ray said we'd had enough. Blood was trickling from one of his nostrils and he seemed disgruntled as we removed his gear.

It's no fun if you run the whole time, Ray said, wiping at his nose.

I nodded my head and wondered what he was talking about. It was my first time; of course I had backed away.

You did good, though, Ray said, not seeming to mean it. I got mad at you and had to hold myself back when your punches were landing.

I couldn't understand why Ray seemed so upset. I felt like Superman, Ali and Hercules in one skinny white body. Ray told me that my ribs would be sore in the morning and I should take some aspirin. I did no such thing. I felt no pain the next day: I was a warrior with corpses piled at my feet. I didn't realize, then, that Ray's tone showed dismay at himself, at the realization that he was slowing down and even a novice could hit him easily. Ray was thirty-seven and probably hadn't been very fast to begin with. I remember Bernie coming out of his office and cackling at one of Ray's sparring sessions.

Ray's blocking punches with his head, Bernie said, laughing.

Yet Ray wasn't beaten into retirement. The gym was filled with his friends and no one exploited his weaknesses. Still, he would not admit even the slightest deterioration in his skills. Another veteran asked Ray how old he was. When Ray told him, the man suggested he consider coaching.

No, I'm not ready for it, Ray said fiercely. I just can't stop boxing yet. If I had to stop boxing, I wouldn't want to be alive.

As for me, my second whirl in the ring dissolved all my superhero dreams. My sparring partner was a bearded Irishman who came to the gym every evening in a blue suit. He'd been a serious kickboxer in his home country, with over twenty fights. The second or third time I threw a jab he timed it, his hook sweeping over my extended arm. I went stumbling across the canvas in sudden dark.

Are you all right? he asked, a look of quizzical concern over the beard.

I'm fine, I lied.

That same hook followed my jab another ten or fifteen times in the next two rounds. I don't remember how I reacted, only that it ended with a bell and there I was, taking off my gear and shaking my head. I had a lot to learn before they gave me the Superman cape. I was still exhilarated, however. I felt enormous and full of life. I was in it now, as real as a head-on collision. My own pain proved to be a remarkable stimulant.

I remained in that boxing necropolis for a few more months. I learned how to hit the speed bag and hesitantly jump rope. I sparred when I could, usually with the same dismal results, once hyperextending my left elbow so badly it never completely healed. As we trained, derelicts and prostitutes from the neighborhood would press their faces to the windows as if we were Chinatown carp in a tank. My first impression, that I had found myself in an insane asylum, faded; I was now a model patient, grunting, leaping and striking the air. Cast sweat patterned the floor around the bags and where we jumped rope. Sometimes you would slip. Old Bernie pushed a mop and complained about the mess. I came to know the sadder figures of that little gym. There was a Mexican drunk who would run in off the street sometimes. He would hit the speed bag and boast about how he'd fought Julio Cesar Chavez, then run out again when Bernie threatened him with the mop. There was a Vietnam vet named Lou, a heavyweight, who lived in an SRO nearby. Lou would sit in the gym for hours, saying nothing, an amiable expression on his baggy face. Suddenly, we would hear the sound of someone drubbing the heavy bag and turn to see him, in street clothes, striking the bag with his bare hands. Bernie said Lou had been a great kid before he "blew out his mind with the drugs," but Lou remained gentle and kind. Once he appeared bare-chested in winter because he'd just given his shirt and ten dollars to a homeless guy in the street, never mind that Lou was microns from homeless himself.

The gym seemed like a fragment of an old San Francisco, the blue-collar city of the longshoremen's general strike or the San Francisco where the Fillmore was Harlem West. I left gray and white San Francisco for Germany and New York. When I returned to do an interview for a journalism piece in 1998, everyone told me the city on the hills wasn't the same, not even the same as five years earlier, when I had shared a three-bedroom Victorian for $240 a month. Vacancy rates were under 1 percent, my friends said, and rents were as bloated as Manhattan's. I went down to the Tenderloin to visit the old gym but the windows were cased in newsprint and the doors padlocked shut.

MUNICH

Locating the boxing gym in a new town can be a challenge. One summer I spent two months in Asheville, North Carolina, and could not find the gym. I searched diligently but in vain; everyone I met who I thought might know insisted the town harbored no such thing. They had dojos and judo, health clubs and tae kwon do, but no straight-up boxing. So my gloves mildewed in my gym bag, and I shadowboxed in my yard beneath an angry Southern sun. In my last days there I met a white teenager with wannabe dreams (he insisted that the place in the world he most wanted to visit was South-Central Los Angeles) who said that yes, there certainly was a boxing gym in Asheville, beside a housing project in a black neighborhood I passed through daily. In the hundred-odd times I walked down the street, I had never noticed the small building that held the gym.

Once every city had its central gym where aficionados gathered to watch prospects and champions preparing themselves for fights. Stillman's and the Times Square Gym in New York, the Fifth Street Gym in Miami Beach where Ali trained for Liston, the New Gardens in Boston, all closed now, although you can still see the decals advertising the Times Square Gym on the windows of its old location across from the bus terminal. Today the old-style gyms are elusive, relying for clientele upon a communication network that predates the telephone (a musician who boxes told me that when he is on tour, he finds gyms by contacting the local police). The gyms didn't need a listing in the yellow pages; they relied on their district for fresh talent. Every local could tell you where his gym was, if he wanted to (and he might not). Even today (although things are changing), gyms remain hidden away, in abandoned mills and factories, as afterthoughts in sports clubs, the shrines of a dying cult with grizzled priests and their cant and the rare young acolytes upon whom so much love and care are expended and upon whom so much depends. Those gyms are dank caves with floors of damp concrete or wood grayed by shuffling feet. Naked bulbs for light. Heavy bags creaking on chains.

In Munich, I found Horst and his team through the friend of a friend who knew someone who had once trained with him. When I called, Horst arranged to meet me on the plaza in front of a McDonald's near his gym. I stood for a time beneath the golden arches until a slender man with a crooked nose approached and asked my name.

I walked around here for a while, he said, but I didn't see anyone who looked like a fighter.

I didn't know what to say to that.

How many stripes do you have? he asked after we got into his car.

Stripes?

Stripes. You know, fights.

None, I confessed.

Horst looked disappointed. I don't know if there had been a misunderstanding and he never spoke of it again, but Horst had the air of someone who'd been promised a Porsche and received a Pinto. I wasn't the real American boxer he'd obviously expected.

One of those southern Germans with tight dark curls and tawny skin, Horst conformed to the model of a certain kind of trainer (the Milton model), lean and sardonic with a vibrancy, a living intelligence that kept him talking, watching, moving. I remember him barking criticisms in his T-shirt with Tyson's face and famous quote "Next to boxing, everything is boring."

Horst trained in a storage room above a big state sports complex, the extra gear from soccer, basketball and swimming shrinking the space. Horst didn't charge his fighters for training and must have had an arrangement that gave him the space rent-free, for he never spoke of money to us. Most of his fighters were big white men different from the Germans I'd met in the bars and cafés of bourgeois Munich. For one thing they spoke little, if any, English. Educated Germans speak excellent English, it being on the curriculum for the university-bound from about age eight. Horst's fighters hadn't gone to university, however. They were tradespeople for the most part: masons, carpenters and factory workers, who lived in the industrial suburbs outside the posh city center.

Lacking skills and language, I was lost among Horst's fighters. I couldn't tell if they liked, tolerated or hated me: the handsome cruiser-weight fond of practical jokes who would pat me on the shoulders like a mascot, or my regular sparring partner, a middleweight, who rode a motorcycle and looked like a cross between a Hell's Angel and Thor. When the sports complex closed for August, I traveled with the team in search of places to train. We practiced in parks, running back and forth in fields and sparring in the shades of oaks. We went to shows in little country towns, driving through the undulating Bavarian countryside with its green fields, low hills and clumps of forest. I watched chauvinist crowds scream for their German boys against woolly-headed Turkish fighters. In a medieval town Horst led us to an ultramodern health club nestled in a stone building. The machines stood there, gleaming and incongruous, although none of the Germans operating them seemed affected by the gulf between centuries. Above the health club was, yes, the boxing gym, an afterthought, unfinished, a place of cracked plaster and dust. I felt like a pioneer. A lot of Americans had been to Munich, but how many had penetrated into the quotidian fastnesses of those old towns?

I couldn't speak but stood watching and tried to imitate the movements of the better fighters. At twenty-seven, I still didn't get it. Sparring sessions were a confusion of rage and exhaustion, blood mist clouding my eyes as I gunned it out with the larger Germans, slinging wild punches as hard as I could. I remember Horst shouting, "Breathe, man! Breathe!" as he tried to take me to the next level, past the violence, where my eyes would clear and I could see that it was all a game. Horst understood the game. I watched him move with his experienced fighters, a jab flicking out from his easy stance. I saw him casually lean back to let hooks pass, leather fans blowing wind in his face. The African pro who came to Horst understood the game. He was a heavy-weight although little taller than I, a black beach ball of muscle who could slip under the Germans' punches and quake them with body shots, smiling all the while. I didn't understand. I shadowboxed before the mirrors and did the drills. I ran through the sculpted ground of the Olympiazentrum near my apartment. Tough and healthy among men, among boxers I was neither. Discouraged, I refused to jump rope in front of the others because Horst once pointed out my awkward hops and laughed. I didn't show my face in the attic room for weeks at a time because I was afraid, afraid of the language I didn't speak, of the bruis-ing indifference where I could train for hours without a word of direc-tion. Still, I kept up the drills, hoping that boxing knowledge would illuminate me in some sudden and mysterious way, enlightenment between one blow and the next.

PROVIDENCE

I returned to the United States no more of a fighter than I'd left, but the desire remained. I found my next gym in my hometown of Provi-dence, Rhode Island. The yellow pages did not list one gym in the city, population 170,000, where as a boy my father could walk half a block to Meehan Auditorium on Friday night and watch Rocky Marciano and Willie Pep. I called a listing for a boxing club in Warwick, a few towns away. After the owner gave up trying to talk me into going there (to discourage him, I said I had no automobile), he told me about a new gym in South Providence.

We'd love to have you come out here, the voice said, but if you don't have a car, it probably won't work. Ollie Kreuger's got a new place. I think he just opened up last week.

Ollie's gym was in a warehouse on a bleak lot in South Provi-dence, "South Providence" being synonomous with "slum" in the city since before I was a boy. The block around the warehouse was mixed use: other commercial buildings and three-floor wood-frame multiple-family houses, black and Latino children spilling into the street. The entrance to the gym was on one side of a crumbling loading dock.

Painted around the gym door was a big mural of an American eagle framing a fighter who looked like Tyson with acromegaly. Inside, the gym, open a week, looked as old as Jericho with the standard-issue naked bulbs and gray wall-to-wall smelling of mold.

Ollie was a retired mason and a trainer of the Bernie variety albeit a few hundred years younger (there are only four or five current models of trainers). He had a wattled neck and a smoker's rasp. Many (many) years earlier, Ollie had been a top amateur prospect in New England, until the day he'd been demoing a chimney and a brick splinter pierced his right eye, blinding it. The sightless eye jarred me, damaged pupil dripping into the pale blue iris like the broken yolk of an egg.

First among Ollie's prospects was Samson, an enormous black man with the physique to fit his name. A West African, Samson was generally trailed by an entourage of admirers and family members, many of whom wore black silk jackets with "Samson" embroidered on the back. Samson frustrated Ollie, who complained about his poor work ethic and appetite for nightlife. None of Ollie's sharp comments dismayed Samson, however, and his muscles, his humor and his followers enlivened the gym. Ollie's other prospect was Sammy, a lean half-Mexican kid who had already won the regional Golden Gloves. He rarely spoke and seemed older than his twenty-one years (except when he launched into enthusiastic descriptions of video games). Although Sammy had been in boxing just a few years, he moved with elegance and dignity in the ring, a boxing cavalier. Ollie had great hopes for his future. "That Sammy is a good little fighter," Ollie said approvingly, after a dinner at the Harvard Club where Sammy fought before the besuited swells.

Within two months of my arrival, Ollie was forced to close. He told me the sad story as he dismantled the ring, a wrench in one hard hand (to settle some of his debt, he had arranged to sell his equipment, the bags and the ring, to a boxing club in Connecticut).

I just can't make the nut on the space, Ollie said, unbolting braces and stays beneath the canvas. I'm only charging the kids in the neighborhood twenty-five a month, and they can't come up with that. People like you, I'm charging fifty, but not too many people like you are going to come down to South Providence to box.

Ollie was sanguine for a man unbuilding with his own hands a lifetime dream. In this he was like most former fighters, a resilient and fatalistic group. Fighters grow accustomed to disappointment.

I asked Ollie what he was going to do.

Well, I've still got Sammy and Samson. We're going to start working at some other gyms until we find a regular place.

Do you think maybe I could go with you too?

Sure, Ollie said, I'm always willing to train a prospect, especially if it's a white guy.

For the next few weeks, we became the Ollie's Nomadic Boxing Road Show. We would meet at twilight (it was winter) before the warehouse and carpool to whatever gym Ollie had chosen for a training site that day (Sammy acquired a handsome black eye at the Petronellis' gym in Brockton, courtesy of a local pro). The group usually consisted of Ollie, me, Sammy, Samson and a few family members or friends (Samson's entourage had been greatly diminished by the loss of venue). In our caravan, we made a round of area boxing clubs. Ollie was on good terms with the various owners (gruff, muscular middle-aged men), and there would be a fanfare of greetings and handshakes as Ollie introduced his prospects.

And what about this guy? the owners would ask, pointing at me.

He just started with me, Ollie would say. Green as grass.

It made me wince; two years of intermittent training and still green as grass in the fighters' world.

One afternoon Ollie told me he had found a new home.

We're moving down to Leo Correnti's place off Charles Street, he said. I mean, permanently. They're not going to charge me an arm and a leg, and they got guys that Sammy and Sampson can go with.

We stood on the frosted tar in front of the warehouse.

Kid, Ollie said, we've got a fight later, and we're not going to be coming back this way, so bring your car.

I got the directions from Ollie and made my way down to Charles Street. The name had a resonance for me. When I was in high school, the Charles Street Gang had the reputation of being the toughest street gang in the area. They had been at the edge of my teen world but not of it, showing up occasionally to discipline whatever group of jocks had claimed that *they* were the toughest gang in town (on one occasion a Charles Gangsta had pulled a gun on Thayer Street and been canonized in the next month's gossip). While I made my way along the rutted street at ten miles an hour, I wondered where gang members would live, as all I saw were picturesque shattered factories and mills along the wooded banks of the Mosshasuck River. In the lot of one of the old mills, I recognized Ollie's big sedan and parked beside it.

The mill was being converted into lofts and work studios, but the conversion had barely started and Dumpsters stood in ranks in gutted rooms. A sign pointed the way to the gym. I walked through the rough wood cradle of the mill to the gym door. In front of it stood a large, shirtless, muscular man in leopard-pattern trunks.

What can I do for you? he asked in the nasal Rhode Island accent.

I'm looking for Ollie Kreuger, I said meekly.

Ollie's in the office. Are you here to box? he asked dubiously, looking me over.

Yes, I squeaked.

The dressing room is over there. He pointed. Beside him, I felt like a child, puny, pale and weak. He didn't belong to the same species as I did. The leopard shorts seemed like animal hide or his own skin, not any store-bought fabric.

I changed and returned to the floor. In the ring Sammy waited to spar with a fighter whose nose had been fractured into a fishhook. The bell rang and Sammy started quickly, backing his opponent up and knocking him against the ropes with body shots. Sammy moved like a swashbuckler, his body expressive and balanced. An uppercut pinned Fishhook as he tried to dance off the ropes and then Sammy drilled him with a straight right to the face. A squirt of blood painted Fishhook's lips and spritzed down his shirt. It didn't look like boxing to me; it looked like murder. I had seen sparring like this a thousand times but it was suddenly new. I had phased out of the compact of boxing where I could judge—good round, bad round, nice combination. Now I saw acts of inhuman violence, a lion grappling with a wildebeest on the Serengeti. I had to watch. The lion twisted the wildebeest's neck and it bellowed.

Fishhook improved in the second round. Instead of covering up, he began to counterpunch against Sammy, who had perhaps tired himself in the first. Leopard Shorts shouted encouragement. The two men sparred for about four rounds.

Later I changed with the two fighters in the locker room. They had never spoken or met before. There was no animosity. The sparring had been clean, if hard. It was boxing. Fishhook began talking of the women at a certain bar. I had never heard a more vulgar human being in my life.

There are some good-looking fucking cunts there, I'll tell you, he said. You sit there watching one piece of ass and you're thinking, "I'd like to tap that," when all of a sudden, another cunt walks by, and you forget about the last one.

Gentleman Sammy didn't seem to mind the course the conversation had taken.

Hot bitches, huh?

Like you wouldn't believe.

And you show up with a couple of beers in you and they stay friendly?

Friendly like you was made out of chocolate, the cunts.

What jarred me most about Fishhook's harsh tone was its familiarity, the accent of the white Rhode Island working class. An accent without ethnic leavening, the accent of my parents' past and one I had left after high school (driving it from my own voice with American Standard). An ugly voice, uglier than Sammy's (he had been raised in Colorado), ugly and close to me.

The conversation turned to boxing. Sammy wanted to know about Fishhook's pro debut. Fishhook had lost. Badly.

Well, let me tell you, it was pretty hard to take, Fishhook said, discouragement weighting his face. You work so hard at something for so long and then have that happen. I didn't do too well. It gets you down. I didn't feel like fighting for a while. I almost quit for good.

Fishhook seemed burdened by the failures of an older man. He couldn't have been more than twenty-four.

But here I am—he shrugged—trying to put it back together.

Ollie's road show was the end of my boxing prehistory. I trained once more at the Charles Street Gym but I had been offered a job and a place in New York, and I knew I was gone. Sammy said he would visit me in the city, that we would party, but I didn't really expect to hear from him and never did. About four years later, watching an Atlantic City fight card on TV, I was surprised to see Sammy, opposite Floyd Mayweather, Jr., in his inevitable rise to the title. "Sizzlin" Sammy had a loser's record of 17-4-1 (in professional boxing, even two losses can end a career) and was a blood sacrifice to the talented Mayweather. A safe opponent (he lacked the power to win with a lucky punch), my old gymmate went out in the second round on a TKO. Sammy had been as good as Ollie claimed, good enough to serve as stepping-stone for one of the stars of his generation. It was the highlight and the biggest payday of his career, a career nearing its end. My own career as a writer had barely started. Sammy was all of twenty-six.

N E W   Y O R K

In New York I took the first apartment I was offered, a share in an old co-op in the heart of "Dominican City" at the convergence of 169th, Broadway and St. Nicholas. It was so far out my friends called it upstate Manhattan. When I first lived there, at twenty-three, New York was hard for me. I had few friends and lived in Bedford-Stuyvesant, a neighborhood where my white face made me an occasional target. Now, almost twenty-eight, I hoped things would be different. With more friends and a finished first novel, I moved through the world less fearfully (the skin toughens; the disguises become more convincing).

I actually found Julio's Gym in the phone book (a first). Of the three listed (this in all of Manhattan), it was the cheapest by far. It was also in the East Village, where I would have lived if I'd had the money. To reach Julio's, you had to pass through the lobby of a senior center, where ancients milled around and watched the doors like guardians of the underworld. Sixty-eight stairs brought you down through one basement to a subbasement and the gym. The ceiling must have been forty feet high, and the heavy bags chained to it swung pendular when struck, long arcs back and forth across the room. Buckets had been placed at strategic locations on the floor to catch the endless drip from the distant ceiling. The room flooded often and Julio, who had a crippled leg, could usually be seen limping behind a mop. The showers lacked hot water most of the time and were infested with roaches and a particularly necrotic genus of ringworm. Dues ranged from $50 to $150 a month. According to gym lore, Julio would determine your rate from the quality of your footwear. My scuffed oxfords were assessed at the $50 minimum.

Except for the heavy bags (heavily taped and misshapen as if packed with corpses) and a few rusted free weights, all the equipment—ropes, speed bags, double-end bags, medicine balls—belonged to individual trainers. On my second visit to the gym I was hitting a speed bag when a short black man approached me. I'd noticed him watching me from across the room.

That's my bag, you know, he said.

I'm sorry, I said, and stepped back. I thought it was gym equipment.

In this gym? There ain't nothing you don't bring yourself. You can keep hitting it, though.

When he spoke, I saw a few of his front teeth were missing.

I began to hit the bag and he continued to watch me. After a few minutes he told me to stop.

Here. Why don't you try it this way? he said.

He stepped to the speed bag and began to hit it at an angle. When he stepped back, I tried his style for a few minutes. He continued to watch.

You've done some boxing, huh?

I admitted that I had.

You ever had any fights?

I admitted that I hadn't quite. Not quite exactly.

Do you want to?

Yeah, sure.

You're pretty fast on the bag.

Thanks, I said, flattered.

So you are training with anyone here?

No.

Because I train a few fighters. If you were going to fight, I'd train you for free.

Really? I said, noticing thin pale scars clustered around his eyebrows.

Yeah. We could give it a shot. I think you might have something. You ever think about turning pro?

I don't know. Not really.

Well, we can talk about it later. Follow me.

He led me to an open space on the floor. For the next half hour he had me throw punches and corrected my style. In that time he became my trainer. It was the tender coupling of two delusions: mine, that I was a quality warrior, and his, that through him I could become one. We agreed to meet the next day. As I changed, he had one other question for me.

You haven't talked to Milton?

Who's Milton?

He's another trainer. He's got most of the young guys around here, but he's not in today. If he was here, you'd be with him now instead of me.

Darryl gave a philosophic shrug.

That's the way it goes.

· 4 ·

SEPTEMBER

February, March, April, I kept meaning to go back. I still had money problems, however (and work problems and life problems), and time, in youth a bottomless hole, was always slipping through my fingers. Three hundred boxing days until the Golden Gloves, then 250, then 225 and it was summer. At some point I began to date a witty, elegant writer. Who liked to drink. Our affair featured vodka gimlets and savage conversation about our friends as we sailed from bar to bar through the Williamsburg (Brooklyn) night. That summer Williamsburg was a perfect place to be . . . young, or if no longer young, then not yet old, its night world of new bars and clubs set in a scenic, wasted industrial landscape along the East River, the bars filled with attractive people. I would go to certain bars to work late or to meet the writer (as I'll call her). Some of the managers and bartenders welcomed me by name. I felt indecently proud of the occasional free drink. A child's delight: I could go out at night and see people I liked, people who liked me.

My training continued. I ran three or four days a week. I shadow-boxed in my apartment and practiced the new Milton tricks. I would return to him in August, but August was six weeks off. Then four. Then two. I heard from actor Dave that Milton had lost his super job at the building on 14th and, with it, his apartment and gym. The building had been sold in the spring and Milton clashed with the new owners and that was that. Actor Dave also told me that Laura had turned pro and won her first fight. I called Milton soon after to find out if I would have a gym for the Gloves.

Yo, Supreme, came his voice.

Milton, it's Bob Anasi calling.

Yo, Anasi, what's up? You disappeared.

Yeah, I owe you some money too. I want to pay you.

That sounds good. Sounds like a white guy paying his debts. If you were a black guy, you'd be gone. And if you were Puerto Rican, forget it. You would have left the country already. Yo, yo, yo. Anasi, you know what street has the prettiest women in the city?

Somewhere around Union Square?

That's a pretty good guess. As a matter of fact, I'm on Fifteenth right across from the park.

He shouted to a passerby.

Hey, hey. How are you today, sweetheart? Boricua?

Milton was in a celebratory mood and the world agreed with him, August outdoor café lounging, the sidewalk parade of women wearing summer little. Idle hours, time suspended in the long days. I imagine him at his table on that afternoon, looking like a lighter-skinned O. J. Simpson, long legs pointed toward the street (although, as I came to know him, I realized that some specific scheme must have brought him there. No senseless idling for my trainer).

I've been talking to Mazzeo, and he said your gym closed down.

Yeah, but we got a great new space. You're going to love it. It's about five times the size of that closet I had. Nice and clean.

A shower?

Showers, everything. It's just down the street too.

Still on Fourteenth?

Yeah. We'll be ready to go by the first of the month. It's a good thing you didn't go into the Gloves last year. Stupid idiots changed the rules again, so now you got to go open after one Gloves.

So a guy can get knocked out in the first minute of the Gloves and not fight for another year and have to fight open in the next Gloves?*

---

*In amateur boxing, fighters are divided into two classes: novice and open. Historically, a novice boxer was who had never won a major tournament and had fewer than ten fights in his U.S. Boxing book. Into the 1980s, however, many novice fighters would participate in smokers—that is, unregistered bouts that would not show up in their books. They were also allowed to continue entering the Gloves as novices until they had reached the ten-fight limit or made the finals (it was not uncommon for boxers to turn pro after winning a novice

That's right. There's gonna be a *lottt* of beatings this year, Milton said reflectively.

I heard Laura turned pro.

Yeah, after she won the Gloves again. Her second fight is next week, out at some state fair in New Jersey.

I'd like to check it out.

All right, call me next week. I'll give you the details.

We talked for a while longer. Milton informed me that he was displeased with the behavior of black and Spanish women in New York. The subject led him to wax philosophic, Socrates stream of consciousness on the topic of *la femme*.

I tell you, Anasi, these women have attitudes. They want the car. And the house. And the money. Then the Puerto Rican women are trying to hit you upside the head with a frying pan every five minutes. White women, they just want you to love them. Pretty soon you white guys can have all the black and Spanish women because they're going to be all alone.

He laughed.

Hey, I should get a show talking about black women, he said, the Puerto Rican Howard Stern. I could be the most hated man in America.

I found my way to a scale in August and gaped as the needle swung to 139. One hundred thirty-nine! Couldn't be right. Tried again. Too true to be good. Summertime and that easy living. Still, I remained far from tubby. Had definition in my abdomen and the same lanky arms and legs as always. With a little discipline, I believed I could shrink down to the 132 I had fought at four years earlier.

My diet for years had been pure Blue Ridge Mountain bachelor: peanut butter by the tubful, bagels and pita bread, canned tuna fish, cream cheese and knishes, rice and pasta, pasta and rice. I liked Campbell's soup, ninety-nine cents for the red and white can. Throw in some

---

Gloves title). To control such behavior, the rules were changed to force boxers to fight open after participating in two major tournaments (or ten fights). The decline of the smoker also reduced opportunities for young boxers to gain experience.

oregano, a little olive oil, a handful of ziti, *et voilà!* instant gourmet. Breakfast was frosted flakes in whole milk. Something would have to change.

The writer, who was fabulously thin, swore by protein powder fruit juice smoothies in the morning. She subsisted entirely on these, boiled artichokes, coffee, vodka and guilty cigarettes (she was five-ten and 118 pounds; it seemed to work for her). I decided to pay a visit to a local vita store. The abundance of products frightened me: Stocking the shelves were fortified alfalfa pills, bee pollen, bonemeal and royal jelly. There was Korean ginseng, guarana and kava kava; there was creatine, yohimbé bark and Saint-John's-wort. The potions, powders and pills promised hair growth, sexual potency, soothed nerves, better digestion, lowered cholesterol—live forever. Products endorsed by gurus, doctors, dietitians, famous athletes (no boxers, though). I reached for my credit card and bought a vitamin-bolstered protein powder (one of over twenty brands crammed with muscle boosters and brain stimulators). I bought a box of meal substitute bars that contained unique muscle-building amino acids (packed with twenty-three grams of protein! Real chocolate fudge brownie flavor!). This was shrink-wrapped alchemy, alchemy for the masses in a color-coordinated corner store on Seventh Avenue (not slopping over the side of a witches' foul tub). I spread my purchases across my apartment floor. Now I would be thin.

The next morning I emptied two tablespoons of protein powder into a glass, added orange juice and stirred. This gave me a thin, sour gruel, with lumps of undissolved powder suspended in the solute. Didn't taste very good. Still, I choked down the lumpy broth that morning and every morning for the next few weeks. The unpleasant substance only reinforced the fact that I was in training. Training was *supposed* to be a struggle. If it were fun, everybody would do it.

The Tuesday after Labor Day I took the L train to the Supreme Team's new home on Sixth Avenue and 14th Street. Four flights up from the street, Revolution Studios seemed no place for a boxing gym. The lobby looked like a showroom, with fitness machines in sleek array: tread-mills, stationary cycles and Nautilus contraptions. Head shots of the personal trainers smiled across the freshly painted walls. Signs by the water coolers advertised classes in belly dancing, Pilates, hip-hop, spinning (whatever that was), high-impact aerobics, low-impact aerobics, aerobic kung fu, aerobics on trampolines. The trainers were young, handsome and fit. In the sprung-floor studios they prompted their classes with upbeat exhortations over the thump of up-tempo dance music: "Everybody! One, two, three! Kick! Stretch, reach, turn! Do you feel it? Do you? Feel it!" The locker room shone and the showers geysered hot water. In the fifth-floor hallway a magnified magazine cover showed the owner's head and named her "Fitness Diva."

Yet in a studio on the fifth floor, the boxing gym looked like . . . a boxing gym. But a *nice* boxing gym, easily five times larger than Milton's last space. Between mirrored walls, heavy bags and kick bags swung over an expanse of polished wood. Gear hung from a pegboard. There was a large new ring, a padded bench and, in the back, a fat body bag and wall mount for a speed bag. I found Milton on the bench and a sun-browned Laura stretching on the floor. The week before, I'd called Milton for directions to Laura's New Jersey fight only to have him tell me . . .

She ain't fighting.

No? What happened?

She started complaining about the contract, he said in disgust. She said it was supposed to be for one thirty-two, and instead it was one twenty-nine, and she didn't know if she could make the weight and this and that. So I told her to stop whining. Two pounds here, three pounds there, we're still gonna beat the bitch's ass no matter what she weighs. But Laura doesn't want to hear that, so I told her to either shut up or quit. And she quit.

I understood immediately. Laura had succumbed to a fear that seizes on the smallest detail and inflates it to an excuse, allowing a boxer to avoid the very thing he has looked forward to for months: his fight.

That's the way it goes, Anasi, Milton had said.

I offered my regrets to Laura about her canceled fight.

Oh, I fought, she said.

What?

The promoter said if I didn't fight, he would have my license suspended. They said I could fight at whatever weight so . . .

How did you do?

She beat the bitch's ass, rasped Milton from the bench.

Great. Congratulations.

It was the same girl I fought in my first fight.

No kidding.

Yeah, said Milton, arching his eyebrows. We were surprised that she came back after the first time.

He turned to Laura.

I told you it wouldn't be a problem.

Well, said Laura, maybe if I had a gym to go to, I would have been less worried.

I questioned Laura about the fight for a few minutes only to be interrupted by Milton.

So, Anasi, get dressed and warm up. You're going to spar Laura tonight.

Tonight?

Yeah. Laura's got another fight coming up in a few weeks and we got to get her ready.

I went to the bathroom and changed. I hadn't intended to spar for weeks, but I didn't want to complain or question my trainer on my first day back.

This sparring went worse than the last in December. In the preceding six months, Laura had won the Gloves again and her first two professional fights, while I had performed mixological experiments on myself. Laura hit me with double jabs, hooks off jabs, two-three combinations. I fell for every feint, and Laura hit me. I lifted my gloves to protect my head, and Laura hit me in the stomach.

Milton proffered advice from the bench.

C'mon, Bob, don't plod. Let's see some bounce in those legs.

Bob, enough of that robotic shit, already, Jesus Christ.

Bite down on your mouthpiece, Bob.*

Bob, punch to her. *To* her. You're punching to yourself. Let your hands go. Let them be free.

My only success came when Laura pushed straight ahead (trying to "walk through me" in box-speak). Then, at least, I could hit her while

---

*As boxers tire, they tend to open their mouths, risking a gashed tongue and broken jaw.

she was hitting me. Otherwise my punches fell short. If I reached too far, I lost balance with the same, by now tedious result: She hit me.

Between rounds, Milton encouraged me.

You're following your two with your hook. That's good. That's how you'll keep 'em off of you in the Gloves.

Adrenaline carried me for a few minutes, but by the third round I was a cadaver. Laura slipped under a jab and made an incision with her left, about three inches below my arm. Suddenly I couldn't breathe. I had to ask for time.

Lift your arms up, Bob, Milton said. Lift your arms up and inhale.

I stood in the middle of the ring, gasping. Gee, it was great to be back. The bell finally brought an end to my suffering.

Hey, Bob, has anyone ever told you that you look like Elvis Presley? Milton said after he tugged off my headgear.

No, no one ever did [except for a modest pair of sideburns, I look nothing like Elvis Presley].

Laura?

She studied me.

Maybe a little.

Elvis! Milton said. Sing to us! Well-uh, well-uh, well-uh . . .

Milton bellowed and swung his hips. The thing was done. In the months to come, "Elvis" I would be.

Laura and I worked the floor, and then she left. It was getting late, nearly nine P.M. I said good night to Milton and headed for the door.

Oh, Anasi? he called.

Yes?

I need you to spar every night for the next couple of weeks. You're the right size for Laura and she likes working with you. Can you do that?

Sure, I said ("Every day!" I thought. It seemed a horrible, impossible thing).

I waited for the subway, my thoughts scattered and flat, time stretching into a dull brown tedium. After looking left and right to make sure no one was watching, I stuck a forefinger in my nose and began to scrape dried blood from the septum and nares. The blood surprised me; after five years of boxing, I hadn't thought my nose could still bleed.

The next day Milton said, Come here, Bob.

He led me down the narrow hall from our boxing gym to another studio.

It's pretty nice, he said, isn't it?

I took in the white room with its free weights, Nautilus machines, exercise mats, medicine balls and treadmills. Revolution occupied two floors in an industrial building with a dingy façade but windows that ran to the high ceilings and filled the north-facing rooms with light. Over the floor lay a black perforated rubber mat, the kind put in the backs of bars to keep the bartenders from slipping on their booze, suds, water. A few young trainers coaxed their clients through sweat-yielding repetitions and life-affirming contortions, using soporific hospital voices to encourage the stiff white struggling bodies.

You can come in here and use the equipment, Milton said, lift weights, do sit-ups, use the treadmills, whatever.

Really? I exclaimed. It's cool?

I had never had access to a real gym before and couldn't believe that I would be permitted into this clean white space, this shrine to fitness.

Oh, sure, Milton said, it's all part of the deal.

The week passed in a general ache marked by flashes of intense pain. Laura had bruised my ribs so that sleeping was uncomfortable, I damaged my hand throwing the Milton-style hooks incorrectly and the thumb on my right hand swelled to twice normal size. The toughness that had taken me through my first session with Laura faded before my injuries. Laura had learned from our first encounter. She no longer tried to slug but needled me at a distance with jabs and hooks (her arms were unusually long for her height). Unwilling to lose a sparring partner, she tried not to strike my injured ribs, but even the lightest jab to my right side made me gasp in agony. In our third session, I stopped in the middle of a round and shouted at Milton:

What good is this doing me? I'm injured and I'm not learning anything.

Milton shrugged.

That's the way it goes. We got to beat you back into shape.

After training, Laura handed me her business card so that we could call each other about sparring. The card read: "Laura Kielczewski, accountant."

One night after sparring, I sat across from the writer at a bistro table. Her words came through layers and depths, as if I'd been wadded in cotton, weighted with iron and sunk in an ocean canyon while she called me from a sunny beach. As far as I felt from her, I felt equally removed from myself. The words I spoke were extruded by a distant mechanism to which I felt only vaguely connected. The world lacked vibrancy, its colors muted and sound muffled. I was a dim soft padded thing in the gloom.

Are you okay? she asked.

I'm all right, just tired and a little beat up.

We drank wine. The cottony feeling dissolved in general inebriation.

Physically and psychically, I was not prepared for that sparring. Sitting at the table, I wondered why I needed to stimulate and stress my body to the point of breakdown. It was just sparring, "work," as boxers say: "You want to work today?" "You want to work a little?" It had never been "work" to me. Yet even injured and in poor condition, I loved being in the ring again. "Next to boxing, everything is boring." There was truth in Tyson's words. The world did seem less interesting after the ring, from color to black and white.

Fortunately my penance at Laura's hands had few witnesses. In fact, there were so few boxers in the gym those first weeks in September that I wondered if Milton would stay in business long enough to take me through the Gloves. Milton reassured me when I asked him where the fighters were.

They haven't found their ways down here yet, he said. I need to start making some calls. But they'll show up soon.

Milton was right: As September progressed, the gym began to stir. Summer is a fallow time in amateur boxing. There are no major tournaments and young men's minds are on the beaches, the girls and all the dramas of the street. They work summer jobs and visit scattered families. Autumn draws them back.

One evening the middleweight Dave Marrero appeared, sleepy-eyed and golden-skinned, with a nascent Buddha belly. He lifted his shirt and pinched his jelly roll with a warm smile.

Hey Marrero, Milton teased, what happened? Are you pregnant? Got to lay off those cervezas, papi. You want a garbage bag? How about two? (Milton's panacea for every weight problem was to wrap it in a Hefty bag and set it jumping rope.)

The next night Joey Colon returned, a good ten pounds over his fighting weight but hiding the extra bulk well on his solid frame. He brought one of his sons with him, a boy of five or six, who ambled ringside, by turns awestruck and restless in the adult world. Joey donned a garbage bag also, and his sweat fell to dapple the floor.

Milton summoned me ringside for a personal introduction to another fighter.

Watch this, he said.

A white fighter moved with a much taller black man in what seemed a terrible imbalance in weight class.

Isn't that black guy too big for him? I asked.

No, no, Milton said. They're both about one sixty.

I couldn't believe how much taller the black man was, looming over his opponent like a mantis scrutinizing dinner. When he punched, his arms extended halfway across the ring, but when the white fighter pressed inside, the long arms scissored against the body and he flowed off the ropes, out of danger. He moved with the elegance of a young Ali.

This kid is serious, Milton said. He's been here since ten in the morning.

How old is he?

Seventeen. I've only had him six months.

And that, I discovered, was Will.

Although his head was shaven and he had added a small mustache, I recognized Victor Paz, the glowering middleweight. Track lighting burnished his brown skull.

Are you ready to go? Milton asked Victor on his first day back.

Yeah, the doctor said it was okay to spar, Vic answered in his soft voice.

Well, get dressed.

Vic sparred shirtless, and I saw he had added something besides a mustache. A fresh scar sectioned him from navel to sternum, and another, smaller scar arched a few inches below his armpit.

Last to return was Julian, sometime near the end of the month. His presence filled the gym as he exhorted Victor to attack a heavyweight.

Come on, Vic, hit him! Hit him behind the elbows! Drill that body! Come on, Vic, you got him!

The loud voice followed me as I worked the floor.

That's right, Vic, he's tired now! He's tired! Finish him off! Take him out, Vic! That's it!

Julian was another middleweight, with a dark, round face that made him look even younger than his twenty years. I discovered that his late return stemmed from a trip to the National PAL (Police Athletic League) tournament, where he'd lost a fight and missed an opportunity to make the Olympic Trials.

Well, that's over now, he said pensively. I got one more chance, though. You know what my problems was, Milt? Those body punches don't score.

They score, Milton said, if you knock the motherfuckers down.

The two men were addressing the electronic Olympic scoring system, which awarded a point for each scoring punch, unlike the traditional amateur scoring system, which scored rounds on a twenty-point "must" system (the winner of a round must be awarded twenty points; the loser, a smaller number). The Olympic system was instituted following a series of officiating scandals that culminated at Seoul in 1988. It was thought that the new system would reduce corruption among the judges. It didn't. The electronic system also tended to only award points for head punches.

I'm telling you, Julian said. That's why all those guys got their hands up.

Listen to me, Julian, Milton said. These black guys *will* go down if you hit them to the body.

Yeah, but the judges . . .

Black guys don't like getting hit. That's why they move their heads so much.

I'm a black guy, and *I* don't mind getting hit to the body.

Julian was a force, loud enough and large enough to balance Milton.

That's why you got an advantage, Milton said. You can take the body blows *and* you got good head movement.

Milton turned to me.

You see, Bob, everyone wants this [he pointed to his head], but it's small and hard to hit. I'm gonna teach you to show it to them, then take it away. Guys'll get frustrated after a while.

What weight are you going to fight at, Bob? Milton asked.

I don't know, I said, I used to fight at one thirty-two.

One thirty-two. Milton sucked on the number. Do you think you can get down to one twenty-five?

I don't know. I'm one thirty-nine now, so don't expect any miracles.

'Cause you'd be good at one twenty-five.

That started the doubts, termites gnawing my confidence to pulp. I'd fought at '32 before and won and lost. Still, in my three fights I hadn't encountered anyone any bigger than I was, or taller. I know they were out there, though, great white sharks in the ocean vastness. One-hundred-thirty-pound six-footers with incredible reach. The five-eleven Oscar De La Hoya had won a gold medal at 132 and his first professional title at 130. In one of his early fights, I watched him dice a five-foot-six-inch Jesse James Leija with his jab. Thunk, thunk, thunk, the knife plunged into meat, blood streaming down the Mexican's face while his shorter arms futilely flailed air. I remembered that Darryl had wanted me to stay at 139 when I couldn't get down to '32 four years earlier. "You're thinking about it the wrong way, Bob," he'd said, but I didn't see how thinking that guys at 139 were too big for me was in any way wrong. And now Milton wanted me to go down further.

Milton kept my doubts fresh.

What do you weigh now, Bob? he would ask on a weekly basis.

I'm not sure, I would say. I have to check.

You can make 'twenty-five, he said, no problem. You'll be walking right over guys at 'twenty-five.

I resolved to wait and see how far the protein powder took me.

———

I want you to see this, Bob, Milton said, calling me ringside.

Laura and Dave Marrero were preparing to spar. It was Dave's second day in the gym. In the 1997 Gloves finals, I had watched him display incredible bravery. He'd been matched in the novice division against a junior champion with over two hundred bouts who shouldn't have been fighting novice at all. The kid had great skills and impressive hand speed; in the first round, the fans around me were predicting a knock-out. Yet Dave didn't surrender, and although outclassed, he wore his opponent down and won most of the exchanges in the third. When the decision went against Dave, the Garden crowd booed the winner, who so clearly was an open fighter. For his courage, Dave received a tremendous ovation.

Now I watched Dave rub Albolene (a lubricant that "opens the pores" and brings sweat) on his chest and don his garbage bag and belt. There was something Native American in Dave's golden skin, in his long waist and solid frame. Drawing a headgear from the pegboard, he stopped, then wrinkled his nose and held it as far away from his body as possible, like a man holding a dead cat by the tail.

I can't wear this, he said.

Why not? Milton asked.

That black guy was wearing it.

What black guy?

That black guy yesterday. I can't wear it.

Just wear it.

I can't.

Why not?

Where's the new headgear?

That *is* the new headgear. Brand-new.

Behind Dave, Laura caught my eyes and laughed into her hand.

I can't wear this, Dave said, with final certainty.

Why not?

That black guy was wearing it.

Dave finally found a headgear that met his standard and joined Laura in the ring.

Gym etiquette called for Dave, as the heavier and more experienced boxer, to go easy on Laura. He jabbed at her and threw genial counters. Laura, however, did not throw lightly at all. The punches came like bullets from an automatic, rat-tat-tat-tat, filling the air, her gloves in motion like fists flying out of a whirlwind in an old cartoon. I was astonished at how few of these hard, accurate punches actually landed, although Dave stood directly in front of Laura. He dipped an inch to one side and a punch blazed through the space just vacated by his head. He lifted a glove and a hook detonated harmlessly on his forearm. He stepped in and out of range with a slow nonchalance, the lunch bucket attitude of a man going about his day's work.

The next day, Joey took Dave's place. Joey had won Gloves titles at '25 and '32, and he wore his trophy, a gold medallion of boxing gloves, on a gold chain around his neck. As much as I wanted anything, I wanted a pair of those for myself. While Joey wrapped his hands, he joked with Milton and Laura, his smile making the room glow. I had never seen him fight. Years earlier, at Julio's Gym, I had listened as he plotted to jump a fighter who had knocked him out. I'd sat in the locker room as Joey and the Supreme Team fighters made extravagant ambush plans that were probably just talk. We were the same height; I might have been a little broader through the shoulders, Joey thicker in the torso and legs.

You're about to see a totally different style from yesterday, Milton said.

In a way, he was right. Joey was more mobile than Dave; he broke from the waist more, bobbed, crouched and stuck his chin out, daring Laura to hit it. Yet there were as many similarities as differences between the two. Both used Milton's nonchalant style, lead hand held low. Both relied on slipping, and both threw hooks in the same unorthodox manner (Milton's style, joined with his disdainful air, demonized him in New York boxing).

Since Joey was also a lightweight, he had more freedom to hit Laura than Dave (although he was far above 132 on this day). From his crouch, he threw powerful hooks and strong lead jabs that pushed her back. Against Joey, Laura's punches lacked conviction. She moved tentatively and jerked away from his slightest feint; fear pinned her arms and sent her stumbling around the ring. In one flurry, she lost control and rushed Joey, who retreated behind a series of ones and twos. They were light punches, but Laura, panicking, practically impaled herself on them. When the ropes brushed Joey's back, he spun to one side, and

Laura, blindly reaching for him, plunged through the ropes, her head crashing against the wall. It was a strange moment: Laura the boxing diva, as awkward as a novice.

Laura righted herself and began yelling at Milton. I can't move with him when he's hitting me like this!

Joey was smiling and incredulous. Laura, I was just tapping you.

Laura glared at the audience that had gathered around the ring.

Isn't anybody else here working? she shouted.

Don't you worry about what everybody else is doing, Milton said. Worry about what you got to do.

Milton had them spar another round. Joey allowed Laura to regain control of herself. He jogged around the ring, stopping to pivot and dip. Joey, who started boxing at seven or eight, had been with Milton since age thirteen. More than half his life.

You see how he controls Laura, Milton said, just like she controls you. Nobody likes to be controlled.

The suggestion that Laura controlled me made me furious. But what could I say? He was right.

My education in Miltonia picked up where it had left off the previous December—with me in the corner, wearing the dunce cap. I could not learn how to throw his hooks, not to save my soul. Milton deployed all his teaching aids. "Circle, Bob. Like you're stirring a bowl of soup. Circle." He grabbed my right arm and pushed it around. "Stir the pot. Stir the pot." I circled and stirred. Milton handed me a three-pound weight and had me rotate until my arm burned. He stood me before the uppercut bag and had me hook it (his hooks) round after round.

Is that it, Milt? I said when I thought I finally mastered it.

He cocked his head to watch.

Nope, he said. Keep going.

The traditional hook depends on a pivot of the hip and lead foot as the punch is thrown. The elbow turns over so that the palm of the hand faces the body and the forearm parallels the floor. Thrown correctly, this punch has great power. Joe Frazier was a classic hooker, holding his gloves high, slipping inside to where he could unleash his hook;

just one could end a fight. The problem with these hooks, however, is that you have to be close to your target to use them. So you get hit a lot—like Joe Frazier. Milton wanted something different. He didn't want me to pivot and turn my elbow.

Throw it like you're pimp-slapping someone, Bob. Look.

He plucked a towel from the bench and wound it.

Now if I push the towel, he said, shoving in the motion of a traditional hook, nothing. But if I snap it— He flicked the towel like a kid at the beach.

Snap!

You hear that? Now what would you rather get hit with?

Of all the unusual elements of Milton's style, his hooks were the most outlandish. Most young fighters carry power in their dominant hand, the two hand. They use their jabs to position an opponent to receive a right cross. Milton's style reversed that order. A jabbing amateur would find the right hook of Milton's fighter sweeping over his punch.

The *Daily News* called us hook shot artists, Milton boasted. They called Dave Marrero the Happy Hooker. Amateurs aren't ready for a hook like that.

As with every magical object, Milton's hook has an apocryphal story of origin.

A girl slapped the hell out of me, Milton said. I thought, Damn. How come I didn't get away from her? I was like, "What did you hit me with?" So I tried to figure out how the hell she slapped me. Then I went to the gym and started practicing that on the guys I was training. Just to see the reaction. All of a sudden I started clocking these guys so damn easy. So then I had to figure out what was the actual motion to make them learn it. It's "stir the pot."

With the traditional hook, your elbow crooks at the hip pivot, thumb pointing in toward your chest. Turn your wrist over throwing Milton's hook, however, and you will smash the base of your thumb into your opponent's head, agony to follow. I did this innumerable times in my first months with him, my thumb inflating to a fluid-filled bubble of grief.

Yet while Milton claimed that his punch had derived from a slap, he also insisted that it was not a slap, that unmanly thing. Other trainers insisted that it was, and mocked it, even as the Supreme Team used it to render their fighters senseless. (Since the Milton hook could be thrown while leaning backward, and without cocking the shoulder, it could function as a "trick" punch, coming from a stance where the opponent wouldn't expect a hook.)

Laura swung her hook to fabulous effect, hooking off her jab, jabbing off her hook, doubling it up, fast and snappy and clean. No matter what I did, though, I couldn't find a rhythm. Trapped in my old patterns, I would turn over my hand halfway through the punch and crush the base of my thumb against hard heads. Then I would stand cursing and shaking my ruined hand as Milton intoned: Circle, Elvis, like you're swinging that microphone around. Come on. Circle. Let the arm go!

The gym was alive and hungry; Milton needed fresh meat to toss to his lions. Now, along with Laura, I had Joey to spar. Both of them requested my presence. I was good practice, an excellent utensil for flaking away summer ring rust. So I went into the ring and took more beatings. Joey's hooks chimed off my head.

We got to beat you back into shape, Mickey Blue Eyes, Milton said (my eyes are hazel).

During a rest, I insisted that Joey step up his attack (adrenaline had obviously affected my judgment).

Throw more rights, I said. Throw more combinations. Come on, Joey, put the pressure on.

Joey hesitated.

You got to push him, Milton said. He's getting ready for the Gloves.

Okay, Bob, Joey said. But if I'm gonna hit you with rights, you gotta bite down on your mouthpiece.

Each night Father Milton narrated my boxing sins while Laura and Joey flagellated me. The list was long: I left my chin exposed after throwing crosses; I fought scared or I fought wild; I threw only one punch at a time because I was generally off-balance; I was robotic; I punched "to myself," in Milton parlance.

You got to let your punches go, he said, and gesticulated. You got to reach your opponent.

I did not know what he meant by this. I *was* trying to reach them. I wanted nothing more than to reach their heads and knock them off, but whenever I extended, I threw myself off-balance.

You know who you remind me of, Bob? Milton said.

No.

Busdriver.

Busdriver?

Yeah, we call him Busdriver because he drives a bus for the city. He's about your size, Italian guy. When he came to me, he was even more handicapped than you. He couldn't even walk in a straight line. You'd put him in the ring and he'd be falling over his shoelaces. He'd be falling over the *other* guy's shoelaces. So we took him, worked with him, taught him the style. His first fight in the Gloves, he knocks the kid out. People were coming up to me afterward, saying I performed a miracle.

That's good to know, Milton, I said.

Days in the gym continued with their lessons of pain and strain. Milton had me practice his drills: one-foot hops down the hallway across a tapeline, jabbing into the air with a weight from a prone position, bouncing from foot to foot on an automobile tire. My bruised ribs were only good for a few days off from sparring. Mostly I was beaten. I won a few moral victories. As Laura knocked me around one day, I fell against the ropes, crouching. She moved in, and I hoisted a left from down around my knees. The punch split her guard and clubbed her on the point of the chin. Laura was durable, however, and this only slowed her for a moment. The next day she pointed out the bruise the punch had left on her face.

I thought it was dirt, she said, but when I tried to rub it off, it kept aching.

The presence of the bruise gave me secret pleasure, but it was small consolation in the face of so much hurt.

One afternoon I watched one of the Revolution trainers, a Thai boxer named Lamont, work the bag. Shirtless and hard, he danced around the leather heavy bag, striking it with knees, elbows and fists. Whump!

Whump! Whump! Whump! The bag jerked and cringed, the heavy thuds filling the room with sound. As he worked, he talked to Victor.

When I fight on the street [thump!], I rely on my elbows [wham!]. It's too easy to [wham! smack! bang!] fuck up your hands on someone's head. You got to use your knees too [whump!], 'cause they aren't expecting that.

Lamont was of mixed race, skin with an olive luster over trim muscle. He was ten years younger than I and strong, poised and confident. Beside him, I felt as if I were fondling the bags with fists made of soggy bread. He was the mixed-race *über*man of the future, and I was white and obsolete. My body, so solid in the world of café smokers and coffee drinkers, dissolved into a suety puddle. Beside Milton's warriors, I felt unmanned, a hermaphrodite who couldn't fight.

So, Bob, how is the style working for you? Milton asks.

I don't know.

You're getting hit less with your hands down, right?

Maybe so.

I wasn't convinced, however. Less or more, I was certainly getting hit plenty.

Let me put it this way. When you were with Darryl, you were always coming out of the ring with red T-shirts, right? And now your T-shirts are staying white, at least.

Milton looks at me.

Why don't you wait until next year, Bob? You keep coming in for the rest of the year and we'll have you sharp. You'll walk over them, no problem.

My head drops. I have heard this before. Next year is uncertain, further away than I can think. For me, there is no next year. I mutter something noncommittal and walk away.

Sundays at the gym were pleasant. On Sundays the health club closed early and most of the boxers stayed home. It was the one day of the week I didn't have to listen to Hot 97 or to the three DMX, Nas and Jay-Z discs that we maintained in endless rotation.

Milton might appear briefly.

Are you gonna be here for a while, Bob? he would say.

Sure.

All right, keep an eye on things for me.

You bet, boss. I got it under control.

One Sunday I was alone in the gym. I walked down the hall to finish my workout with calisthenics in the white room. Halfway through a set of pull-ups, a harsh voice slashed through my gerbil repetitions. What are you doing?

I turned to face a woman a few years older than I was, sausaged into spandex.

Uh, pull-ups? I said.

I've told you guys a thousand times, you're not supposed to be in here.

Although I had never met this woman in the flesh before, I knew her. I had gazed into her distended face a thousand times at the end of my hallway tapeline hops. It was her face on the magazine cover. This was the Fitness Diva.

I don't know what you're talking about, I said. You've never told me anything.

You know exactly what I'm talking about, she rasped. You people are not supposed to be here without a trainer.

The voice—hard to do it justice—acid blended with ash and gravel, trucked to 14th Street from northeastern New Jersey. She had spotted me on the monitor above her desk on the fourth floor and run up after me.

Well, I am one of Milton's trainers, I said. Although, strictly speaking, I was not. But Milton *had* told me to watch the place when he was gone.

The Fitness Diva was not mollified.

Milton can only have two other trainers, she said, and as far as I know, that's Julian and Will. You need to have one of them in here if you want to use the space.

Okay, fine, I said, I'm gone.

I walked back down the hall, enraged.

Before leaving the building, I stopped at the front desk and made peace. Seeing that I needed to be in her kingdom for the next few months, and I couldn't afford to have her as an enemy.

She's a goddamn racist, Milton said when I mentioned the encounter. It's okay for the nice white girl Stella to be running backward on their treadmill, but let Vic go in there and they start dialing nine-one-one.

Milton had also told me a story about Victor's interaction with one of the clients: So Vic's doing sit-ups on the incline bench, he said, and after he's done, some white guy wants to use the bench. So he says to Victor, "Can you wipe off the bench?" And Victor just stares at him until the guy walks away. I thought Vic was going to kill him.

Soon signs stating that no one could use the space without a trainer were posted on the white studio's walls. Since no one came to Revolution simply to use the equipment, it was hard to feel that the signs were meant for anyone except us (Stella continued to run on the treadmill without complaint).

A re you going into the Metros this year, Dave? Milton asked.

I don't know yet, Dave answered.

I want to send in the form for you, so I need you to tell me.

If I'm feeling ready, okay, but right now I don't know.

Dave seemed a little irritated by the pressure from Milton. He had been training with us but irregularly, present for a few days, then out of the gym for a week or more. On this particular day he said, "I'm not feeling too good" to the room as he came in and said that he wasn't going to spar. He appeared unhealthy, somehow, his bronze skin tinged gray. He moved slowly in his polymer warm-up suit and garbage bags: slow as he shadowboxed, slow on the rope. Later I watched him drop onto the bench and slump against the wall.

I crawled around patched with rags. All I wanted was to be lost in the shuffle, anonymous in the gym, ignored and alive. The fact that Milton said, "We need you for sparring" made it a point of honor. I was beset by a weary fearfulness, the old man's fear: fear of an all-too-foreseeable future. Bodies have a vivid memory for pain. Adding shame was the fact that I was afraid of a woman. "Nice going, tough guy," a little voice whispered. I went around the gym remarking on how strong Laura was, seeking reassurance. Everyone readily agreed with me. Laura was no ordinary woman boxer. Milton pointed this out at every opportunity. "Laura, show us your muscles," he would say, or he would point at my abs. "Bob's got a six-pack, but Laura's got a twelve-pack."

When a new fighter walked into the gym, it would be "I want you to get in there and go for a couple of rounds with Laura," or "Laura don't hit like no woman," or "You should have seen the expression on their faces when they saw Laura."

In the newly minted world of women's boxing, Laura's talent, which should have only made her a star, also tarred her as something of a freak. "Laura looks like a man," people claimed, but this was not true. Laura looked like no one I had ever seen before. She had hit the jackpot in gene pool Lotto and then conditioned herself to the highest level (the truly frightening thing was that she didn't even lift weights for all her blue-veined muscle). She was a woman of a type that had barely existed a generation before and had never existed in boxing: the woman as world-class athlete, demanding a new frame of reference. With her warm hazel eyes and her graceful manner she was certainly a woman. A woman who had cracked my ribs.

I began to duck her. Upon arriving at the gym, I might say, "Oh, I forgot my gear," usually the mouthpiece since that was unlikely to be loaned. Or I would ask Laura what time she planned to come in. If she said, "Seven," I would act dismayed.

"Oh, seven? That's really too bad. I have a meeting then. If we could only meet a few hours earlier . . ."

If she said, "Five," I would answer, "No, five is no good for me. I told my boss I'd stay late that night. That's too bad."

Or I would say I felt sick. I don't imagine I was actually fooling anyone, but it made me feel better. In boxing that sort of charade is necessary. Fighters cannot admit that they will not meet someone in the ring—no matter if that someone is fifty pounds heavier, twenty years younger or the current world champion.

On the last day I was to spar Laura before her fight, a tropical storm rampaged along the coast and flooded the city. Most businesses closed, including Revolution. No one has ever been so gratified by dangerous winds and driving rains. Three days later Laura knocked her opponent out in the second minute of the first round. This made me feel better.

You should have seen the other girl, Milton said. When she walked out of her dressing room and saw Laura in the ring, she turned around and walked the other way. We could see her arguing with her trainer. "I ain't gonna fight her." It was over before it started.

Another trainer would have been delighted. Miltonic reasoning, however, operated on a different level.

Laura didn't play it smart, he said. The fight was on TV. She could have done something with the opportunity. She had four rounds to play with this bitch and look good; instead she puts her out right away. She should have had some fun. Thanks for giving us the sparring, though.

Oh, no problem, I said.

I walk into Julian on the rope alone at the gym. He's zipped up in a polymer warm-up suit translucent with sweat. The bell rings, and Julian makes a last double swing on the rope before stopping.

Kind of dead in here, I say.

Well, you know, when Milton's not around.

Julian's mouth tightens in his dark face.

Like, I got the Metros coming up soon, but I haven't been getting any sparring. That's all right, though. I'm in shape.

Julian removes the top of his suit and the white wife beater beneath it. Because Julian's face is so boyishly padded and he always wears baggy clothes, the heft of his arms surprises me. He's not as bulky or cut as Victor, but the arms signal power. Julian takes the wife beater and begins to wring it into a bucket beside him to a steady plashing.

So have you been with Milton a long time? I ask.

Well, I was with him from about age nine to age twelve, Julian says. Then, you know, I moved around a lot, so I kind of got out of it.

So you didn't box at all.

No. I got into trouble instead.

What kind of trouble?

Drugs, that sort of thing. I was on Rikers for a while.

Oh, really?

Yeah.

He gives the wife beater a final squeeze. We look down into the bucket, a quarter filled with murky fluid. It can't all be sweat. Can't be.

A lot of water, Julian says.

Joey tried to cheer me after yet another beating.

One time you hit me with a straight left to the body, he said, and it knocked the wind out of me. I just had to stop and take it until I caught my breath.

Anasi, you hit hard with those little hands, Milton said.

So . . .

I have small hands (and small feet) for a man. Wrists and ankles — Popsicle sticks. Well into my twenties, I wore my shoes too large with the thought (the hope) that my feet would eventually "grow into them." As for the hands, however, I remained in blissful ignorance of their inadequacy until a kind girlfriend brought it to my attention.

You have such small hands, she said.

I do?

Yes, but I love them. Your hands are the most honest thing about you.

Nothing compares with the faint praise of a lover. Honest, meaning . . . ? My hands spent the next two years in my pockets. I squeezed rubber balls incessantly and dangled from pull-up bars by my fingertips. Knowledge had sullied my blissful ignorance. I remembered reading a mystery novel as a teenager that described a character with "strangler's hands." From that day forward, I'd wanted strangler's hands, murderer's hands: blunt, calloused instruments of punishment. Alas, it was not to be. My "condition" has led to expressions of surprise and ribald jokes from women who have assured me that while folk wisdom may not be true in *my* case, it generally is.

My hands may be so small that I wind up my wraps an extra pass or two, but once they are swaddled, strapped, locked in the gloves, no one can see how small they are. And they hit hard. Since I discovered they weren't going to make me a great guitar player, battering seems to be the only fate they deserve. Even though I've punched brick walls, metal doors, hard heads, my small hands have never broken.

At night I was still drinking with the writer. White wine and vodka gimlets, summer hangover into fall. One night, we were wrestling about in bed when a stray elbow struck me in the ribs. I pressed my face against the wall and gasped until the pain subsided.

At the end of October I collapsed with the flu, a two-week Niagara of vomit from my heaving guts. When I did begin dragging myself into the gym again, I felt that any progress I'd made had been erased.

· 5 ·

LAURA

The muscles, the skills, the punching power—we all agreed: Laura was no ordinary woman boxer.

After training one night, I am eating sushi with her on First Avenue near her building, home for thirty-five of her thirty-five and a half years. We get to talking about her life before boxing. In the time Laura went from toddler to woman, her Lower East Side transformed from a working-class Polish, Puerto Rican, Ukrainian neighborhood to a dreadful heroin slum to its current incarnation as bohemian theme park, streets thronged with tourists from faraway New Jersey and Japan. Born in 1964, Laura was a child of that first, ethnic Lower East Side. Her Polish-American father and Ukrainian-American mother both grew up in the neighborhood (her father in the same apartment as Laura); they met and married there; her father became a driver for the nascent UPS and her mother an office worker. They lived in an immigrant world of Polish and Ukrainian bars and diners, some still running today, Veselka, Leshko's, the KGB Bar (former headquarters of the Ukrainian Communist party), primped and made over for the tourists long after the Eastern European voices have disappeared. Laura went to neighborhood schools and played in Tompkins Square Park as it filled with debris and runaways and homeless men with blear faces, the city at the edge of collapse with summer brownouts and spiraling debt in the 1970s.

As Laura talks, she lifts decorative hunks of protein from her plate. Yuppie hamburger. I ask Laura if she was athletic as a youth, expecting yes.

No, she answers.

Not even in high school?

Not even in high school.

This surprises me. Laura tells me she did martial arts, karate, for thirteen years before she started boxing. I ask her how she got started.

I was in an abusive relationship, Laura says.

Physically abusive?

Physically abusive.

I stare as she keeps packing the sushi away. Perhaps Amazons are made, not born, but an abusive relationship? Any man who hit Laura now would be facing an extended hospital stay.

And . . . I kind of felt trapped, she says. You know, I was very young. In love. And thought, you know . . . and he was an alcoholic. I was into playing housewife and cooking and baking. My mom got married when she was very young. I guess I kind of thought that was going to happen to me. My mother was married when she was eighteen. And you know, my friends in high school were out partying and going on ski trips . . . and I had a boyfriend. I'd run home after school.

Again surprise. Seventeen is a long way from thirty-five, but Laura seems to have traveled farther than most.

The relationship wasn't a good one, Laura continues. He was an older guy. Eight years older than me? Nine years older maybe. Quite a bit of difference. He was Ukrainian. Ukrainian-American. He was a plumber, a hard worker. And I admired that. He would come home drunk, you know, and complain about this or that, knock me around a little. And then I'd wake up the next day and, you know, feel sorry for him, 'cause I would say, "Oh, it's not his fault because he's an alcoholic, he didn't know what he . . ." And then he would wake up and apologize. I guess I just wanted to take care of him. We were together three years . . . or four years. It started when I was a junior in high school. My parents were living in the same building. They were not very happy about it at all. My father would come home and start banging on the door. And you know, "What are you doing to my daughter?" They'd get into arguments. Actually, what made me leave him, he almost got into a fistfight with my father, and the four of us, me, my sisters and my mother, had to hold my father. Had to pull my father off of him. But my father didn't know he hit me. I tried to hide it. I think my mother might have known. My middle sister, Lisa, knew. And then when things really got bad, she used to stay with me. Down in the apartment. Because I didn't want to be alone with him. Finally, I got fed up, and I said, you know, "I'm not going to take this."

And so I started martial arts to kind of build myself up. And I just loved it, loved the discipline of it. Working out, sweating, it felt so great. I don't know if I broke up with him first or if I started the karate first, but it all fell along the same, you know, like, "I'm going to take care of myself." And I just got into this fitness craze. Working out, taking karate three times a day. I'd go in the morning; then I'd go to work. At lunch I'd go and take the afternoon class; then I'd go back to work, and then I'd go again in the evening. I got a black belt eventually.

Before karate, the idea of being athletic had never occurred to Laura as something she might do. Had never been presented to her, perhaps. Wasn't necessarily an option available to Polish-American girls growing up on the Lower East Side in the seventies.

Got into a little trouble with karate too because I lost too much weight, she continued. I was anorexic for a little while. I just got obsessed with body image. I think one hundred forty-seven was the most I had weighed. It must have been where I dropped down to one hundred fifteen pounds. It actually hurt for me to sit down. 'Cause, like, the bone, in my ass. Like I had no meat on me, whatsoever. I stopped getting my period. I looked like a little boy. Even my legs, *my* legs, were thin. I mean really. I'm one thirty now. So fifteen pounds lighter. Then one day I passed out. I was lying down on a couch and I got up and I blacked out. And that threw me. So I got up and I had something to eat. That scared me. That really scared me. So I started eating more, and I started putting on the weight. And then I started throwing up my food. I was bulimic, for about a year or two.

And then I think slowly I kind of got out of that stage, Laura says, and again, that was a self-esteem thing, you know. So I think I'm very disciplined, and I think I'm very strong, when I want to be. But I also think I'm self-destructive.

Laura's next step toward boxing came a decade later in a karate sparring session.

We'd do round-robin sparring, where you move to your left and you fight the next person next to you and they have different levels. So as a black belt, you know, you're supposed to control who you fight. And

I was boxing—fighting a green belt, and she got angry because . . . I don't know. I kicked her to the face, but with control. But she turned around and punched me right in the face. And what do I do? I turn around and look at my instructor, like, what am I supposed to do? And that really bothered me. You know, here I am, a black belt, and I'm getting hit in the face and suddenly I'm defenseless.

"With control" in martial arts means hitting to make contact without causing injury. Yet in a truly dangerous situation, injury will be exactly what your assailant will be trying to cause. And what will keep you from flying out of control? The same dilemma I faced with kung fu after three years confronted Laura with karate after twelve.

In 1990 Laura went to a major karate tournament in England. Unlike most styles, which rely on elaborate point systems and restricted blows, her style, oyama, allows full contact (except to the head). "Which is why I liked it," Laura says. The tournament featured two weight classes for women, divided at 140 pounds. Laura missed the lower class by 2 pounds.

I ended up fighting this woman who was about one hundred eighty pounds. And it was a full contact tournament. We had no protection on our hands . . . like bare-fist. It turned into a wrestling match. She was throwing me across the ring.

Fortunately for Laura, such brute antics count for little in karate, with its strict scoring system. In fact, Laura had the better technique and began to build a lead.

I scored a good low kick. I got a half point for it. I was just trying to stay away from her. After that happened and it looked like I was going to win, she came out and deliberately punched me in the face. She broke my nose. There was blood all over the place, and I was hysterical crying. My friend was, like, "Get up! Stop crying! Get up!"

Laura laughs and shakes her head.

And I was, like, "Stop, I'm bleeding." Hysterical. I used to go crazy when I saw blood. Especially my own blood. I just couldn't handle it.

Though the woman was disqualified, Laura, a second-degree black belt with a shelf full of trophies, had found herself undone by a single punch.

I belonged to New York Sports Club, and they had this boxing fitness class. I saw this sign for boxing, aerobic boxing, and I thought, "Oh, let me check it out." And that's how I really started boxing.

In the early nineties boxing began to gain a following outside its old ghetto walls. What differentiated this from boxing's mini surge in popularity following the success of U.S. fighters in the '76 Olympics and the first *Rocky* film was that the nineties upswing included women and white-collar men. There was aeroboxing, boxing fitness, boxerobics, the first yuppie boxing gyms, the first women amateurs, women's boxing for the first time as something more than a tank top circus.

The instructor saw me and thought I was great, and he asked me if I'd be interested in teaching. So I started teaching boxing. I went to a fitness seminar at the Hyatt or something. You paid like twenty-five dollars to get in. That's where I met Michael Olijade.

Michael Olijade, Jr., had been a middleweight contender, losing two title bouts (to Iran Barkley and Frank Tate) before a severe eye injury ended his career. One of the first boxers to recognize the money in white-collar boxing, Olijade (sporting a pirate's eye patch) designed his own "aerobox" videos and taught classes to models and lawyers at the swank Chelsea Piers sports complex.

They have a beautiful boxing setup there, a nice-size ring. I started teaching some classes with him. And I loved it. He said, "If you're really serious about this, you should join a boxing gym and quit the karate." He recommended that I go to Kingsway, which his father owned. You know, I thought, "Let me give it a shot." I think I was thirty-one. And I thought it was the last year I could fight in the Gloves, but then they raised the age. So I quit karate and I started boxing.

Laura's conviction that she could do well in the Gloves came from watching one of her students win.

When we found out she had made it to the finals in Gloves, all her boxer friends went down to see her. And she won the Gloves. I remembered her trainer from the Gloves too and thinking that he was really good-looking. And I remembered his name, Milton.

It was 1996, Milton's banner year in the Gloves. Six finalists, five titles. Like Laura, I sat in the audience at the Garden that night as Milton, banned from corners, stalked outside the ring, screaming instructions.

At Kingsway, Laura started working with Takunbo, Michael Jr.'s younger brother (himself a Golden Gloves champion and now professional). He had her wrap her hands and shadowbox in the din of blows falling, men's grunts and whistling breaths, the yammering of the speed bag. She moved under his gaze, and then the bell rang.

Okay, rest, Takunbo said.

She noticed the silence that dropped on the gym with the ringing of the bell.

Rest? Laura said.

Around her, the men who had been brutalizing the heavy bags circled aimlessly or slurped water. The once-chattering speed bag rocked slightly on its swivel.

I remember that clearly because the gym got so quiet for this one minute. And everyone stopped. I was like, "What's going on?"

I guess Takunbo wasn't really sure what I knew or how much I knew. We did, like, two rounds of shadowboxing, hit the bag for two rounds, hit the mitts for two rounds, speed bag for two rounds. He was like, "Okay, you're done." And I'm like, "That's it?"

Wanting to spar, Laura was disappointed and decided an explanation was in order.

I've been working with your brother, she said. You know, he's put me in the ring before.

Oh, okay, Takunbo said, and nodded. Let's go then.

He stepped up to the apron and held the ropes for her to enter.

Okay, he said, and bent over. Get on my shoulders.

What? Laura said.

Get on my shoulders.

Laura straddled his neck and he lifted her in the air.

Okay, he said, I want you to do five sets of sit-ups from this position.

Laura was stunned. I don't need to do sit-ups with you! she said. That's not what I wanted to do in the ring! I want to spar!

Sitting across from her in the restaurant, I laugh and Laura shakes her head.

Takunbo was what, seventeen? Sixteen, seventeen. I could have been his mother.

The comedy of the first day marked only the beginning of Laura's difficulties. The culture of boxing, transmitted orally for the most part, is extremely conservative. Female boxers are common now in the United States, with over fifteen hundred registered amateurs and three hundred pros, but for most trainers in 1996, no paradigm of a woman fighter existed.* I had never seen one before I came to New York, and even there they were all kickboxers, a sport that is more white and suburban, more accepting of women.

At Kingsway, a real boxing gym, Laura found it difficult to move forward. She sparred with two women and threw punches at some of the male fighters. In sparring, however, she encountered an unusual training tic of the burly Michael Olijade, Sr. For some reason, he would allow very few of his clients to spar outright. Instead he had them jab and block. Back and forth across the ring, jabbing and blocking, for rounds, days, weeks, months, while he trundled around the gym, giving instructions in a thick Caribbean accent: "What are you doing, man? I want you to jab-jab, block-block." Those at Kingsway who knew how to box had learned it somewhere else. It seemed that the only people allowed to move to another stage were teenage boys—that is, the people who might traditionally become fighters.

As Laura stretched one day, she noticed a new trainer, a tall, slender man with a sardonic expression scripted upon his handsome face. The trainer had brought a group of fighters with him, younger men, black and Puerto Rican. The new group made little effort to ingratiate itself with the Kingsway crowd. They whispered and laughed among themselves as they watched the other boxers.

Over the next week, Laura realized that the new trainer was watching her. Soon he found an excuse to approach her, leaning against the wall as she hit the heavy bag, giving her one of his sly, considered gazes.

So this Spanish guy came over to me and said, "You look great," or something like that. And I said, "Are you referring to my boxing or—" And he said, "Oh, you can hit. But you can't punch." And that really bothered me, you know. I got really angry. And I think he said, "Well, who are you?" Or "What's your name?" And I said, "Well, who are *you?*" And he said, "Milton." And I said, "Milton! Did you train Amy Berg?" And he said, "Yeah." So we started talking, and I thought, "If Amy Berg can go in and win the Gloves, there's no way that I can't do it."

You know, Mike and all the other trainers were coming over to me and saying, "Watch out for this guy. He's no good. You can't trust him."

---

*The first sanctioned amateur women's bout in the world took place in Sydney, Nova Scotia, on July 29, 1991.

People would say, "Oh, you know, his style is no good." And I'd get very defensive. Michael was always watching him, and finally he kicked Milton out.

Milton's flirtation with Laura may have brought him to the end of the line at Kingsway, but there were plenty of other reasons. He'd already begun preparing the midget gym on 14th in the building he supered, where he'd have to pay no rent and no trainers' fees. Laura left Kingsway soon afterward, walking the fourteen blocks and three avenues over to Milton's new gym.

With his collector's eye, Milton had found himself one of the best female prospects in the city. A women's division of the Golden Gloves was created in 1995. For the first time, women were able to earn a title men had been awarded since 1927.* The small number of female boxers made it relatively easy for women to win. Where a man might have to fight five times to reach the Gloves finals, a woman boxer could arrive there without a single bout. And Milton liked to win. Soon enough, he was bragging crazy on his new girl: She was rock-diesel; just the sight of her flexed biceps would terrify her opponents; she was going to litter the ring with corpses on her way to a victory.

To Laura, however, Milton expressed reservations. She intended to fight at 132, but at that weight she would face Melissa Salamone, sister of the former light heavyweight champion Lou Del Valle and a former kickboxer.

Milton told me that I should drop down to one twenty-five because I could not beat this girl. Being the insecure person that I was and am, hearing that gave me doubts in myself.

Do you think you can get down to one twenty-five? Milton would ask her. At one twenty-five you'll knock the shit out of everybody.

But I won't at one thirty-two?

Milton sighed in the way he sighs when confronting those who doubt the truth according to Milton LaCroix. And on it went over the weeks.

Are you under one thirty yet?

No. You still think I should get down to one twenty-five for the Gloves?

---

*Unlike the men's division, the women's did not have a novice class. It also had a new weight category—ninety-nine pounds and under.

Well, if you can make that weight, you should. You'll have an easier time.

But that girl who won last year at one twenty-five is fighting again.

Yeah, but she's not that good. You can beat her.

But you don't think I can beat Melissa Salamone at one thirty-two?

I didn't say that.

You didn't say it, but that's what you think?

Well, she's better than the girl at one twenty-five, so if you can fight the easier fight, why not do it?

So you don't think I can beat Melissa?

That's not what I'm saying.

Well, that's what I'm hearing.

Laura's first match came in the semifinals at Holy Cross Church in Brooklyn. After the weigh-in she sat in a little room with her three prospective opponents for the night, one of them being the previous year's champion. While matches in preliminary rounds are made by U.S. Boxing officials (who in theory try to match opponents by experience), in the semis, bouts are decided by lot.

I was sitting there saying, "I don't mind fighting this girl, this girl and this girl. I don't want to fight *her*." And sure enough, we pick the pills, and I get *her*. And I walk out of the room and my face was white. "I got Alicia." That's what I said to Milton. And it's before the fight, and we're, like, warming up, and I start crying. And Milton freaks out. "What the fuck are you doing?" Yelling, cursing and screaming at me. And I'm like, "I don't want to fight this girl." Hysterical crying.

An official called them to the ring and they stepped into the crowded hall. Laura's friends clustered around, shouting encouragement. She couldn't look at them, sniffling, her face red.

I lost the fight before I even went in there. I fought with people in my corner more than I fought in the ring. I was arguing with them between every round, just looking for a reason not to go out there and fight.

It was a close fight. It was a 3–2 decision. I wish I had known that, you know. And I would love to—I haven't seen this fight on tape yet. And I would love to. I came out of the ring and Bill Farrell, from the *Daily News*, asked me if my left hand was okay. And I looked at him like, "No, my hand is fine. What are you talking about?" And my friend told me afterward, he's like, "You didn't throw your left. So he thought your hand was broken." All I did was throw my jab and hook.

Milton didn't come up to me after the fight. He didn't call for the next couple of days. I think I finally called him. Afterward I keep throwing it in his face that it was his fault, he told me that I couldn't beat Melissa Salamone, and that started me off on the wrong foot. He said it was my fault because I never told him what happened in my last fight, when I got my nose broken.

Laura went on to win two Gloves titles and her first three professional fights with Milton, clashing with him all the while, even leaving him for months at a time. At thirty-six, she sees herself facing the end of her career.

Melissa Salomone is the IWBF [International Women's Boxing Federation] champ in my weight class right now. She's actually very good. And I would love to fight her. But you know, I'm getting tired of it. I run in the morning, I work all day and I go to the gym every night. It's a lot of hard work. My last birthday was a wake-up call: Where are you and what do you really want? Do you want a family, do you want to settle down, do you want to keep doing the boxing? How much longer can you do it? You know, there are a lot of young girls getting involved in the sport, and I'm jealous. I wish I was twenty-five getting involved in it. I wish I started this ten years ago because I love it, but it's a lot of discipline.

My friends tell me now that I take this too seriously. You know, "You've got to have fun!" But I like the discipline. I like that I'm good at it. So I'd like to try and push it as far as I can. You know, I worry sometimes about getting hurt. I'm like, "Why are you doing this?" But I can't let that stop me. You risk getting hurt just walking down the street too. Boxing is a big sacrifice. Sometimes I think, you know, "All right, enough of this already. I want a normal life. It's hard work." But I want to, you know, give it maybe another year. See if I can get a shot. Get a belt.

· 6 ·

HEAD SHOTS

On November 20, 1999, Stephan Johnson and Paul Vaden met in a junior middleweight bout at Donald Trump's Taj Mahal Casino in Atlantic City. The fight was on the undercard for a main event featuring heavyweights Andrew Golota and Michael Grant and televised by HBO. The winner of Johnson/Vaden would receive the minor United States Boxing Association belt and, more important, the chance to fight for a major title. Thirty-one, Johnson had retired in 1993 after suffering a detached retina and had lost the first two fights of his comeback three years later. Still, he was a durable fighter and perpetual contender who had once gone the distance against Roy Jones, Jr., while Jones was a super middleweight. Realistically, the Taj Mahal bout was his last shot at a title. In the tenth round of the fight, ahead on points, he collapsed following two light blows and was taken from the ring unconscious.*

In the following days, as Johnson lay in a coma (QUEENS PUG IN JERSEY HOSPITAL—*New York Post*), reporters learned that he had been knocked out seven months earlier in Toronto. The pattern was the same. Winning the match in the eleventh round, Johnson had fallen after a few light blows and remained dazed in his corner for the twenty-some minutes it took for an ambulance to arrive (as he sat unresponsive

---

*Trump, who watched the fight from ringside, had this to say: "I've seen a lot of fights. The Golota/Grant fight that night was murderous, but it wasn't as good as this one. I've seen fights where the fighter goes down and they help him to the dressing room and then he collapses, but I've never seen a fighter carried out of the ring like that."

on his stool, drunk fans took photos in the ring pantomiming the knockout). Following provincial law in Ontario, Johnson's boxing license was suspended for sixty days pending the results of three different brain tests. He took only one of the tests, a CAT scan that showed "slight axial bleeding," a "borderline" result that called for further testing. Meanwhile, he received permission to fight in South Carolina on August 7 from the state athletic commission. After winning a decision there, he fought and won again in Georgia on October 2, a victory that set up the Atlantic City match.

Laura and I met to spar the week after Thanksgiving. We had the room to ourselves; Milton was out of town, visiting a son and ex-wife of whom he almost never spoke. In his absence the studio remained lifeless, the boom box inert in its corner. It is common for fighters, even the most dedicated, to stay out of the gym when their trainer is away.

Did you hear what happened to Dave Marrero? Laura asked me as we warmed up.

I said I hadn't.

He called me over the weekend, she continued. He'd been having bad headaches. You know, like migraines. I knew he'd been having them. But he told me that he collapsed a few days before Thanksgiving. He just collapsed, his head was hurting him so much. And then it happened again the next day. So he went to the hospital to have all kinds of brain testing done.

You're kidding, I said.

No, they told him that the tests showed he had brain damage.

That's terrible, I said.

I had thought about brain damage in boxing without really thinking about it. Without worrying about it. "What are you, punch-drunk?" was one of Milton's favorite remarks if you did something particularly awkward or witless. I remember how ill Dave had seemed the last time he came to the gym.

Yeah. He said he'd called me because he thought it was something that might make me . . . that I might want to reconsider my career.

Yeah, I bet. What is he going to do?

He told me he has to have some more tests done.

So that's it, huh? He's finished with boxing.

If he's smart he is.

Laura and I stood in the ring with our belts, headgear, mouthpieces, caparisoned for battle, our hands enveloped in cotton and leather, nostrils and brows slathered with Vaseline. The bell rang. We looked at each other.

I feel a certain doubt about this, Laura said. She'd heard about Stephan Johnson, of course; every boxer in New York had.

I feel the same way, I said.

We laughed, tense and reluctant.

Let's just take it light, I said, and watch the shots to the head.

We began to shuffle and paw with our jabs. This once we restrained our blows, barely tapping when we reached for the head, the only sound our gloves clashing.

I'm going to bash your brains in . . . ring your bell . . . crack your skull . . . smash your face . . . split your wig . . . knock your block off . . ." It's right there in the language. In the natural world (playgrounds, schoolyards, bars) punches are inevitably directed at the head. In boxing, this inclination is known as head-hunting. "Everyone wants the head," Milton says. "So you give it to them and then take it away." He instructs you in how to expose your head, briefly, and then withdraw it as the punch comes, with your counter to follow. "Make them miss, then make them pay," goes the apothegm. In boxing, fighters must be trained *not* to throw at the head. The logic is simple: The head is small; the body offers a much larger target. Also, the damage from body punches is believed to accumulate over the course of a fight while the effect of a jarring head shot can often be shaken off in seconds. Yet most amateurs cannot aim at anything other than the moving, bobbing head, the carnival target with its grand prize promise of an instant KO. Even skilled professionals often break discipline and forget the body in their quest for the skull and its sweetmeats.

To strike at the head may be human nature, but what happens in a few rounds of sparring has little to do with natural combat. In a street fight, a punch to the head generally breaks the hand of the person who throws it (it's said that the average street fight is over in five seconds, the loser going to the doctor with a fractured nose and the winner going to the doctor with a fractured hand). Skulls are harder than hands. In the bare-knuckle era, fighters made substantial efforts to protect their hands, soaking them in brine and following special "bone-hardening" diets. In bouts, bare-knuckle fighters had to be circumspect about the velocity and force of their punches, knowing that a blow struck too hard would result in fractured metacarpals and a lost battle. Padded gloves were adopted to protect hands, not heads, the padding allowing fighters to hit harder. Even today the most common boxing injuries are to the twenty-seven small bones of the hands. Headgear, a late development in boxing, appears to protect the brain but mainly guards against facial lacerations and ruptured eardrums and does little to prevent concussions. In fact, headgear, by making a more sizable target of the head, makes it more inviting.

A few days after I sparred Laura, the usual routines had returned to our studio: hip-hop blasting, boxers in motion, Milton slouched in a director's chair. I stood ringside and watched Julian and Will stalk each other.

Hey, Milt, I asked, what happened to Dave?

Silence.

I considered asking again but did not.

The first few times I confronted Milton with direct questions and he failed to respond, I assumed that he hadn't heard me and asked again. To continued silence. His eyes fixed on some middle distance in a perfect aspect of incomprehension. So when he ignored my question about Marrero, I let it go. Maybe you weren't supposed to talk about brain injuries in the gym. But, then, where were you supposed to talk about them?

Boxers train to throw punches fast, hard and in number. Central to success is the ability to deal, and deal with, frequent and severe blows to the head. A head shot is something boxers learn to endure, even enjoy. It braces, the first jab that slips your guard and rebounds from your cheek, a jump into chill water on a summer day. A hard blow to the head can even serve as incentive. When someone catches you good, you settle into the rush of the shock and seek revenge.

In nine months of serious training, I sparred, on average, say, four days a week, five or more rounds a session. At first, the dings came often ("We got to beat you into shape"); as I became slippery, they fell in number. Estimating at least one fairly hard blow to the head per session, that figures to over 130 blows of real force (as well as dozens of minor blows*). The human brain is fragile, with a consistency akin to gelatin. Place a naked brain on a tabletop, and it will, like a Jell-O mold, collapse under its own weight.

I grew accustomed. After a while being punchy didn't seem unusual. In the wake of hard sparring, I would feel euphoria and be mildly dazed. I would meander around the gym for a few minutes, slowly returning to Earth from interstellar space. By the time I finished my workout and took a shower, the euphoria would have vanished. On the subway I'd feel tired, irritable, still a little spacey. I'd read a paragraph in a novel, then catch myself reading it again and realize I hadn't retained a word. Once home, I'd eat quickly and try to boost myself with coffee (I had a book to write). A part of the sluggishness was simple physical exhaustion.

After the more grueling sparring sessions, you come to expect a certain constellation of effects. Immediately following the very hardest punches, the world takes on a distinct yellowish tinge for several minutes. A low-level "boxing" headache accompanies the daze, often extending into the next day or two (longer when you face harder punchers). You need a nap the following afternoon, even after a full night's sleep. More subtly, the pounding seems to affect your mood. You become irritable, and your attention wanders (this may be why Mike Tyson finds everything outside the sport boring). The organism adapts; I established a routine to accommodate my headaches and shortened temper. Yet the aftereffects in no way made me want to quit. I wasn't

---

*Testing on animals suggests that light blows delivered at close intervals have a more deleterious effect than heavier blows spaced at wider intervals.

getting beaten anymore, was no longer "a punching bag with arms and legs." Everyone told me that I was getting better.

Dave Marrero possessed the essential boxing virtue of heart, and that put him at risk. I heard Milton brag on his toughness more than once: "Marrero is something else. He comes into the gym overweight, drunk, and he starts knocking guys out." A middleweight, and a short middleweight at that, he would regularly climb into the ring with heavyweights. I watched him spar endless rounds, standing erect and imperturbable. During the 1998 Golden Gloves, as he pounded his way through his bracket, he endured a nightstick drubbing from a New York cop in a brawl. At the time Dave had already won his quarterfinal match; as the semifinals approached, and his sparring intensified, Dave began to suffer terrible headaches. An X ray revealed a skull fracture (most likely a souvenir of the nightstick kiss), and Dave was forced to drop out of the tournament. On his first day back in the gym with us, Milton threw him into the ring. Out of shape, fat. "We've got to beat you back into shape" was always Milton's mantra.

In the months following Dave's disappearance, his name was never mentioned in the gym. It was as if he had—not died, because then we would have spoken of him—not died but never existed, never boxed with Milton, never gone to the Gloves finals. In this we followed Milton's lead. We were to regard what happened to Dave (and to Stephan Johnson) as nothing more than an occupational hazard.

A concussion can occur when the head strikes a hard object or spins violently. It is not a brain bruise and rarely results in bruising or swelling (you don't have to lose consciousness). Rather, the impact or shaking causes brain cells to stretch and tear. The cells short-circuit, as in a seizure, and flood the brain with chemicals; neurons are poisoned and paralyzed. The injured areas block the normal transmission and processing of the messages of the brain and deaden certain receptors linked to memory and learning. In other words, you have trouble thinking.

Doctors recommend that athletes avoid all contact from a week up to a year after a concussion. The more pleasant aftereffects include severe migraines, headaches, memory gaps, reduction in creativity, fatigue, lowered tolerance for alcohol, slowed reaction times, difficulty in concentrating and personality changes, including increased aggression, irritability, inattention and depression. All these are present in concussion sufferers without any detectable alteration in the structure of the brain, and they can last for up to a year. The brain heals slowly because the chemicals that flood injured areas also constrict arteries, making it difficult for blood to reach damaged cells. Having once suffered a concussion, a person is four times more likely to sustain a second. The brain needs a smaller impact to be concussed and requires more time to heal. After even a single concussion, some function may be permanently lost.

In recent years, top athletes like Eric Lindros (hockey) and Steve Young (football) have had their careers threatened or ended by repeated concussions. This has raised awareness of the dangers of postconcussion syndrome. Yet very little attention has been given to concussions among boxers. While boxers who are knocked out in sanctioned fights are generally suspended for at least thirty days, most boxing injuries take place during sparring. In the gym, mismatches are common. Pros slam rookies and heavyweights drub welterweights, all in the name of "work." Boxers are knocked down or out in the gym and rise to spar the next round. My own experience after being knocked cold was to awaken—out on my feet—as my trainer shoved me out of my corner for more punishment.

It remains a mystery to doctors why boxers, who regularly endure concussions, are not more affected by them. Part of the answer lies in the fact that boxers adopt behavior to buffer themselves from the most severe concussive effects. They learn to "roll with the punches"—that is, move the body and head in the same direction as the blow to diminish the jarring action. They strengthen their necks and backs and shoulders to absorb more of the force passed by the fist to the head (a good boxer's head rarely snaps back after a blow). Finally, boxers just get used to walking around dazed and irritable and unable to focus.

There is a boxing axiom that aging fighters "lose their legs." Anyone who follows boxing has seen the spectacle of a former champion, perhaps only twenty-seven or twenty-eight years old, staggered in the middle rounds of a fight by routine punches, his legs seemingly unable to carry him (this seems to have happened to the Olympic gold medalist David Reid at twenty-five). But the idea that these men have "lost their legs" is ludicrous; the muscles of a young athlete don't rot away. What these unfortunate boxers lose is the ability to endure blows to the head. This loss is a variant of the glass jaw syndrome, in which a boxer cannot recover from a hard punch, even during the rest between rounds (Tommy Hearns comes to mind). Other fighters "leave a part of themselves in the ring" after a brutal fight and never compete at the same level again. Successive concussions can also create second impact syndrome (SIS), in which rapid, massive swelling of the brain leads to coma and death. There is no way to predict who might be vulnerable. Some version of SIS killed Stephan Johnson.

On December 5, fifteen days after his collapse, Stephan Johnson died in the Atlantic City Medical Center without having regained consciousness. His death received international attention and dominated the back pages of the New York City tabloids. TRAGIC BOXER WAS A DEAD MAN WALKING (*New York Post*); BOXER DIDN'T HAVE A FIGHTING CHANCE (*USA Today*). It provided a grim finale to yet another ugly year for boxing, a year that featured the Mike Tyson circus, the infamous Holyfield/Lewis "draw"* and the indictment of four top boxing officials on racketeering charges. It also brought the usual calls for interdiction (BOXING SHOULD BE BANNED, JUST LIKE DOG FIGHTING [*Greensboro News & Record*]) and the usual promises of reform (FIGHTERS SERIOUSLY NEED HEADS EXAMINED — MAKE BRAIN SCANS MANDATORY [*New York Post*]). South Carolina enacted a series of regulations to protect fighters (Jim Knight, a spokesman for the state's overseer of boxing, explained, ". . . in the future, when a boxer comes to South Carolina, we want to do everything to ensure the boxer doesn't die"). The South Carolina board did not, however, accept any responsibility for permitting Johnson to fight

---

*Holyfield was awarded a draw in his heavyweight championship match with Lewis, even though Lewis clearly won every round, the swindle taking place before millions of people worldwide who had paid up to a month's wages to see the fight.

in the first place, even though it had been aware of his troubles in Canada.*

The death shook the little colony that is New York City boxing. Johnson had been raised in Bedford-Stuyvesant, Brooklyn, lived in Queens at the time of his last fight, and trained at Gleason's Gym under the Manhattan Bridge. Yet even the people closest to him spoke as if what had happened to him were an unavoidable accident. After the Toronto fight, Johnson told friends that he suffered dizziness, but he (and they) apparently thought little of it. "He certainly felt comfortable," said a friend, Charles Jamison. "Clearly, from our talking to Stephan, he felt he was qualified to get in the ring." Mercer Cook, the spokesperson for Johnson's family, said, "We are not blaming anyone for what happened." Nobody's fault. It was just boxing.

In retrospect, and only in retrospect, I will say that I was more affected at times than I believed. I did have memory lapses, more tip-of-the-tongue straining than was normal. I'd catch myself wandering around my apartment and realize that I'd forgotten what I was looking for. In the shower, with the shampoo bottle in my hand, I would wonder if I had just washed my hair and run my fingers through my wet scalp, looking for soapsuds. It seemed that I lacked a mental edge, that I didn't feel like myself exactly, for extended periods of time, noticing that I didn't feel like myself later only when I felt like myself again, when I had energy, when my thoughts jumped and I wasn't irritable or tired. Boxing or just normal disorder? It's hard to tell. The brain is a subtle organ and generally goes wrong in subtle ways. At first.

That winter I returned to my alma mater for an awards ceremony that an old professor had established in poetry. Prior to the event, there were the usual wine and canapés. I had a quick glass of white wine and, going for a second glass, found myself dizzy. By the time the ceremony

---

*Donald Trump had his own analysis: "Look, I went to the Wharton School for finance. If boxers went to the Wharton School, they would be at a disadvantage in boxing. Let's face it: Tough kids are the best fighters. The nicest environment they know is the ring. What would they be without boxing?" Alive, perhaps?

began, I felt stumbling drunk. Afraid that something embarrassing was about to happen, I tried to clamp down on my staggering senses. I listened to the award winners recite their verses as high winds buffeted my mind from different vectors. This was new. I didn't know what to think. The next time I had a cocktail, a few days later, it happened again.

A fighter never admits to being hurt by a well-aimed punch. He (or she) will remark upon a self-inflicted injury—broken hand, dislocated shoulder—or on an injury caused by an illegal blow—head butt, elbow gouge, fist to the groin—but never on an ill effect from a legal blow. The better the fighter, the less likely he is to admit injury. After a sparring session, a boxer might say, "That's a tough kid you got!" or "You hit pretty hard!" in a gleeful tone, as if there is nothing he enjoys more than being hit by someone who really knows how to hit (and the fighter is so high on adrenaline he really does feel a happy exhilaration). The boxer's model is the Stoa: the stiff upper lip and iron jaw. Acknowledge that someone has hurt you, and you are admitting that he can hurt you again, moving you one step closer to defeat. And if one person can defeat you, then there must be others who can as well.

To witness real damage done in the ring, then, one must observe the fighters closely, study the involuntary reactions of the body: a hiss of breath, a snapping back of the head, a doubling over or a retreat. Good fighters learn how to conceal these reactions as well, knowing that to show hurt is to offer opportunity. "You've got to learn to watch their eyes," Milton told me. "You can tell by their eyes when you've got to them, when you're in with a hurt fighter."

It is left for the trainers to judge when their fighters are in danger and need relief. However, trainers are as reluctant as fighters to say "enough." They think their fighters need the experience, have to toughen up, will shake it off, or they want to give them another chance, or they refuse to recognize the extent of the damage, or they are punishing the fighters for failure, or they are ashamed of them. Trainers aren't exactly health care workers either; all that is necessary to obtain an amateur trainer's license is a short class and a passing grade on a multiple-choice exam.

Milton takes rudimentary precautions when he oversees sparring, especially if there is large disparity in weight or experience between the fighters. He'll shout, "Watch the uppercuts," or restrict the dominant fighter to a jab and tell him to concentrate on defense. In competition, boxers are taught to return immediately to the fight after being dropped (one knee on the canvas as the referee counts over them). In sparring, however, there is no referee and no physician to step in. Sparring in New Jersey, Julian knocked down a pro and was later knocked down by him in the same round. To succeed, a boxer learns to battle while stunned or dazed. It is a necessary, thrilling part of the sport; great fighters rise and go on to win matches. In fact, surmounting this adversity is exactly what makes fighters great. For the same reason, the last person to ask whether or not a fight, or a career, should continue is a fighter. The answer will always be yes.

Whenever a boxer dies the way Stephan Johnson did, the American Medical Association howls that boxing is a barbaric deathtrap for the poor. Ring death, however, is rare, and boxing proponents inevitably counter by pointing out that the mortality rate in boxing is lower than in any number of other sports and that the AMA doesn't shout itself hoarse about outlawing NASCAR racing or downhill skiing.* Boxing opponents then argue that unlike other sports, boxing is directed toward physically incapacitating the opponent. This makes a rather weak argument, however: If the result of your driving a car faster than anyone else is injury and death, it doesn't really matter what your goal is, does it? All this op-ed wrangling, however, does not address a danger that many boxers fear more than sudden ring death, a danger that may not affect them until years after their careers have ended.

I am referring to punch-drunk syndrome or pugilistic dementia, the most horrifying impairment that can affect fighters. Everyone is familiar with the stereotype of the old boxer and his slurred speech, shaking

---

*The call to outlaw boxing is not new. The sport was actually illegal in the United States for most of the nineteenth century and the first quarter of the twentieth. Fights were held in barrooms, on barges, in fields, the venues kept secret until the last moment to deter police raids.

hands, shuffling gait and inappropriate behavior. Everyone also knows how it happened: "Too many shots to the head." Muhammad Ali, once all grace and mouth, is now a mumbling block of wood (although his doctors claim that he retains the full use of his intellectual facilities, it's hard to believe they would be saying that if Ali weren't the most adored icon in the world). Jerry Quarry, an undersize heavyweight who twice fought Ali (and every other top heavyweight of his generation), died in 1999 of syndrome-related illness. For years he barely recognized even members of his immediate family, and he spent his days in front of the television watching tapes of his old fights.* After a magnetic resonance imaging test in 1995, doctors told his brother they had never seen a brain as deteriorated as Jerry's. A shot fighter at the age of thirty-two, the former heavyweight champion Riddick Bowe was found mentally incompetent to stand trial for the kidnapping of his wife and children (IQ 79; mental development of a ten-year-old boy). Hundreds of other former boxers, champions and pugs, show signs of mental and physical derangement by early middle age.

From 9 to 25 percent of former professional boxers suffer this syndrome to some degree. Medical symptoms include ataxia (loss of muscle control), slowed movement, awkward gait, Parkinson's type syndrome (which Ali is said to have), memory loss and dementia. A British study published in 1973 examined the lives of fifteen former boxers. The grim details include anecdotes of violent behavior, an inability to remain employed, failed marriages, vagrant lifestyles and early death. With some of the boxers, visible decline had set in as early as their late twenties. Postmortem examinations of their brains revealed extreme cortical atrophy; in the most extreme cases, the brains had shrunk to chimpanzee size.†

In recent decades, the number of cases of severe pugilistic dementia has declined. In part, this is due to changes in the sport, including shorter fights, better organization, closer medical supervision, forced layoffs and retirement. The decline of boxing has also played a role. Through the first half of the century, boxing was ubiquitous in the

---

*In an unpleasant irony, Quarry was used as an example of the fighter who had escaped the ravages of punch-drunk syndrome in an essay Budd Schulberg wrote defending boxing in the early eighties.

†The loss in cerebral capacity is caused by rattling of the brain inside the skull following a blow. The friction damages surface matter, which scars and sloughs away.

United States and Britain. Every street and country fair had a boxing tent, and local boxing clubs existed in every neighborhood. Fighters could get fights easily, no questions asked. Some of the fighters in the British study mentioned above had over five hundred professional bouts and a three-hundred-bout career was not uncommon; in a week one of the British fighters fought a twelve-round bout each day, Monday to Friday, and a fifteen-rounder on Saturday. However, more sophisticated medical testing has revealed damage to fighters that would hitherto have gone unnoticed. In a study of forty-two licensed New York professional boxers, two had frankly abnormal brain scans, and another seventeen showed borderline brain atrophy. In a study of fourteen national champion boxers, both amateur and professional, six had abnormal EEGs, and nine had other physical signs of brain atrophy.*

Ringside, the boxing equipment company, publishes a pamphlet titled *Amateur Boxing Is Safe*. The booklet makes its case by noting the dangers in other sports (the cover illustration is a gruesome montage of newspaper headlines about death and injury in soccer, football, gymnastics, racing, etc.). It draws a hard line between amateur and professional boxing and notes that amateur boxing reports fewer yearly injuries than cheerleading. While I appreciate Ringside's efforts to defend my sport, the pamphlet both exaggerates and distorts (among other things, it claims amateurs are given physicals after every match, and that isn't true). It didn't agree with my experience of daily headaches and the pressure to pit myself against the best competition available, amateur or professional.

At age thirty-three, I never considered brain damage a potential danger. If the thought did occur, I assured myself that I hadn't been boxing very long and wasn't fighting top-level competition. Yet as I read through medical abstracts and monographs, I felt a chill, a spreading fear when I matched the symptom lists to my own symptoms and looked at the photographs of dissected brains of boxers, the tissue shrunken and torn. Although I doubted I was a candidate for punch-drunk syndrome, I had to accept that I had suffered a series of con-

---

*Recent studies suggest that vulnerability to pugilistic dementia may be related to a gene allele linked to increased risk for Alzheimer's; former boxers possessed of the allele showed a much higher incidence of the syndrome.

cussions. Anyone who boxes regularly will. Moreover, the longer one boxes, the greater the neurological damage. How much brain function was I willing to lose to a sport? Had I increased my chances of getting Alzheimer's? It's one thing to strain your arm throwing curves or blow out your anterior cruciate ligament on the basketball court, quite another to dim the light of your mind. I felt as if I were playing a game of Russian roulette in which I wouldn't find out for a decade if the gun had gone off; at the same time, I believed that as long as I was reading about brain damage, I couldn't get brain damage. The new knowledge would protect me.

On the Supreme Team, we did discuss brain injuries: the injuries our fists inflicted on the brains of others. At times, Milton acted as a pied piper, luring other boxers to our gym by plucking on the strings of their egos. Later we gleefully recounted the beatings the least qualified received at our hands.

You should have seen it, Bob, Milton said. This trainer was talking all kinds of shit to me at the Gloves weigh-ins, telling me that he was going to show us how a real professional fights. "Well, come on down," I said, "and bring your friends." So first I put him in with Julian, and they start going at it. First round, Julian's on him, bap-bap-bap. And he's rocked.

Milton pantomimed the distress of Julian's victim, walking with wobbly legs around the room.

So the guy says, "I wasn't ready. I need to get warm." All right, so we start again, and Julian gives him a two-three-two. And there he goes, staggering around the ring.

Again, Milton performed the wobble walk.

So this guy says, "Let's just work the body." Okay, so Julian starts ripping fours to his gut, and he's doubled over. Then he starts complaining, "This guy is a champion. He's too good." Okay, so I give him Victor. Victor, I will say, does *not* take it easy on him . . .

And so it goes. Some days I stood at ringside and winced at the terrible beatings overmatched fighters absorbed. "That's boxing," we say, and "they should have known better." In fightland, nothing signifies and satisfies as much as a knockout, even for the experts. It get us off our feet and shouting in a cluster around the television on those days we watch tape.

"Oh, Bob, you should have seen it. That motherfucker was *out*. They could have counted to a hundred."

On those rare occasions when *we* got staggered (and they were rare; Milton manufactures good fighters), the incident was addressed quickly and soberly.

I ain't gonna front, said Julian, after being knocked down by the Jersey pro. He caught me with a good left hand when I was doing something stupid. I saw it coming too, but I couldn't get out of the way.

On March 6, standing in front of the gym, I was surprised to see Dave Marrero walking toward me on 14th Street. I shook his hand and asked him how he was.

I'm good, he said in his soft voice. Is Milt around?

I told him Milton had gone to get the van, that we were going to a Gloves fight that night out on Long Island.

Who's fighting? he asked, smiling. Dave looked much better. Healthier. The gray banished from his tawny skin. His eyes were clear; his mustache and soul patch immaculately trimmed.

I just got out of work up the street, at Old Navy, and I wanted to see how Milton was doing.

He should be here any minute, I said. I told him about our luck in the tournament and asked him about his health, if he planned to box again.

Dave shook his head.

I don't know. After all I been through, the EEGs and the MRIs and this and that. I still miss it, though, you know what I mean? I get the urge to go in there. It's addictive, you know? But after all that stuff . . . I'm okay, my faculties are okay, but I got white spots on my CAT scan that shows I took some shots. You can tell by looking at the scans that I boxed. Nonboxers don't have those. But since my tests came back clean, I started working out again. Running, you know, and doing some weights. I miss boxing, but—it's bad for you. The doctors are telling me this, and some of them are huge boxing fans. It's bad for you. Even sparring. And with Milton, you spar all the time. Right?

Right, I said, both of us smiling.

And Milton will put you in with anyone. I sparred heavyweights. Milton's crazy, yo.

I shook my head in agreement.

You can't blame Milton too much, though, he said. You're the one who chooses to get in there.

We talked about Laura.

I need to give her a call. She does my taxes, and tax time is here.

Then the van drew up to the corner and Milton was leaning across the seat.

Marrero! he said. How's it going? You look a lot better.

Yeah, I been training a little. I just got out of work and I wanted to see how things were going. I hear you're headed to the fights.

Yeah, I gotta drive out to Long Island for this fucking fight. I tell you . . . all the fighters live in the city and yet we got to go out there and fight in front of a bunch of white assholes.

So I want to come down and work some corners for you.

All right. First you got to work yourself into coming to the gym; then you can work corners.

All right. Dave smiled.

Hey, Anasi, Milton said, unless you want to walk, get in.

We were late. I opened the door, climbed aboard, and we drove away.

NOVEMBER

Spirits, porter, gross feeding, stimulants, tobacco, onions, pepper, and *the sexual intercourse*, must vanish, and be no more heard of.
—Pierce Egan, *Boxiana*

Bob's getting diesel, Will said as I walked shirtless in the studio.

Bob's the Mini-Me Mike Tyson, said Milton.

It's crazy, I said, looking at my body in the wall mirror. I've lost fifteen pounds since September.

Yeah, but Bob, Milton said, crack kills.

Things had changed in a few months of boxing. Of necessity, I had left the bars, the gimlets and the wine. At thirty-three, I couldn't party and train. I didn't miss it, however. Boxing was more engaging than any cocktail hour I could remember. The writer had also departed, her blue eyes shining on someone else. Her I missed. I had started to date a dancer (not the sort of dancer in a place named Shooters, or The Foxy Lady), who also worked as a personal trainer. Thighs like artillery. Sick with health. She did not smoke, drink or use drugs. Never had. She claimed hippie parents had cured her of all such desires by encouraging them.

One-three-eight to one-two-three. Weight lost by methods both devious and direct: blender drinks, spinach, cabbage and carrot salad, red vegetable paste, protein bars, pickles, coleslaw, low-cal matter to fool my stomach into thinking it was full. Subsisting on coffee and water, I left carbohydrates alone. A primitive concept of nutrition made me believe that if I focused on protein, I could pack my stomach (protein doesn't break down into sugars the way carbohydrates do; the superfluous is eliminated). No carbs: Pasta remained in the package, and two bagels moldered at the bottom of my refrigerator for more than a month. Exercise cemented the change: two-plus hours in the gym every day and roadwork besides. My body altered, from under my skin sprouting blue river systems against the white, veins spreading up the back of my calves, across my hips, over my stomach and chest; I stared at my hollowed face in the mirror, cheekbones sharpening, eyes growing large. I could follow a single vein from my ankle through swerve and brachiation as it undulated up the length of my leg and crossed my hip. Unfamiliar pain as I sat or did sit-ups because my ass had grown too bony to take the weight. Junkie thin. Acquaintances passed me on the street without the spark of recognition.

"I didn't know it was you," they said. "You look . . . different," as if I had joined a severe cult that shaved and scarred my body. A Russian friend put it more simply: "Bob's face collapsed," he said, "but it's okay." Two months into my training I bought a scale and stepped on it. Couldn't believe it when the needle froze at 123 and had to check it again. I had never been so thin, hadn't seen that weight since freshman year in high school. The whole shape of my body was different, my face gaunt in photos, the muscles swollen in my arm. I would stand on the scale three times a day, gauging the movement, up and down.

I don't know, said the dancer's roommate. It sounds like your boyfriend has an eating disorder.

She was right. But my eating disorder was for a cause, a higher-level disorder. I loved it—the evidence of strength, the flexion of will against flesh, inscribed upon the self, shaping. Hunger was a tool to sculpt the body. I came to appreciate the extremities of hunger. I had almost never been hungry in my life, didn't know what real hunger was; as an American I hadn't felt its edge. I was stronger than hunger; I liked being thin.

Maybe I'll go down to one nineteen, I told Milton.

One nineteen! he said. If you can make one hundred nineteen, you'll fly through the Gloves.

In the center of the room, Vic swings a giant ball on a tether, the muscles of his arms and back swollen, Atlas preparing to cast away the world. I have teased out the story of his scars over the months, juicy details included. Apparently, Vic was riding the number 6 train in the Bronx with some of his boys when they saw another group wearing Crips color blue. Since the other boys were not Crips, they were not allowed to wear those colors on the number 6 train in the Bronx. An argument ensued; Vic began to punch one of the other boys, who responded by pulling a knife and slicing him. Vic in turn drew an ice pick from the big pocket of his baggy coat and began poking holes into the boy. The battle ended in arrests, and Victor spent the night handcuffed to a hospital bed. Assault charges were dropped, however, as neither group would testify against the other.

Hey, Vic, Milton shouts over the music, you think you can get down to one forty-seven for the Gloves?

Vic scowls in his strain.

If I'm 'fifty-six, he says, I'll fight 'fifty-six.

In the center of the room, Vic swings his tetherball, hurling the world into void.

I'm overweight, Will says in the dressing room, distress across his long face, I don't know what happened. This morning at home I weighed one fifty-nine, but on this scale I'm one sixty-five.

The dressing room is in a city-owned gym in the South Bronx, where I've arrived with Will, Julian and Milton for an early round of the Metropolitan Boxing Tournament, the other annual amateur tournament in New York. Although Will isn't fighting until tomorrow night, he's come up here to check the scale, with this disturbing result.

You been eating steaks, Will? You make a pit stop at McDonald's today?

No, nothing, he says, shaking his head. Oh, well, looks like it's apples until tomorrow night.

The gym occupies a cinder-block subterranean annex to a housing project. Around us, muscular '57s and '65s wander in wife beaters and briefs, trainers among them like the tiny, wrinkled nurses to a race of warriors. Except for two whites from a club upriver, the boxers are all black and Hispanic. One of the white fighters has hair everywhere on his body except for his head and looks older than I do, making me feel better. From across the room I can hear Milton, boisterous in Spanish and English, shaking hands and making sarcastic cracks.

If you want the scale, you better hurry, a U.S. Boxing official in his ice-cream uniform tells me.

No, I'm not fighting tonight. I smile and look around. I'll wait until they get a little smaller.

In fact, I won't be fighting in the Metros at all. Milton has pointedly not asked me to enter, reinforcing just how not ready I am. While I know I'm not ready, it would have been nice to be asked (it would have been horrible too, because I would have had to say yes).

Will sees me writing in my notebook.

It's gonna be tough taking notes when you're in the Gloves, he says. "Hold on a second. That was a right. That was a left."

I'll just take notes between rounds, I tell him.

Sitting in that room among the athletes, I know how sports journalists feel covering the exploits of younger, darker, higher-paid athletes through the years, fading and fattening as the athletes stay forever young. How unpleasant to try to elicit interesting copy from a twenty-five-year-old after yet another game while all he can think about is getting out to do what twenty-five-year-olds do.

I can't get a fight, Julian says as he walks over to Will and me. New York is supposed to be loaded with 'fifty-six opens, but the only people who showed up was me and one other guy.

No one wanted to fight you?

I guess not. I'm number one in the state, and he's number one in the country, so it looks like we're just going to have to meet in the finals.

It's hard to believe that Julian, who wasn't even in boxing two years ago, is now one of the top middleweights in New York. Victor, who won the Metros last year at 147, hasn't rehabbed from his injury long enough to compete.

All right, everybody, announces the official. All fighters need to weigh in again. The scale has been recalibrated. Everybody needs to get back on the scale.

As the fighters complain and shuffle, I notice Milton's absence. The room is quieter and larger; his vividness crowded us.

Will returns happier.

I knew that scale was wrong, he said. I only weigh one sixty. And I can weigh a few pounds extra 'cause it's the first round. If I go running tonight, I'll be fine. Let's go upstairs and watch the fights.

Unlike the more renowned Golden Gloves, which are managed in an uneasy alliance between U.S. Boxing and the *Daily News*, the Metros are solely the purlieu of the former. While their tradition lacks the resonance of the Gloves, the Metros carry equal weight in giving fighters access to national tournaments and the Olympic Trials. Their position in late autumn also makes them the perfect perpetual tune-up for the Gloves.

A group of white cops stands at the doors to the hall. There is that tension around them that cops always bring to these neighborhoods. As the young toughs swagger by, they draw their caps down and talk louder. The cops stiffen and grip their Sam Brownes. The hall has a high ceiling and looks as if it were once used for basketball, at center court the ring raised and painted red, white and blue.

As Will wanders with Milton, I sit beside a large young black man named Maurice who tells me he's there to watch a friend fight. When I ask him if he's a boxer, he says, no, he's not a boxer, but he's a fighter.

He explains: I live on Sugar Hill. You know where that is? We have these fights in my neighborhood. All the drug dealers up there, they put up money on their guys, and the other drug dealers put up money on *their* guys. So the two fighters get eight-ounce gloves and start going at it. The first man down loses. They have the fights right out there in the street. You know the Ma Bell building up there, takes up a whole city block? Well, the sidewalks are wide, so we can have the fights on them. Sometimes the police even block off the streets for us. They know who's putting up the money, but they're getting paid off too. Everyone in the neighborhood comes to see, and people walking by and shit. Only problem is, drug dealers don't have money now like they used to, so the fighters don't get paid like they did.

Along Maurice's bare arm winds a scar raised and segmented like a fat annelid or bullwhip. He tells me that besides the name fighters, Tyson, Bowe, Holyfield, he has never followed the sport. He says someone up at the Sugar Hill fights "saw something in him" and wanted him to start boxing, so he's come to a few shows. I mention the commitment, how a one-fall street fight is a little different from three rounds in the ring.

I know, he says. That's why I don't think I'm going to get serious about it. I'm too interested in money right now [I notice the thick gold chain around his neck] and sex [he smiles].

In a few minutes, Maurice is off his chair, screaming for his man in the ring.

C'mon, Carlos! he shouts. Flurry to the body, Carlos! He's tired! Straight to the body!

From my seat, I watch Milton in action, showboating, working the room. Somehow he gets his hands on the microphone and begins to MC, employing suave hand gestures and an entertainer's voice. Milton keeps moving, from the ring to the judges' tables to offer unsolicited advice on decisions, then over to the boxers with further notes ("You have those long-ass arms, what are you doing fighting inside all the time?").

The upcoming bout and his weight concerns have snuffed Will's glow, so he and I leave early. I sense his anticipation and dread, the fear of receiving what you so much want to give: a knockout, sent *through* the canvas, manhood taken. We emerge from the basement and into the South Bronx night. Across a small park the projects loom, three dark towers made strange by a full moon rising between them. Victor lives just a few blocks away. This neighborhood isn't the disaster area it was fifteen years ago; all the storefronts on 149th Street are tenanted and people crowd the street. Different worlds mix up here: New York in the gray tenement blocks, Latin America in the patterns and language of the awnings, in the cassettes sold from the tops of folding tables, in the merengue from store speakers and the bright, tight clothing. We pass lots packed with the corpses of buildings, no fragment left larger than a fist. Starving guard dogs behind fences whine after us, scrabble across the debris and excrement wagging for a friend. Will leads us into a bodega.

What can I eat, he asks, that won't make me any heavier?

On the 4 train downtown, Will and I are an odd couple: the young giant and the skinny white guy talking boxing (well, I think I've gotten thin, but there Will is, nine inches taller and only thirty pounds heavier). On the edge of eighteen, Will has started his first semester of college (the only Supreme Team fighter in school). Although he's spent most of his life in New York, he was born in Guyana, and there's something of the immigrant uplift to him, a separation of expectation.

Will shadowboxes on the platforms and shows me little tricks as we stand on the cars: how to hook over a right-hander's jab, how to feint and go under a counter for a body punch. There's the grace of the natural athlete to Will, fluidity, the movements so natural going one into the next. It's a grace that's rare in a boxer as big as he is, not because America lacks natural athletes over six feet but because those athletes are practicing other sports, sports with a future. Will's clowning on the subway reminds me of how young he is, a thing easy to forget when I'm staring up at him.

The week after Halloween, a new face appeared among us.

Giuseppe Peña! Milton shouted as a man with a small mustache and bright green eyes entered the room.

Bob, Milton said, I want you to meet Busdriver.

Busdriver.

You're both 'twenty-five, so you'll be good work for each other.

How many fights do you have? Busdriver asked.

A couple, I said, but I never fought in the Gloves before.

How old are you?

Thirty-three.

Me too! Giuseppe exclaimed, breaking into a smile. And you're 'twenty-five, same as me. I need the work. I haven't done nothing since the Gloves last year. I usually start coming in after Thanksgiving, but this year I decided to come back early.

You haven't worked out since last spring? I say, amazed.

No, my fight was in March, and since then nothing. Eight months. Nothing. Hey, I got three kids at home, and I'm paying child support for two more in Orlando, so I take a lot of overtime.

A smile lit his stubbled face. I don't have much time to watch television.

My fistic education continues every night as I move with Laura and Joey or let some of Milton's white-collar women punch at me while I slip and weave. In less than three months, I've sparred more rounds than in all the preceding years. Milton throws me the occasional bone of praise. After one session with Laura, he pulls off my gloves and points.

Bob, look in the mirror, he says, and tell me what you see.

I look. I see myself, tousled and sweaty.

Look at your T-shirt. No blood. Am I right?

I look down. No blood.

You're getting better. I should have put you in the Metros. It would have been good experience for you. You still gotta work on your punches, though. Every time you throw a two, you lift your shoulder. If you want to start knocking guys out, you got to turn your hand over and keep your shoulder down. Otherwise you leave yourself open.

Milton is right about the improvement. The drills and sparring have made me a better fighter. A smarter fighter: a boxer. I have rounds where I'm even with Laura, exchanges when I score well against Joey. Of course, the better I get, the harder they work to control me, the more and harder punches they throw (to be in control in the ring means you are safe).

Am I so perfect? Laura interjects.

What? Milton turns toward her. Laura removes her headgear and her hair stands in blond spikes.

Well, you just came over here and told him what to do, but you never say anything to me. So, am I so perfect?

Kielczewski, I do say stuff to you. The problem is, you don't listen.

I always listen.

Well, how about when I was trying to tell you to throw a three-four, and you went over and got the water bottle from Julian. Is Julian your trainer?

At least Julian talks to me.

I was talking to you but you were listening to Julian.

Hey, you guys, I say, and make a joke, which is ignored. I have the feeling that I am standing beside something old and intractable, a struggle my amelioratory words cannot touch.

Every night between midnight and one I would put on running shoes and go out to do roadwork. Midnight is not the customary hour for roadwork. "It's better if you go in the morning, Bawb," my old trainer, Darryl, told me, but roadwork was impossible in the morning for me, the air viscous as mud, clutching my arms and legs as I churned along. If I told myself, "Oh, fuck it, I'll go running in the morning," experience said I would be lying. So, better to run at night than not at all (and Darryl had never said *why* it was better). I liked night runs for other reasons. I drank much coffee after dark and running helped adulterate the caffeine in my system so I could sleep. Running also quelled my appetite: no midnight snacks when I was marking laps. More important, impending roadwork kept me out of the bars, running with wine sloshing in the gut being even more unpleasant than running in the mornings. Finally, after midnight the streets and parks were relatively quiet, and quiet time was precious in a city of eight million plus.

North Williamsburg was a most convivial neighborhood; in the four blocks from my apartment to the park, I passed five bars and three restaurants. Drunk, merry people steamed the glass in those big rooms or bumbled in the streets. Occasionally a local wit would shout the *Rocky* theme at my heels. The nearest park was a Robert Moses creation on several dozen acres between Williamsburg and Greenpoint. It was a disciplined place, with ordered rows of trees and regulated paths. There were tennis and handball courts, baseball fields and a track surrounding a sodless football field. Across from the track, an abandoned outdoor swimming pool lay within hulking walls and sentry towers of red brick festooned with graffiti. A chain-link fence topped with razor wire ran around the outside of the wall. The pool was an archaeological wonder, airfield enormous with diving platforms and sculpted lagoons. Its pale blue interior was contoured with cracks and mosaic rubble from deep end to shallow. Weeds and gray bushes proliferated between the fence and the wall.

The park served as a crossway, a liminal zone between the neighboring ethnicities. Mexican and Dominican families Sunday-picnicked in the grass and watched soccer leagues play on the former football field; Polish marriages were launched in tuxedos and lace, complete with accordion polkas; pregnant women pushed baby carriages; men grunted in their reps in the exercise yard; bicycles, babies, lovers, joggers and the doddering old circled the track, a promenade turning on a loop. With darkness, crew-cut Polish teens dragged in the bordering streets and brawled in the playground. In marijuana clouds Mexican kids listened to metal and Puerto Rican boys from the Southside walked with arms around pale Polish girls who spoke city jive and their own Slavic tongue.

I ran in near silence, the only sounds faraway cars, my footfalls and the jounce of glass on steel as homeless men with shopping carts scoured bottles from trash barrels, squeaking wheels and the musical clash of the bottles. The later I ran the quieter it was, although in the warm months the handball games went on forever. At night it was safer than you might imagine; people stepped out of my way, warned their friends, "Watch out, this guy is running." But sometimes when fifteen teenage boys stalked by, I'd feel a helpless chill. For the most part, people barely noticed me, isolated in my purpose, not to be disturbed.

Pre-Milton, I had run on the same track three nights a week, three and a half miles each time (twelve laps). Roadwork for boxing required a little more. I pushed my nightly laps up to fourteen and began sprinting on the straightaways, one-quarter of every mile. The inspiration for sprints came courtesy of Evander Holyfield, who executed them as a part of his regimen. "A boxer isn't training for a marathon," he said. Far from it. The rounds rage like a vacuum storm, sucking the oxygen from your lungs, from your corpuscles and cells. Very often when fighters collapse late in fights, they do so less from the effect of punches (which grow weaker with every round) than from absolute physical exhaustion. There is nothing worse than being tired in the ring. "A tired fighter is a scared fighter," a truism proclaims. I was an old fighter; at least I could be a well-conditioned one.

Go, Elvis! Milton would shout when I sparred. People are gonna think you're this white Elvis impersonator. Afterward they're gonna say, "What was up with that?" And you'll tell 'em, "It's a black thing."

Although being "Elvis" did not please me, I soon learned that I was not the only soul in the gym to wear a Milton-designated nickname. There were Monica Lewinsky and Gloria Estefan ("Gloria," Milton said, in full fantasy mode, "I got a plan. We'll all go into some top-class restaurant wearing dark sunglasses and say, 'Hey, we want a table for Gloria. Table for Gloria.' We'll be your bodyguards. People'll be bugging out"). There was the Professor (a graduate student in anthropology), Big Mama, aka Mama Cass, and Spiderman (for a web tattoo on his upper arm). Born Crazy was a temperamental heavyweight whom Milton also referred to as Born Stupid, when Born did something that displeased him. Milton was the jester uncle everyone suffers in his childhood, an inexhaustible storehouse of bad jokes. Besides being Elvis and Mickey Blue Eyes, I heard Bob and Weave and, if I did something well, White Lightning.

C'mon, Bob, Milton would yell as I sparred, weave! Weave, Bob, weave!

On a monitor at the front desk, Joey and I are watching tape of his 1996 loss in the Gloves finals. At 132 pounds, he's fighting a Long Island kid who has a braided tail of hair dangling from the back of his headgear. Joey deploys his usual cute tactics—slipping, spinning, pulling back from a jab and countering with a hook—but his opponent is awed by none of it. He forges ahead, punching, punching, punching, his jab a torch in Joey's reddening face. "That's Rich Mantovani. He reminds me of you, Bob." I take the compliment with glee, although Joey probably only means we're both white and short. The tape draws an audience and questions. Joey looks up, abashed.

No one wants to see me getting my ass kicked, he says, smiling his golden smile, and pokes the fast-forward button to another fight of the same night. It's the middleweight finals, and a wide-bodied Puerto

Rican is efficiently dismantling an opponent who looks as if he's about to cry.

That's my cousin Efrain, Joey says, happily. All through the tournament that kid was talking shit about how he was going to beat Efrain's ass. I didn't say nothing. And Efrain almost knocked him out.

Joey's smile draws you in, welcomes, puts you at ease. I can never get him to sit down and talk about himself, but I've learned that he was raised and still lives in the projects on Avenue D on the Lower East Side, that he's a high school dropout, that his immediate family has been devastated by AIDS. Sometimes on the weekends, Joey brings one or both of his young sons to the gym. The boys dash around or swipe at the heavy bags that dangle inches above their heads. In minutes of rest, Joey holds up his gloves for his older son to hit. The boy can't be more than five or six but he already throws swift and liquid combinations.

Even when we stayed in our room, the Supreme Team generated conflicts at Revolution. Certain of the trainers felt defrauded because they had been promised full access to the boxing studio but found the atmosphere made their clients uncomfortable. Not because Milton's fighters were hostile or unpleasant to the clients (they weren't, usually), but because the feel of an operating boxing gym was very different from that of a fitness club. The spandex crowd would stand at the doorway as vulgar men brawled and shouted, What's my name? What's my name?

I'm the champ! I'm the champ!

Is that all you got? I'm just playing with you, boy!

Bring it on!

The boasts and shouting were a part of the sport, as visiting teams tried to psych themselves up in hostile territory. The contact was hard; the occasional blood and knockdowns were real. It was an intrusion of street into the sprung floors and padded seats of white-collar privilege.

As it happened, the Revolution trainers resembled the fighters more than their clients—that is, they were young, working class, ethnic. The expansion of the health and fitness market in the 1980s had presented new opportunities, and the city kids had come running. Many of these youths had learned to "code shift" and navigate the customs of the white, moneyed world. Lamont, the Muay-Thai kickboxer, lived in the same South Bronx neighborhood as Victor and had known him since childhood (he referred to Vic as Dogface when Vic was out of the room). Around the boxers, Lamont's speech was the customary profane braggadocio about screwing, fighting and getting into trouble, but with his clients (most of them white women) he became charming, seductive, playful, nearly effeminate in manner. Lamont could switch as his friend Victor could or would not. Lamont could thereby make money.

And there was money to be made in personal training (although not, it seemed, at Revolution). A successful trainer could bill at sixty to seventy dollars an hour or more. In fitness, trainers were less handicapped by substandard schooling; the culture of sport is strong, and many of the trainers had received their higher educations in weight rooms or dojos. However, the market quickly became saturated (even as it fragmented into hundreds of disciplines, from Pilates to Tai Bo), and prospective trainers found themselves hyperexploited. The big franchise gyms had new trainers work the floor as "advisers" at McDonald-land wages. The gyms told these advisers to push "private lessons" on the clients, which would earn them commissions and a chance to escape from wandering the floor. Most of the trainers ended up working long hours as salespeople without ever developing lists of private clients. Ultimately, the only trainers who did flourish had either the money to tough out the lean months or a rare combination of connections, luck and charm.

At Revolution, the owners relied on young trainers—nineteen, twenty, twenty-one years old—to teach most of the classes, paying them four dollars per student (classes often drew three students, or two or none). "Is that all they pay you?" Milton asked after one of the trainers mentioned what she earned. "That shit's worse than *Roots*." Revolution also seized forty-five of the sixty dollars per hour charged for private lessons. When the young trainers complained, the Fitness Diva told them to be patient, said they were gaining valuable experience, promised that the clients would come. I would see them in the gym, killing the hours between one underattended class and the next, young and hopeful and waiting.

Julian, Will and Victor are sparring, round-robin, two rounds in, two out. The work is quiet, with none of the boasting that comes with outsiders, just heavy breathing, the concussive thud of blows and Milton's dry commentary: "More than one punch, Victor." "Don't wait on him." "Two-five. Two-five."

I've come to know our middleweights. Victor often seems distracted. Not glaringly so, just a little distant, less than focused on his strategy. In the ring he appears to be marking time instead of making time. Yet no matter who he is in with, he never complains, never trash-talks, just stands there, skull shaved and shirtless with the silent boast of his scar. Will at times is also passive. He stands back and measures with the jab—paw, paw, paw—waiting for his chance to flash that plastic man left hand. But passive, letting lesser opponents push him against the ropes. And Julian. Julian . . .

Physically, Julian is the least prepossessing of the three, lacking Victor's bulk through shoulders and chest and Will's skyscraping height. Yet in the ring Julian has the most . . . presence. A good athlete, yes, but it's more than that. Focused, intense, yet loose as he weaves forward, his mouthpiece shoving out his lower lip so that it juts bright pink against his skin. Of all the boxers, Julian shows the most creativity. He switches effortlessly from offense to defense, "throws punches in bunches," takes punishment well, doesn't become discouraged. Outside the ring Julian is quiet much of the time so that my first impression of him has changed.

After the sparring, he settles on the bench and picks up the *New York Post*. He begins reading aloud the cover article about the vicious beating of a tourist by a homeless man.*

The way people look at this guy, Julian says, homeless, no job, on crack. And you got this nice successful white girl from Kansas. Well, there's Mr. Homeless. Of course he looks familiar. Oh, he confessed? Guys will admit to anything. Man, I had cops pounding my head on a table in an interrogation room for twenty-four hours. Another con turned him in? Shit, those cons will say anything. Well, he's better off in prison anyway. Three hots and a cot.

---

*Although the beating led to a major police crackdown on the homeless, it was later discovered that the attacker was not homeless at all.

After Julian leaves to shower, I turn to Milton.

So, Milton, I say, what kind of trouble did Julian get into?

Oh, Julian, Milton says, Julian just killed somebody.

After our sparring, Laura stands in the ring with me, and we run drills. I'm still having problems with my hooks, and we play pitch and catch until I finally begin to endow them with some snap. Milton, the virtuoso, has little patience for drill; the best I can hope for is a round or two of pad work, a few fine adjustments, a gnomic utterance and job well done.

Why don't you guys take this next door? Milton says. It's as empty as my wallet over there. All the space you could ever want.

He wants to see contact, so Laura and I surrender the ring to the next contestants and take ourselves to the adjoining studio. Laura works with me on details: hooking off jabs, throwing flurries, blocking, then punching with the same hand. It's calibration I've never received from any of my trainers. In my years of boxing I never had a sparring partner whom I could work with regularly and trust.

You never met Rudy, Laura says, Dave Marrero's older brother. He won the Gloves with Milton. He used to go into the gym with me and work for hours. All the little things. It really made a difference when I won my titles.

In the evenings Vernon often came to the gym and sat in the director's chair or on the bench. Who was Vernon? Vernon was a rounding middle-aged black man with the gruff bass tones of a trial lawyer or a singer of midnight soul. Languid from happy hour, he sprawled and watched the action. Milton's gym as spectator sport. Who was Vernon? Vernon worked days for a company that rented lighting for commercial shoots and moonlighted as an events electrician. Who was Vernon? Vernon was Sancho Panza to Milton's Don, Robin, Tonto—the sidekick, second man. Vernon and Milton operated a partnership of sorts in Milton's cleaning business and worked event security together. They made a dangerous combination. Julian shook his head over one of their hustles.

We may be the Supreme Team, he said, but when we're not around, those two are the Scheme Team.

Vernon was a window into Milton's past, the flash Milton of the seventies with the big Afro and mack-daddy vines.

I worked in the music business. I hung out with the Temptations and Berry Gordy, all those guys, Vernon said. And Milton worked in the music business too. We were . . . rivals, I suppose you could say, working for different promoters around Harlem. Then we started hanging out.

So you two got to be pretty good friends?

Well, let me put it this way, I arranged Milton's whole wedding. Milton was a completely different person in those days. A completely different person. He wasn't into boxing at all. His thing was cars. He always had the hottest sports car. You'd be somewhere, at some music event, and Milton would come cruising up in a flash car. He had this Stingray Corvette that was in a car show and everything. I'll never forget the time . . . one day, I'm walking down the street, this was many years ago, and a car starts talking to me, "Please stand back from the vehicle, please stand back." It was the first car alarm I ever heard, and I thought immediately, "This has to be Milton's." Sure enough, Milton comes walking out into the street a few seconds later. That was funny, man. But he's a totally different person now.

Busdriver wore outsize silk shorts over his skinny legs, red and green shorts, colors of the Italian flag. Spectacular shorts, Tyson patch on the front, Italian flag on one side and the names Giovanni and Giuseppe sewn one to each leg.

Why do you have those names there? I asked him.

Giovanni and Giuseppe, he said, those are my two oldest sons. I haven't seen them since their mother, my first wife, took them to Florida six years ago. She won't let them visit me. Can you believe that? Six years.

Giuseppe shook his head (how many men born in the United States are named Giuseppe?).

And I'm still paying child support every week.

Although he had been in the gym for almost a month, we had not yet sparred. At first he needed a few weeks to get ready, then a crisis.

What's really bothering me, he said, I got this kidney stone.

He had tried to work through pain, sparring Joey, but every body blow left him gasping.

When I'm driving the bus, Giuseppe said, it feels like someone's kicking me in the back all day. The doctor says I can't spar until I pass it. I've heard about that, it's supposed to be . . . I mean you feel it. Agonizingly painful. It's hereditary, you know. That means you get it from your family. I know you're not a doctor but . . . maybe you can give me some advice.

I confessed my ignorance. We agreed to spar as soon as he was feeling better.

On my way out of Revolution one night, I met Laura in the stairwell. It was her birthday, thirty-five—"and can you believe it?" We shook our heads. I congratulated her and asked her why she was training on her birthday.

Oh, I'm not training, she said. I'm picking up my stuff to bring to Gleason's. My manager is coming up from Pennsylvania to watch me work. Do you want to come over there and spar?

I don't know if my hand is ready yet, I said (I had reinjured my right thumb the week before). I wish they would let us use the other studio so I could do some weight work because I can't really hit the bags. Milton should hire an assistant, so we can train in there. But that would mean he'd have to pay someone, and I don't see that happening.

Yeah, because Milton's such a cheap bastard, she said with disgust on her face.

I remembered their argument of a few weeks earlier, but her vehemence surprised me.

You know, Bob, if you weren't here to work with, I might not come in at all. It's so dead in here it's not worth my while. Milton sits on the bench eating Cheez Doodles. Half the time he's asleep. He never says anything to me anymore. What's the point of my coming here? I can hit the bags and jump rope anywhere. You saw the argument we had.

It wasn't always like this?

No. My new manager doesn't like Milton, and ever since they started disagreeing Milton's been weird with me. I think it has something to do with that. Milton feels angry or left out or something. I don't understand. He should be happy. He's the one that got me to turn pro. I don't know, Bob, I'm really thinking about leaving for good. Besides you, there's no one for me to work with here. When I spar Joey and he starts hitting me with those hooks to the head . . . I go home every night with a headache. What is that? What have I learned?

Yeah, sometimes I think Milton spars his guys too much.

And everyone has the same style. Milton tries to train everybody the same way. It doesn't matter what they're like naturally. And he's so arrogant about it. He doesn't respect any other trainers. To Milton, everyone else is a bum.

Well, maybe Milton has to get used to handling pros.

I don't think he'll ever be ready to train pros, Laura said. He's a great amateur trainer, but I don't know if he has what it takes to go to the next level. Joey lost his first three professional fights.

Joey lost his first three pro fights? I said, astonished. You're kidding?

No, Laura said, body shots. Don't say anything to anyone about it. Joey didn't want to make a big deal about turning pro. He's really sensitive. I think it affected him up here [she tapped her head]. My manager—my manager was going to get Joey a fight where Joey would get beat. Because he hates Milton. I asked him to get Joey a fight, and he said, "Yeah, I'll get him a fight, all right."

How old is Joey? I asked.

He's twenty-seven now, I think.

Twenty-seven? I thought he was younger.

I'd always believed him to be twenty-three or twenty-four. Twenty-seven years old and an 0–3 record. Joey had been one of the top amateurs in the city. I wondered how he'd gone wrong.

No. And he doesn't get good work here either. Milton just throws him in with the girls and has them hit him. They don't hit like guys. I just don't think Milton has the mentality to deal with pros.

You sound pretty sure about leaving.

My manager wants me to leave. He wants me to go down to Pennsylvania every weekend. I don't know; I haven't really made up my mind yet.

I told her she shouldn't worry about it on her birthday.

When I asked Milton why I hadn't seen Victor in the gym, he told me that Vic hurt his leg. A few days later I walked in to see Vic warming up.

Hey, Victor, I said, you were out for a while.

Yeah, I injured my leg.

He pointed to his Achilles tendon.

Still bothering you?

No, he said, it's better now.

After three months of training together, this was our longest conversation.

At Metro Finals in Brownsville, I await Julian's match. To one side of me Will sits eating a candy bar and smiling. A few days earlier he had won the Metros in the 156 Novice Class, an excellent accomplishment for a seventeen-year-old who has been boxing for nine months. In the weeks leading up to the finals, Will was tense and gloomy in the gym, but victory has relaxed his tongue into its old wisecracking ways.

I'm tired of eating like an Ethiopian, he says. For the Gloves, I'm going up to 'sixty-five.

On my other side is Stella, ranked number three among American women at 125 pounds. Looking at her, you would have difficulty believing this. Her freckled pale arms in her sleeveless top aren't particularly muscular, and her red hair drawn back in a ponytail makes her seem even more slight and girlish (she is in her mid-twenties). Soon, however, Stella and I will spar regularly, and I will discover exactly why she is ranked number three in the country.

Have you seen Milton? I ask Stella. Julian wants him to wrap his hands.

I had just left Julian in the almost empty dressing room, a contrast with this bustling, bright hall, loud beats buzzing from taxed speakers.

That's just like Milton, Stella says. He always has to be everywhere at once . . . except with his fighter. But what other trainer is there?

Stella has also won the Metros, although, unlike Will, without a fight. A week earlier Laura had met Stella's opponent and bragged of Stella's prowess. Minutes before the weigh-in the woman dropped out ("Why can't Laura just keep out of something that doesn't have nothing to do with her?" Milton grumbled after the walkover).

I find my trainer near the judges' table at ringside. He has nominated himself MC for the evening's events and is running a sound check on the microphone.

Milton, I say, trying to gain his attention, Julian wants—

Milton ignores me to greet an overweight Puerto Rican in a suit.

Hey, Milton says, pumping the man's hand, you look sharper than a mosquito wearing a white tuxedo . . . chasing a cockroach with a can of Black Flag.

Julian did not have a single bout on his way to the Metro Finals. In a city filled with 156 open-class fighters, no one wanted to face the state champion or his nationally ranked opponent. For the previous month Julian had talked of the bout and how a victory would open his way to the Olympic Trials. He trained hard, preparing for what should have been an epic battle between two styles and two champions, each hoping to use this to leap all the way to Sydney. It should have been something.

It wasn't. Neither man looked anything like a top boxer. They flinched, they held, and when they did punch, they waited until they were so close together that the blows deflected harmlessly. Julian received several warnings for ducking. It was a case of respect and caution edging into fear. His opponent won a decision.

After the bout, Julian kept asking, I could have had it, right? It was that close, right?

Who cares? Milton said. You should have knocked him around the ring. You got in there, and you didn't do anything that you were supposed to do.

All the next day in the gym Milton complained. I can't believe we went all the way out there for that shit.

When Laura and I sparred at Revolution two weeks after her birthday, Milton would not speak to her. Every time she addressed him, he performed his most frustrating trick, staring blankly into the middle distance. By this time she had clearly switched her allegiance to Gleason's and her former trainer there. Drawn by the promise of a fight and his own frustrations with Milton, Joey accompanied her.

I don't mind coming over there and working with you, Laura said, if Milton doesn't mind.

Milton did mind, however. He would not take her phone calls (recognizing her work number when it came up on his cell), and when she called him from an unfamiliar line, he hung up.

· 8 ·

BAYWATCH

It happened like this: I walked into our studio one day to find a new trainer, a young black man, handsome and fit. In the ring he was directing a Barbie-pretty blonde, all Los Angeles long and smooth and tan, with an impressive chest. The trainer had once fought for Milton. "I tried to help him," Milton later said, "but he went into Cus D'Amato's camp and started using that Tyson style, you know, hands up, peek-aboo. You can't really work with a guy moving between styles like that." It was the D'Amato style that the man attempted to communicate to the blonde (we'll call her Baywatch). Within a few minutes we all realized that the trainer was incompetent. You felt it, and felt that everyone else felt it, a flash through the room. He lectured, he stood stock-still and she stood before him absorbing the gibberish, boxing philosophy 101 from a turgid adjunct. She gazed up at him with unblinking eyes of pacific blue. Every swing of arm, every shift of leg was bordered and bookended and buried in words. We laughed behind our hands.

Baywatch was an actress, in New York to play the lead in a boxing film. It was just a matter of time before she met Milton. I can only guess at the reasons that brought her trainer to flaunt his prize before us, but his fish would soon begin to wriggle away. Whoever he was, he had brought his student to the wrong gym.

By the mid-1990s, every high-power health club *had* to offer classes in boxing to keep pace in the locker room arms race. The requisite heavy bags and rings were installed, making those gyms more . . . gym-like. Unfortunately, the bodybuilders and aerobics instructors didn't know how to use this equipment: Beefy arms swung awkwardly; wrists were damaged, nails broken. So, for the first time since the antiracketeering act stifled the mob and shrank the job market for enforcers, boxers found themselves in demand.* Trainers (and their fighters) migrated away from the few remaining outer borough clubs into Manhattan, where the streets are paved with dead presidents. To these high-rent locales, boxers brought a hint of the street, and while a bit of street serves as a stimulant, an aphrodisiac even, too much of it frightened the suits who exercised there. After all, boxers were indistinguishable from the people who scared them on the subway; they had the same rough voices and dark skins. A cry went up from the yuppie gyms: WANTED: BOXERS WHO CAN TALK TO WHITE PEOPLE.

Enter Milton, who, for all his abrasive arrogance, had charm. He had MC'd parties and events, managed musicians, booked shows and could speak American Standard. Milton hadn't gotten into amateur boxing to make money; directing the Boys' Club program on the Lower East Side was no ticket to the Fortune 500. "I lost everything over boxing," Milton said. "I lost the wife, the kid, my house, the whole nine yards. So I decided I might as well stick with it." He wasn't Nostradamus enough to foresee that within a few years, boxing would become a fitness flavor of the month.

By the time Milton moved to 12th Street, however, a few pioneer white-collar types were creeping down to that subbasement and paying whatever Julio could squeeze them for to learn nothing: corporate VPs who'd boxed thirty years before in their army tours, an art-dealing couple in search of a new thrill, women wanting to melt flab off their arms. Bounced from 12th Street, Milton went to Brooklyn, to Kingsway, to his place on 14th. With his business cards and sales pitch, Milton ran a good game. "Come in and see what we're about," he'd said. "The first lesson is free. We can talk about money later."

Why don't you get a place out in Williamsburg? I asked him once. There are big loft spaces; rent is low.

Milton gave me the look. Who's going to come out to Brooklyn to train?

He had a point. I knew yuppies in Manhattan who had lived there

---

*The one other market that has opened to boxers in recent years is modeling.

for a decade and never been to Brooklyn, who didn't even know it was on Long Island. Milton might not have started in boxing for the money, but he'd developed a taste for the white-collar bread, pan dulce. No matter how much personal charm he had, they weren't going to follow him to a Brooklyn ghetto to box.

In 1999 at least a dozen boxing films were released or in production, and a boxing documentary made in New York was nominated for an Academy Award. (Milton groused about the documentary. Footage of him shot by the filmmakers did not make the final cut although [because?] one of Milton's fighters had twice defeated one of the film's principals in a Gloves final. "She was our very own punching bag with arms and legs, Bob," Milton said. "They should have shown us beating that girl's ass.")

Within two days Baywatch was consulting Milton on the finer points of boxing, and by the end of the week she had jumped to him full-time. A movie had to be made; boxing skills needed to be acquired; there was no time for sentiment. The other trainer simply vanished. We all saw it coming.

Milton became both Baywatch's personal adviser and something of a consultant on the film, which was being shot in a Westchester township a short drive from the city. With his new authority, Milton leveraged his fighters and friends into extra roles and bit parts in the film (some of them speaking parts, which paid impressive day rates). The production was looking for boxers? Milton knew plenty of boxers. They needed equipment? He could help them with that also. His strategy was to rapidly make himself irreplaceable, the man the production could not live without.

I'm not even the main guy there, Milton said. They got this Spanish kickboxer, and he's asking *me* what to do.

I hope you're not telling him, one of his fighters said.

No chance. Whenever he asks me something, I just sit back in my chair and say [he shrugs], "I don't know. You got me."

Baywatch accompanied the Supreme Team to boxing shows (she was "finding the character"). Her presence among us impressed the little world of amateur boxing. At a show in Yonkers, her name was announced over the loudspeaker, whereupon she stood and saluted the crowd to hoots and cheers. Boxing officials fawned upon her like little boys before a queen. She wore a floppy felt hat, jeans and boots—the queen on holiday. Men stood in line to have their picture taken with their arms around smiling her. I was astounded. This woman wasn't Nelson Mandela or Mother Teresa. She wasn't even Marilyn Monroe. She was a B-level actress whose career highlights included a *Playboy* centerfold and something called *Bordello of Blood*. Yet she performed with a perfect air of noblesse oblige, throwing smiles and brushing glances with her admirers.

Milton played it cool, leaning back in his seat or nonchalantly working the room. He must have enjoyed the reflected prestige, but he knew the world of celebrities and wasn't overawed. Even so, he saw an opportunity. No one became rich training amateurs, and it would certainly be beneficial if he became known in Hollywood as the Boxing Guy.

Milton's dalliance with Baywatch created an agitation of a different sort in the community of the gym. One of the woman boxers, whom I barely knew, told me she was leaving Supreme over her.

It was crazy, Milton said. She started crying, saying I was stupid to be wasting so much time on this actress, that I was abandoning you guys for her and that she was going to go back to California after the film.

Milton shook his head. Julian nodded sagely over the narration.

She's a young girl, right? Twenty-three or something? [Julian meant the woman boxer.]

Yeah, twenty-four, twenty-five, Milton said.

Well, you're an OG [original gangsta] and she's a young girl and she doesn't understand where you're at.

Hey, Milt, another fighter asked, is that actress's chest real?

Yeah, Milton said, it's real fake.

His new responsibilities altered the flow of gym life. Three or four days a week he traveled to the set, and when Baywatch came to our studio, his focus contracted to her. Once one of the fighters asked me,

"Bob, don't you think Milton should be getting paid for his work on this film?" I said, "I think he is getting paid, and pretty well," watching a smirk cross Milton's face as we spoke, a smirk that said we would never know.

Yet the work was not easy; Baywatch strained even Milton's training expertise. Although remarkably fit, she was bodybuilder stiff. Even drilling scrupulously, she barely progressed from week to week. When Milton put me in the ring with her, it felt as if I were being belabored with sofa cushions. I couldn't believe she was about to star in a boxing film. Apparently, auditions hadn't required any type of martial exhibition. The fight scenes were sure to be highly stylized or use good stunt doubles (in this straight-to-video production she plays a jilted ring card girl who finds her true calling as a fighter. Caveat emptor). On the other hand, I admired how zealously Baywatch worked to protect her greatest professional asset. She spent hours every day on the treadmill and with free weights, taking nothing for granted.

I'm afraid of losing my ass, she remarked one afternoon.

It seemed in no danger of disappearing.

I'm afraid I'm losing my ass, she said. All this boxing stuff focuses too much on arms and back. I have to do more legwork.

Sure enough, she added another entire set of lower-body calisthenics to her routine from that day forward.

If there was something more to Milton's relationship with Baywatch, well, it remained a mystery to us. He lived with one woman, but that said nothing.

Besides his son in Atlanta, Milton also had a daughter with another woman. This child appeared in the gym at times, a beautiful two-year-old with golden skin, blue eyes and a brown Afro, the edges of which were also touched with gold. Milton didn't seem on good terms with the mother, a blonde who scowled every second she was among us. When the child exasperated Milton, he referred to her as "the mistake." She would crawl among the boxers' feet, a McDonald's hamburger drooping from one tiny fist, the top bun dropping to the floor.

Milton's interaction with Baywatch continued, all eyes upon them. Her celebrity status didn't change Milton's habits; he still talked on his cell while working the focus mitts, even with this lustrous prize.

How can you train me and talk on the phone? she complained.

I'm doing two things at the same time, Milton said. It's okay, I'm Puerto Rican that way.

The southpaw, hands-down style that he was teaching her created conflict on the set. The director wanted her to use a more orthodox boxing approach. Milton of course couldn't, or wouldn't, teach any other way. "Look," Milton told her, "right now it doesn't matter what you learn. You're as stiff as a board out there. If you keep with the style, you'll start loosening up. Then you can give him what he wants." But there was very little time.

I think this girl is after me, Milton said after she left yet another message on his voice mail. I've been running away from her all week.

Yet if he was running, he wasn't running very far or very fast. In the gym, he waved around a video box, the cover adorned by an airbrushed rendition of her face. He played the role of her papi, putting her in cabs, taking her to Grand Central, having flowers delivered to her Port Chester hotel room. He escorted her to the nightclubs where he had entrée and related their exploits with boyish delight. "We saw Puff Daddy, and he bought us a drink." "There'd be a line outside the club, and she'd say, 'There's a long line here.' And I'd say, 'Not for us,' and we'd walk right in."

One day I drove up to the shoot with Milton, along with Will and a Puerto Rican heavyweight named Nelson, who'd been hired to play boxers in the film (he had the good nature of the stereotypical big man). We drove back and forth between the hotel and the set, in movie slow time. In the car, Nelson told us that his uncle made his living shoplifting from chain video stores.

He goes into the store while I wait in the car, Nelson said. He's crazy, yo. He brings in a big sack and when he comes out, it's bulging with tapes. Then we make our getaway. I can get you any new title. For real. Just give me a few days' notice.

As Milton waited for a chance to introduce Will to the director, we drifted around the location, gorged at the buffet, pretended we had a reason to be there. A woman wearing a headset stopped to greet Milton.

Milton, welcome back! Hey, how was your trip? she asked with interest and delight.

I didn't take a trip, Milton said, but she had already disappeared before his answer. Her false interest was so Hollywood, I looked around for palm trees.

The set was in a big church hall and recreation center with basketball courts. Milton wanted to play and we got our hands on a ball. When we divided into teams, it was Milton and me against Will and Nelson. Will, six-three, had been an excellent high school player, having started on his varsity team the previous fall. Nelson was about six feet tall and well over two hundred pounds. On the other side, Milton was in his mid-forties and I, at five-six, had played basketball once in the past decade. Milton adapted to this imbalance by cheating on every play. Whenever he tried to make a move on Will or Nelson and they touched him, he called a foul. If Will made a quick first step to get to the basket, Milton would do anything to stop him: grab his arm, pull his shirt, push. We ran back and forth over an enormous tarpaulin that had been put down to protect the hardwood floors and that bunched at every pivot. Will trash-talked: "I'm gonna break you down, son. I'm gonna pick your game apart." Milton and I actually won the first game, but Milton's tactics were so preposterous that the four of us collapsed with laughter. The movie people stared. It felt like the best of times when I was sixteen and easy among my friends. When all we did on summer nights was chase the ball back and forth. Under the streetlights, chasing back and forth.

Later I watched a conversation between Baywatch and Milton. They both seemed to be performing. Eye play. Whispers. He clasped her hand. She looked away. Milton loomed over her, earnest expression on his face. A leading man. The tall dark stranger.

Bob, did you ever have a girl you liked better than anyone else? So that you made plans with the girl, to travel, to live together? And then, all of a sudden, this girl changed on you, overnight, basically, and you couldn't understand why?

Milton and I were alone in the gym, toward eight P.M., the December night already hours old.

Well, I said, I've had my heart broken a few times.

But suppose, Bob, that this woman told you that she loved you and that she'd never met anyone like you. And then, all of a sudden, a few weeks later, she comes out and says, "No, wait, I've got to step back. This is going too fast for me." Now, Bob, what if you had never met a girl like this, a girl of this caliber, and you thought you would probably never meet anyone like her again?

The conditional, hypothetical voice Milton was using stirred my attention. I had never heard him speak in this manner.

And suppose, he said, that you had never felt this way about anyone else in your life before.

Never?

No, never, he insisted. And now, Bob, what if your friends were always telling you that she was gorgeous, that they envied you, just to give you a little more . . . proof, you know, that this girl is special.

Well, what your friends think isn't so important, Milt. What matters is what you think.

Yeah, but they were saying this to you, while all the time you hadn't noticed. I mean, I never tried anything with this girl.

The voice had changed. We had left the realm of the conditional.

I never tried anything with this girl, Milton repeated, but she wouldn't leave me alone. She kept calling me, paying me all this attention. So you know, after a while, I started to think about her a little more. In a different way. I let everything go for this girl. I let everything go. I ignored the gym, my responsibilities. In all my life this never happened to me before.

It was an introspective episode for Milton, a Hamlet interlude in the gloom of the gym after dark. I wondered how much truth he was telling.

His cell phone began to ring. He pulled it from his jacket pocket and looked at the number.

That's her again. I'm not talking to her.

You wouldn't believe it, Bob, he said, changing tones. This was different. I've got so many women trying to give me things. I got one woman calling me all the time, baking me cookies every week. I had another one offer to turn over her bank account to me. She was ready to write me a check for seventy thousand dollars. I told her to keep her money. Listen, Bob, if I was a real nigger, I'd be driving around in a gold Mercedes. I would have taken her money and said, "Thanks, now have a nice life." I would have played her like an old radio.

He sighed.

You know what they say?

No, what do they say?

In Paris, women walk two steps in front of you. In Hong Kong, over in China, they walk two steps in back of you. In New York, the women walk all over you. And I have the footprints on my heart to prove it.

Milton pulled up his shirt to reveal his scarred torso. He was smiling. I never saw Baywatch again.

· 9 ·

JULIAN

In the mid-1990's, young males in Harlem aged eighteen through
twenty-four had a better chance of dying violently than soldiers on
active duty in World War II.
    —Philippe Bourgois, *In Search of Respect: Selling Crack in El Barrio*

Julian left us in the third week of January to compete in the Eastern
Regional Trials in Pennsylvania. After his September loss in the
PAL Nationals, it was his last chance to qualify for the Olympic Trials
and a chance at the Olympic team. In the weeks before, he'd been
troubled by nagging pain in the first knuckle on the ring finger of his
right hand (his lead hand).

At the gym we received daily postings from Milton on Julian's
progress. His first opponent was Steven Stokes, a marine who had
fought on the national team for years and was ranked third in the
United States. In the second round, Stokes knocked Julian down ("I was
a little intimidated because of who this guy was," Julian later told me),
but Julian rose and went on to win the match by a score of 15–7. He
won the next day also (15–9), and the next (9–7), and the next (8–3),
four fights in four days, to set up a finals match with Jermaine Taylor,
the nation's top-ranked light middleweight, who had already qualified
for the Olympic Trials earlier in the year. Julian's hand had bothered
him through the week, and by the second round of his match with Taylor, he found himself unable to punch without severe pain. He began

to hold, and his corner, fearing he would be disqualified, and thereby banned from the trials, threw in the towel. Julian lost the match but was awarded the Eastern slot for his second-place finish. He would be going to Tampa for a chance at the Olympics.

Less than three years earlier, Julian had been another sort of trial away from a sentence of twenty-five to life in prison. It seemed strange to me on the face of it, that he could have been in so much trouble so young. Julian was probably the most levelheaded of the young boxers.

The first time I went to prison, Julian said, they charged me with attempt homicide. I had a good lawyer at the time. I was still a juvenile, fifteen. So she got the attempt thrown out, and I just got arrested for the gun. That was about eighteen months on Rikers. I was up for eighteen months, and I had time to evaluate my situation. I was like, "Well, I ain't gonna do that again." But I came right back out on the street and got involved with the same type of crowd. The negative crowd. Right? And . . . just basically went back into the same thing. I can actually recall myself thinking, "I just came home from jail. Why? I told myself I ain't gonna go back." And I was like, "Aw, fuck it. I'm just gonna hang with my peoples. They gonna be there for me." And then not even a year or two later I got into some more trouble. And that was bigger. That was for a homicide.

At seventeen, Julian was a successful entrepreneur (a gun dealer) and already a father, with another child on the way.

I was born in Bedford-Stuyvesant, Julian says. I was born in Brooklyn. We lived on Tompkins Avenue in Bed-Stuy. And then from there, you know, my family moved to North Carolina. Then after my folks split up, I moved with my moms to Hunts Point in the Bronx, right? We lived there for a few years at Hunts Point, and then we moved back to Brooklyn. East New York, on Alabama Avenue. And then we moved up to Harlem.

You just named four of the roughest neighborhoods in the city, I say, laughing.

Right, Julian says. It's like me seeing things in these places, it's like . . . I knew that I didn't want to be just stuck in that, you know?

So how did you get into boxing? I ask.

Well, I was in East New York, Julian says, I knew a few people in Manhattan, so they told me about the Boys' Club. I was like, "All right.

I'll come through." That's when I met Milton. I was about eight or nine. My moms always trusted me to travel on my own or whatever, so I was traveling from Brooklyn to the Lower East Side just to go to the Boys' Club. Around that time, my moms moved up to Harlem. One Hundred Twelfth Street and Seventh Avenue. That made the commute from Harlem to the Lower East Side a little bit easier. So I trained there. I liked it. I liked going to the shows and winning trophies and fighting. Then I stopped boxing when I was about twelve because . . . I just got into all kinds of crazy stuff.

What exactly, I ask, do you mean by "crazy stuff"?

I started becoming my own person. And once I became my own person, I made a lot of decisions that . . . wasn't real good. It's like, see, from an early age I was always respected. You know? When people respect you or they fear you to a certain point, you could do something and everybody follow you. So I realized that whatever I do, I would have somebody else that would want to do the same thing that I do. And that's exactly what took me, because no matter where I went or what I did, I always had somebody that wanted to follow me. So I got in trouble, they got in trouble. If I didn't want to get in trouble and I sent them to do something, they got into trouble for me. You know? And me being young and not thinking, I kind of liked that. And then I got involved with my brother, you know, with the drugs and the gun thing and all that. And then, right along with guns and drugs, always come some violence.

So how did you end up getting involved in that life? I ask.

You know how you don't know you're doing something criminal until the act is over? Well, when I was about, like, thirteen, fourteen, I started selling guns. My brothers were the drug dealers, and I was . . . like I said, I didn't want to do what everybody else was doing. You know what I mean? They were selling drugs; I was selling guns. How did I start? Just growing up in the streets, man, talking to people. Once you talk to people, you see what they about and you make a connection and you just use your connections. Once I knew that I could get a certain amount of guns for a cheap price and sell it for a profit, that's what I did. At that time—this was like, '90, '91, know what I mean?—around that time it was easier than selling drugs. It was most definitely easier than selling drugs. I didn't have to stand outside and be on the street all day. I never was a real hand-to-hand trained street hustler. So that's how I was supporting myself for a little while.

When Julian said, "You know how you don't know you're doing something criminal until the act is over?" I knew exactly what he meant. When I was sixteen, I sold drugs for a while, and while I knew it was illegal, I didn't think of it as something criminal. I didn't feel like a drug dealer on TV. Where was the crime in selling my friends something they wanted? It was easy work and paid much better than the loathsome jobs I'd had. I liked having hundreds of dollars choking my pocket; I liked my new stereo.

The first time I went away was May '94, Julian says, I was about fifteen, fourteen. Me being the person I was I never really bothered nobody. I do what I got to do, and that's that. You know? But a few times I got into some things where a dude approached me and I beat him up, knocked him out. So it's basically word of mouth. People were like, "Yo, yo, don't mess with that kid." You know what I mean? "Because this is gonna happen and that's gonna happen."

To make a long story short, I got in a little static with some kids in the neighborhood. So it was a fistfight first, right? Beat the kid up, you know what I mean? Kid felt like he was disrespected or whatever 'cause he got beat up. And it just so happened that the same kids I had problems with my brother Floyd, that's a year older than me, had problems with too. So, like twenty kids came to my house. Thank God nobody was there. They were just banging on the door, looking for me. It was crazy because we didn't even know until the kids came to our house that we had problems with the same people. You know? That was the crazy part about it. What made it so bad—what made it good, actually, was that nobody was home. They was *bold* enough to come to our house, where we live at, you know what I mean? They were from the neighborhood, but certain kids don't leave certain areas. I'm like, "Damn, well, how the fuck they know where I live at?" So I'm trying to figure it out. And then I seen a few of the kids, word? But I tried to stay low so they wouldn't see me. And then one of my boys that was out on the block when they came around was telling me, "Yeah, this kid such and such, such and such," and my brother was like, "Yeah, I got a beef with him too." And I was like, "Oh, ain't that some funny shit?" So now it was the both of us.

So what happened was, being that I had guns, you know, I had got my gun. And I was just walking around with it. This was broad daylight. In those days I took a gun almost everywhere. Everywhere I went, I always had a gun. It got to the point where if you would leave it in the house or something, you would feel naked. Or when it got too hot outside, and there was a bunch of police around, you had to put it up somewhere. But you always put it somewhere close by where you knew you could get it. You know? It was crazy, man. People knew that if they messed with me, that I was the kid who had weapons. But it was always a point of who get who first. That's what made it a war; that's what made it a challenge. To both guys. You know what I mean? My object was to get him before he got me.

So what happened was, they never heard that I had got a message. The kid kept coming around the block, and I seen him; it was in broad daylight, in Harlem, you know. Swear to God, it was in broad daylight, sun was shining, everything, I remember this like it was yesterday. On One Hundred and Twelfth Street. Right? First time, there was two kids. So they walked around the block, and when they came back, there was three of them. Me and my brother, we were standing there. I'm telling my brother, "Yo, yo, these cats keep coming around the block like they trying to set us up or something." And we were sitting right there on the corner. So I told my brother, "Yo, let's break out, before they come back around again, you know, and something pop off." So I jumped on the bike and I just started, you know, riding around town, whatever. And the kid tried to run up on me. I didn't see the kid until he was right in my face. Broad daylight. I swear to God this world, to everything I love. Kid just pulled out his gun. And I had my gun and I was riding a bike so I had to pull out, and we was shooting at each other in broad daylight.

You were on your bike? I ask, trying to imagine.

On the bike. Word. We were shooting at each other in broad daylight. One of the kids got hit in the shoulder. And I just took off. That was one of the times I almost got killed. I almost got killed a few times. That's why I had to leave it alone. It's scary, man. You don't ever know how you feeling until somebody put a gun in your face, knowing that it could be ending right then and there. You know, that's . . . I wouldn't say that's where you touch your manhood at, but that's where you know where your heart is at. You know what I mean? If you really want to live or die. If you really cherish life over death. That's a moment right there where—where your decision is made. You know? 'Cause if you really don't care, it's gonna be easy. But if you care, and you got something to live for, you're going to try your best to get away from it.

Listening to Julian, I realize the young aren't reckless because, as is so often said, "they don't think they can die." They are less afraid to die because they haven't lived long. They don't have so many things holding them to the world.

So there were other times you almost got killed?

Yeah. I was at a party, man, with one of these kids I had a beef with. It was kind of dark; I didn't even see him. Came right up on the side of me, put a gun to my head. But luckily his gun jammed, know what I mean? And I just jumped him up. I just beat him up. Took his gun. Beat him up real bad. And when I did fire the gun after the fight was over? When I fired the gun, it went off. So it wasn't my time to die. It wasn't time for me. You know? 'Cause you can't delay death a minute. Can't push it forward. Anything. When it's your time to go, you gone. You know? Guess it wasn't my time right then and there.

Anyway, while we were shooting, the police rolled up on the scene, and we got arrested. The police was right there. I swear, man, they just appeared out of nowhere. They just popped up like some Houdini shit. You know? I gave chase a little bit, but I couldn't get far. I threw the gun away, but they still found it. Wasn't much I could do about that. That was the first time I been locked up. So they was like, "Well, if we give you a gun charge, you're gonna have to do eighteen months." Like that. "We'll drop the attempt charge, but you have to do eighteen months for the gun." So I was like, "Fuck it, I'd rather do that shit than be sitting up there doing twelve years for attempt. Fuck it. I'll do eighteen months. That ain't nothing." And that's how that one went.*

Upon his release, Julian found himself with a family to support and eighteen months in jail behind him. It made sense for him to return to dealing.

---

*"When you control for poverty, white and black [teens] commit the same amount of violent crime, [but] blacks are arrested at four times the rate of whites and imprisoned at seven times the rate of whites." Vincent Schiraldi, president of the Center on Juvenile and Criminal Justice (*The Nation*, October 27, 2000).

After a while, Julian says, the police started to know about me. They knew who I was. They—put it like this—they knew my whole family. Some of my brothers were drug dealers and . . . So they know who you are. They got the little dots on the board in the police station: This block is for this, and this block is for that. This person lives on that block. Shit like that. They know where everybody is. Especially if they're in your district, know what I mean? District police know who you are. I mean, I never knew the cops personally, but they knew me. They roll up in their patrol cars, be like, "Hey, Mr. Townsend. Carrying any guns today?" and shit like that. Just like that. And I'm looking like, "Naw. You got the wrong person." You know? And they're just waiting to try to get somebody on something.

So what happened the next time? I ask.

Well, not even a year later, I got into some more trouble. And that was bigger. That was for a homicide. It was a homicide that happened on the block with a . . . rival. On One Hundred Twelfth Street, Seventh Avenue. That's in Harlem, New York. You know, that's how they do things up there. It's like real ghetto; it's a thug area. You know? And only the strong survive. Literally. This kid was a rival. He was a drug dealer on the block or whatever. So his crew was trying to push everybody off the block so they could own the block. I didn't really want to have anything to do with that. But it was the fact that my brother had a part to do with it. Then *I* had a part to do with it. I was just trying to be easy on my behalf and just, like, leave it alone. But it's hard to just turn your back and walk away unless you leaving the state. Friends, family, everything was right there. My son was just born, everything. So it was real crazy, you know? And I couldn't just up and leave my family, you know what I mean? And my family couldn't up and leave me because of the situation.

What made the police think you were involved? I ask.

Word got around that I had something to do with it. I was probably one of the most feared persons on that block, so they wanted to get rid of me and a few of my other partners so they could control everything. That's how it is. You eliminate the people that's most feared, and then everything else is easy. So everybody's all, "You know, this kid had something to do with it." And I really didn't have anything to do with it.

What happened exactly? I ask. This guy just turn up dead?

A lot of people turned up dead. Julian laughs. A lot of people turned up dead. It's just one of those things when it's "If you kill one of my boys, I'm gonna kill you." You know what I mean? Or "I gotta kill you before you kill me." That's just as simple as that. I can't explain it no better than that. That's just how it was. A *lot* of people are either dead or in jail right now. Anyway, what happened was, kid got murdered outside or whatever. Right across the street. A suspect supposedly had ran in my building where I was living at. Word? So the suspect ran in the building, and I was coming out of my apartment, 'cause my apartment was on the first floor, right? I was coming out of the apartment; the police was running in. Now, if I was a suspect, why the hell would I be walking right into the police? You know? Why, if I was a suspect and I ran in the building to get away from them, why would I be coming out of my apartment while they still running in? You know? So that's what happened.

They said I was the perpetrator and they caught me in the hallway of the building, right? But yet and all, I was coming out of my apartment, and they searched my apartment, right? Luckily I didn't have nothing in there. All they found was a couple of boxes of bullets. All right. They didn't find no gun. Word? Now, that's just how everything works. They ran in my house; they searched my apartment; they didn't find anything but boxes of bullets. And the bullets that they found didn't even match the bullets that killed the guy. But they had all these witnesses on the trial that said they saw me do it. People from the street, you know what I mean? Police officers, everything.

Unable to make bail, Julian found himself back on Rikers. He sat there for nearly a year, awaiting trial.

It's not a place for me. Jail ain't for *nobody*. It's crazy, man. I was holding my own, I was doing what I wanted to do, but you don't want to be in a place . . . first of all, I love women, right? (That's why I'm in trouble with my girl now.) And to be locked down someplace where . . . it's not even a fact of the women; it's the fact of somebody telling you when to eat, when to sleep—you know what I mean?—when to take a shower, when you can use the bathroom. And then you're around a whole bunch of dudes all day. Around a bunch of stink motherfuck-ers. Niggers that *don't* want to take showers. It gets you aggravated when you used to doing whatever you want to do. When you want to be clean. But jail is mental, man. It do one of two things. It can either make you say, "Yo, I don't like this. I'm not gonna go through this again." The next thing it can do is it can make you like the mentality of that—that prison mentality. It can change your walk; it can change the way that you talk. Know what I mean? You want to feel like you the baddest. Inside of confinement, you know what I mean? How's you provin' your manhood inside a box? The best way you prove your manhood is if you out here on the street doing what a man's supposed to be doing. That's the only way you can prove your manhood, you know? But that's the two things it do, make you love it, or hate it. And I hate it. I hate it. I can't live with another man telling me what to do, at any given time he want me to do it. They come in and do the strip search. How that is, a man telling another man to strip? A man got you standing butt naked; another man got a man standing butt naked with his hands on the wall and his legs spread. Checking up in his butt and all that. If you like that, if a man likes that, there's something wrong with him.

So what did you do to pass the time? I ask.

Read, study, that's about basically the only thing you could do in there besides get in trouble. You know? Had a couple of fights. But once I beat everybody up, nobody wanted to fight me. The first time it was juveniles, but it was general population for juveniles too. That went by pretty easy because they treat juveniles different than they treat the adults. They make the kids go to school. They make them do things to try to better theyselves. You know? And adult prison is just like, "Fuck it, you just wasting time." You know what I mean? They just in there holding. They just give you a little space, and you do whatever you're gonna do in that space. Which ain't shit, you know? And in order for you to occupy yourself, you gotta do something. And what is there to do in prison besides cut somebody up, you know what I mean? Fight, or drugs. The good people read and try to find ways to get out. But most motherfuckers don't give a fuck. They just, in there, just trying to run shit. You know, they try to lock down the phones. "Oh, I own the phone." How the fuck you own the phone? The prison owns it. You know? "Oh, I own this right here." How you own that? The prison own it. At any given time the warden can come and take it away from you.

Now what you own? *Nothing!* You know? You own the same shit you came in here with: yourself. That's it.

So what happened when you finally got to trial? I ask.

The trial was myself and a codefendant. Right? His name was Shawn. Shawn was accused also. But neither one of us had anything to do with it. So I was looking at life in prison. Like, fifty-five years to life. And that was one of the most scariest times of my life. To know that I was being accused of something that I had nothing to do with and being judged by twelve people. And you not knowing what they were thinking. If they were saying, "This kid is already guilty," you know, or what. "Let's just get him off the streets."

People were actually coming up and saying that I did it. That I was a part of this killing. Court eyewitness, eyewitnesses in there lying. And our defense claimed that they was lying. He cross-examined them and everything. The whole thing. Everything like you see on TV, he did. One of the eyewitnesses that said he saw everything that went on was locked up at the time of the homicide. One of the police eye-witnesses was *in jail*, the night of the murder. So how the hell did he see anything from inside a prison cell? But we beat that because the facts didn't add up. You know? And I was like, "Whoa, man. That's crazy, whoa." You know? "That's crazy." They just trying to, you know, put people away, man. And you also got to think about it like this: The prison system is a billion-dollar-a-year industry, man. So the more people they lock up and keep in these cages, man, is the more money they make.

By the grace of God, the facts was revealed that we really didn't have nothing to do with it. But if I didn't have a good lawyer, they would have never found that out. If we didn't have a good lawyer, or myself didn't have a good lawyer to push the fact that I didn't have anything to do with it, I'd be in prison today. Even if I had a state-appointed lawyer, he might have tried to set up a plea for me where I went and served any-way. Like, you plead down to something. I could have gone up for six years on something like that. But thank God that didn't happen. And the lawyer would be like, "Just take it. You're not going to get better." But the facts was revealed, and we was vindicated, and I'm here today. And sitting in that courtroom made me realize that I don't *never, ever* want to be sitting in a jail or a courtroom again. If it's not involving me getting any money out of it, I don't want to be sitting in no courtroom. You know? So I made up my mind.

You think having money made the difference? I say.

If I didn't have the money for a lawyer . . . yo. Unlike some people, I was also putting money away. That's why I'm here to talk to you right now. That's exactly why I'm here, yo. If I had never did that, I'd still be where my brother at. My brother Floyd that's a year older than me, I mean, he probably made way more money than I did, hustling, selling drugs. But he ain't never saved no money. That way he couldn't talk to anybody. He never had a real good lawyer.

So what happened to him? I ask.

He's still in jail. That's what happened. For drugs. He'll be there till 2008. That boy been in and out of jail since since he was fourteen, you know? He's twenty-three right now. You know? He'll be there in 2008. So that's a long time. A long time.

Talking to Julian, I remember that although I never sold drugs after seventeen, I was often around them. My freshman year in college I shared a room with a pot and mushroom dealer; my sophomore year I lived next door to a coke dealer. On my campus it was fairly easy to obtain a wide variety of drugs, or students would drive to New York City to buy them. The summer I turned twenty, friends of mine sold cocaine out of a rented apartment, freebased all night in an upstairs bedroom and had large parties three or four days a week. No one worried very much about getting caught, and no one ever was.*

Everything happens for a reason, Julian says, and I guess that was actually the turning point. You know, it was fast money on the streets, it was good, but comes a time when you know it's either money or death. Death always follows quick money. Especially given the situation of how I was getting the money. Drugs and guns and stuff like that. So death was not too far behind. It went from attempt homicide to a homicide so I was like, "Whoa." The numbers kept getting bigger. I was like, "Man, I'm young." At the time I was like seventeen, eighteen, you know? I got out of jail when I was nineteen. I was turning twenty. Right then I just knew that I had to do something. I always had good

---

*"Over 94% of drug offenders in the New York State prisons are black and Latino" (*Village Voice,* November 14, 2000).

morals, you know, good values. My father raised me good. As a matter of fact, my father never, ever been arrested in his life. My mother never been arrested, you know? It's just being in the areas and the different places. Once you becoming your own person you start to pick up things. You know? And that's exactly what happened.

I nod agreement. "Everything happens for a reason" is something I hear often when I'm around inner-city people. It's a ghetto mantra, born from the desire to make sense of a difficult position. Because if there isn't some hope they can draw from the unpleasant things that happen to them, then there's only nothing at all.

I always had a sense of knowing right from wrong, Julian says, and I used to see things that other people do? That I was like, "I ain't gonna do that." And basically, that came from always wanting to be different. I always wanted to be different. Just 'cause I seen a guy get a lot of money doing this or doing that? It didn't mean that I was gonna get the money the same way, you know? 'Cause I seen a lot of people go down for things that they don't normally do. What I mean by that is, for instance, you'll see a guy that rob and steal all his life, you know what I mean? And never get caught for it. And then as soon as you try it, your first offense, you get caught. You know why you get caught? Because that's not you, that's not in you to rob and steal. You know? And that's the reason why you got caught. You seen him do it, but you really wasn't a robber or a stealer. So when you did do it, you got caught. So I based my life on that. Always trying to be different. Like, I tell people that I never smoke or drink. People find that hard to believe because of where I'm from. You know? Or people that know my brothers, because they smoke like chimneys and they drink like alcoholics.

So that's a life I don't want to have nothing to do with any longer, you know what I mean? And that's one of the greatest things about New York. If you really want to change, you can change. It's not like L.A., or whatever, where you're born into a gang or something like that, and then you really can't get out. See, here we individuals. We make our own path. You know? We do what we want to do. That's the difference between like, a soldier and a general. A general leads. A general do what he want to do. A soldier do what he's told. And I was always a general. I was never a soldier.

For example, I graduated from high school. I knew what I had to do. It was just that I had a lot of distractions and other things were offered to me. And sometimes the company you keep thrusts you into stuff that you don't really want to be a part of, but you like, "All right, I ain't got nothin' to do." So you do it anyway. I was making money on the street and *still* going to school. You know? That was the thing. I guess that was what made me realize that I can change. I can be something else besides this.

I moved out of Harlem into the Bronx, which ain't that much better. But I really don't know too many people there, so it's easy to come and go as I please. It was a conscious decision. I had to go, man. We had to. If I would have stayed, that's like—that's like taking a bath in dirty water. What's the purpose of taking a bath, you know what I mean, if you gonna take it in dirty water? You not getting no cleaner. You already dirty, getting into something that's even more dirtier, so when you get out, you're still going to be dirty. You know? I was like, "Let's get out of here. Let's go to an area where we don't know too many people and see what we can do there. Make an effort to do something right." As long as we got somewhere decent to lay our heads. And go in and out as we please. And don't bring no negativity to our home. That's the best thing.

So that's when I came back to boxing. I think it was like . . . the end of '98. By the grace of God I was able to get out, and I knew that I couldn't keep living the same way that I was living. And I knew the only thing that would keep me out of trouble was me being active in some type of sport or something in the community. I thought about going back to school. I also liked to fight, so I went to boxing.

On Julian's first day back to the gym, eight years out of boxing, Milton tossed him into the ring with Victor.

Vic gave me a pretty nice beating, Julian says, but I know then it would only be a short time before I could come on as a good fighter. Then two weeks later, *two weeks*, man, Milton put me in the Gloves. I did all right for the first two rounds, but in the third round, I didn't have nothing left. But I was coming along.

The next year Julian lost a disputed decision in the Gloves semifinals to the brother of a current professional champion. The following summer, he won the state championship Empire Games and was on his way to the Olympic Trials.

Who would have thought I'd be fighting in the Olympic Trials 2000? Nobody. I've been back in the game about a year and a half. You know? Who would have thought, with twenty-something fights, who would have thought Julian Townsend would be in the Olympic Trials? Nobody, that's who. If you would have had to pick from all the kids from New York who would have made it, they'd have picked somebody like Josiah Judah or Mark Ani, but these guys is nobody on the national team. But this guy named Julian Townsend come out of nowhere. That proved a point.

Right now my money situation is not the greatest. In fact, that is probably almost one of the times when I'm at my lowest points, but I feel good because I'm doing something that I want to do and I'm doing something that makes me feel good about myself. And I'm not hurtin' nobody else to do it. I have two kids, you know? And I'm just trying to pave the way for them. I try to do something positive, for my kids to grow and say, "Yo, my dad was this. My dad was that." Not "My dad was a dope dealer" or "My dad was shooting people for a living." I don't want my kids to ever say anything like that.

· 1 0 ·

THE SHOW

We're driving through the Village on a December day, a season-defying day, skin-weather warm so that everywhere we look women are wearing little in defiance of winter. We are eight men in a van: A.J., Milton, Julian, Will, Nelson, Victor, Professor and me. Our wolf tongues loll from our heads, and we howl.

That girl over there looks *nice*, A.J. says.

The heads swivel.

That girl? That girl right there? Milton is incredulous. The one with the pushed-in face? The one that looks like Herman Munster?

A.J. rushes to defend his sweetheart.

She's all right, man. She has a nice, tight body.

"She" is probably a "he," Milton says. Did you get in this van and go blind? Now that girl over there, now *that* is all right.

Her? A.J. says in a wounded tone. Man, she looks like a St. Bernard.

At least she's a female, you drunk.

But look at *her*, yo, Julian says.

That girl is dark, though, says Nelson.

Like chocolate, says Julian.

More like charcoal, Nelson says.

Laughter.

The scouting mission has been in effect since the van began to roll from Revolution. Now we're cutting east on 8th Street, street of leather, street of shoes, Bengali hucksters cross-armed before their shops.

So does having sex before a fight really affect you? asks the new white guy on the team—the Professor, Milton calls him.

Sure, Julian says. It takes out your legs. It's like getting shot with buckshot. Buckshot to the knees. It makes you too relaxed. I try not to have sex for at least a week before a fight.

Heads nod agreement.

We are on our way to a boxing show in Yonkers, where I will fight for the first time in four years (*if* we arrive on time and *if* a match can be made for me). Milton has allowed that I am ready. No longer does he advise me to wait another year for the Gloves. No longer does he say, "Anasi, you're punching handicapped." Now it's "I can't wait until Stupid sees you knocking guys out. Then he'll be sure to retire."

I just read that every time a man has an orgasm, A.J. says, he has to eat like three bananas and a steak and protein powder to get back in him what he lost. So every time you bust a nut—

I didn't know that myself, Julian says.

Soon after stepping into the van, A.J. revealed that he has been drinking, and the liquor has slowed his drawling voice to syrup. The English/West Indian A.J. is a Supreme Team part-timer who will show up in the gym every day for a week, then disappear for a month. At every return, he claims that this time he is serious, that he's going to get sharp, have some fights, win the Gloves. As much as I like A.J., I don't believe it will happen. Boxing for him is an elective; he has a middle-class sheen and makes decent money as a manager for trade shows.

You know who's been pushing up on me a lot? he says, and names a woman boxer, a heavyweight. If she keeps coming around, I might have to go for it.

Big Mama? Milton says. You're talking about Big Mama?

Milton jams the brake, jolting us against the seats.

All right, A.J., get out. Get out. You're drunk or you're crazy, and I can't have either one in my van.

This ride isn't the first time I've seen A.J. tipsy, and it isn't the first time that Milton has harassed him for it. Milton, night ranger, club player, doesn't drink himself, not a dram or drop, and shows little tolerance for those who do.

Milton doesn't like black women, Will says.

You don't understand, Milton says. I was married to a black woman. Hey, look at that, she looks like a little something that I used to know.

Then I guess she has to be ugly, Will says.

Will, did you ever see me with an ugly woman?

I'd have to say yes.

But that was just your cousin.

Yeah, Will replies, but he's all right.

General hilarity.

Beneath my own laughter, I'm uneasy, almost hoping we don't arrive in time. That we will is far from certain. Although the hour is just past four and the weigh-in isn't scheduled until six, we must drop Nelson off in the East Village to retrieve his car, then stop in Harlem somewhere to get Julian's boxing book, pick up Puni somewhere near Co-op City and finally make our way all the way back east across the Bronx to the show in rush-hour traffic.

At the moment, however, we are on the prowl, mobile and menacing to women everywhere, a thrill-seeking hormone-boosted pussy wagon. In the East Village, our heads spin to follow a woman in hot pants being dragged by three pit bulls with spiked collars. A hush in the van, silent approval of the pit bulls, the hot pants, the posterior.

I can help her! Milton exclaims, and swerving to the curb, he leaps out and rushes down the street. As we watch, he stops her with an urgent call, then runs his game on her, complete with stupid magic tricks. Seemingly from nowhere, a Supreme Team business card appears in Milton's hand with a grand flourish, and he speaks with animated abandon. We have seen this particular trick before but are not unimpressed. He leans over the woman, arms waving, mesmerist's eyes puncturing hers.

That man is a predator, Julian says, shaking his head in admiration.

I thought Milton had a girlfriend? I say.

So? Will, Julian, Nelson and A.J. respond in choral unison.

Sometimes you get tired of the same thing, Julian says, no matter how good it is, know what I mean? A man might love chicken, but that doesn't mean he wants to eat chicken twenty-four/seven. I know you must feel that way with Nadia sometimes, Bob.

Who's Nadia, Bob? Will asks.

Oh, that friend of mine who comes to the gym.

You mean that little girl you're blazin'?

Will gives a suggestive hip swivel as a visual aid.

A rare smile dawns on Victor's face.

Bob's a pimp, he says.

Bob's a pimp, he repeats, delighted by the notion.

Bob's a part-time gynecologist, Milton says, sticking his head into the van. He only works from midnight to four.

As we roll again, Milton tells us he informed Hot Pants that she needed to train with the Supreme Team. Boxing, he told her, would give her the strength she needed to handle the frisky bulls. Milton is earnest in his narration. "I can help that girl!" he says, half convinced by his own patter like any good con man.

We drop Nelson beside his SUV between B and C, the girlfriend already waiting there for him. Then we lurch uptown, in and out of traffic that gathers and clots as we struggle upstream, a condensation of vehicles toward the hour of five, the desperate commuter wriggle to escape the city. To my right, Professor breaks into a McDonald's bag in his lap.

Who wants a burger? he says. Who wants a soda?

Julian reaches back a big hand for a serving of salt, carbs and saturated fat.

Aren't you fighting tonight? I ask.

I ain't gonna get a fight up there, says Julian. Nobody's gonna fight me until the Gloves, when they *have* to fight me.

I stare wistfully as the french fries bolt down his gullet. Oh, how I love that fried meat smell, McDonald's heating-coil-cooked beef! But I'm to set to fight and the idea of combat with grease in my gut gives me pause, as does the thought of weighing in even a half pound heavier. After the weigh-in, I'll have an energy bar for comfort.

As the last event before the Gloves, the Yonkers show will draw fighters from all over the region. Unlike the tournaments—the Golden Gloves, Metros and the Empire State Games—shows do not require fighters to make a certain weight and do not guarantee bouts. Matches are made by a U.S. Boxing official from among the fighters present.

This show is important to me; I haven't fought a competitive round in over four years. A fight is very different from even the hardest sparring. It's in my best interest to come in as close to 125 pounds as I can. I'll get a feel for the talent in this weight class, since every fighter at the show will be looking forward to the big tournament. I have no shame: I want to fight the smallest, the lightest, the weakest opponent I can, a pushover, a paraplegic, anything to get through those terrible three rounds.

Another car, holding a group of Milton's white-collar boxers, joins us on 68th and Third and now we are three.

Just follow me, he shouts out the window to Nelson, and switches on his hazards as a beacon for the others to follow. Nelson ignites his hazards as well, then the third car, to form a blinking caravan in the dusk. Milton whips in front of a cab doing sixty and swerves across two lanes to avoid another truck that's hit its brakes. I turn away from the window. Thoughts of the show pull me into darkness: I want to fight, I don't want to fight, I want to fight, I don't . . .

We cross to the West Side Highway and then cut back into the grid somewhere in Harlem for Julian's book, the hazard lights saccading behind us. I'm on the back bench between Victor and Professor, Victor's head recessed back into a hooded jacket. He looks exactly as he wants to look: a thug from white flight nightmares. Beside me, Professor has slumped forward in his seat with a desperate look on his face.

Professor, are you okay? I ask.

I feel a little nauseous, he says. I get motion sickness sometimes.

After retrieving Julian's book, the caravan decamps, headed north and east. Twilight thickens and figures on the sidewalks turn to gray shades. Victor stirs beside me. He sticks a hand out from his jacket sleeve and scrawls a large *C* in the mist on the window. *C* is for "Crip" (although Victor insists he's been out of the gang world since his stabbing). On Broadway in the 150s, groups of young men loiter on the traffic island.

Oh, shit, Vic mutters, this is Dominican Town.

He lifts his sleeve and erases his mark. I remember Milton's mentioning that Dominicans in Washington Heights were "looking for" Vic.

We fishtail along Broadway as it skews across the island, Broadway once an Indian trail, breaking the grid geometry. Professor stirs beside me, a dolorous expression on his face.

Milton, he says, Milton? You got to stop.

Stop. What for?

I think I'm gonna be sick.

Milton pulls over. The Professor jumps out of the van and stumps up the cross street to the head swivels of the corner boys.

You see the Professor run out of here? asks A.J. It looks like he went out to score.

They was grilling him, son, says Victor.

The corner boys have clustered and are staring down the side street, wonderstruck by the appearance of the bullet-headed blond man. We stare at them staring.

All I know is, I'm rolling out of here alive, says Milton.

That's my man. Julian sighs. I got to go out and look after him. He's like a baby in the jungle out there.

Julian leaves the van.

We might not be here when you get back, Will shouts.

Victor smiles.

If you hear [thump, thump, thump (he bangs his hand three times on the van side)], drive off.

In a few minutes Julian returns, escorting the Professor, who drops to the bench beside me.

We were afraid they were gonna stick you, says Will.

They was *grilling* him, repeats Vic.

We crisscross the grid, north and east, back onto the expressways, the New York expressways designed by Nazi scientists intent on ratcheting up tension and fear. Steel plates, potholes, tight lanes without shoulders, deranged drivers, grand prix curves, a cruel video game. Beside me, Professor gurgles vomit into an emptied soda cup. Out to the brick towers and swamp reeds of Co-op City, where we meet Puni and his mother in the semicircular drive of their project. Puni is fifteen; Puni's mother, a slender woman with tightly braided hair, looks to be a few years younger than I am. Milton brags on Puni constantly: "Bob, you should have seen him with this pro. The guy said, 'I'll take it easy on the kid,' and then Puni's in there, just spanking him, saying, 'Who's your daddy? Who's your daddy?' Fifteen years old!" Puni's very dark, with a long frame to grow on.

Back on the road it's getting toward six and we're a borough away from the show. Puni's mother opens a foil package of fried chicken. The cell phones never stop ringing, both Professor's and Milton's. For a half mile, Milton hooks a ride behind a fire engine running its siren for our very own motorcade. Our hazards flash. I keep waiting for a cop to pull us over.

Milton is talking to the organizer of the show.

Keep the scale open! he shouts. We're on our way. I got two 'fifty-six opens and a 'sixty-five open and a 'twenty-five novice. Hello? Hello! Hello!

Milton's cell has frozen. Crisis. Soon both he and Professor are talking to Sprint on Professor's cell in an attempt to get the code to unlock Milton's phone. The chaos of the roadway reflects the chaos in my head as I waver between dread and hope. What if I'm matched against the next *Ray Robinson*? What if I walk out from my corner and get knocked out by the *first punch*?

Nelson pulls up beside us, and his girlfriend begins hollering.

Milton! You got a call!

Holding Nelson's cell, she stretches her arm into the expressway night. Milton reaches for the phone with his free hand as he talks to the Sprint help line on Professor's phone (the phone shouldered to his ear), his other hand on the wheel trying to match speeds with Nelson at 40 mph in stop-and-go traffic. I read that cell phones damage long-term memory. This might explain why we go through the same confusion on the way to every show: *Milton doesn't remember the last time.* There are always the hazard lights, the confusion, the shuttling around. Then after we arrive too late, we sit in the front row with our arms crossed, telling one another that nobody in New York wants to fight us.

Cars behind us blare at our antics, infuriating Milton, who pumps his brakes.

C'mon, try honking now, he shouts, waving a fist out the window.

Beside me, the Professor is gray and still.

Do you want us to stop? I ask.

No, I think I can make it, he whispers.

I've got to think, I've got to think, Milton reminds himself, trying to fix on the shortest way across the Bronx to Yonkers. The cell phone is brought back into operation, but we get lost once and then again down cul-de-sacs and curving residential roads.

I hate Yonkers, Milton declares to his captive audience. The van makes odd thudding noises and also a rising whine. With the weight of bodies, it scrapes over every dip in the roadway. The vessel filled with Professor's puke lies at my feet.

When we finally slide into a parking space outside the club, we're only an hour late. Inside, the scale remains open; we can fight (just what

I was afraid of). Spectators throng the tight hallway, our wave breaking against them. Only fighters and trainers get in free; I flash my official U.S. Boxing book with its photo booth mug shot of my face. Milton tries to slide everyone in without paying, a breezy "they're with me," as we flow down the stairs and into the dressing room. The room boils with voices and bodies, bodies of men and boys, naked chests and shoulders, black, brown, beige.

Get on the scale, guys, Milton commands.

After stripping down to my boxer briefs, I take a place among the nearly naked: Irish kids with freckled backs, bronzed Italians with bodybuilder bulk and Play-Doh noses. There are black light-heavies with muscles like suits of mail and Puerto Rican beanpoles that look as if you could punch a hole through them. They have come from all over the region: Bronx boxing teams, Bed-Stuy kids, a Harlem team, a club from Rockland County farther north up the Hudson. This show matters. Victor comes in at 160, and Will even heavier. Since winning the Metros, Will has decided the strain of making '56 is too unpleasant. Julian doesn't bother to undress; he won't be fighting. I'm on and off the scale, "126" scribed on the cover of my book. The doctor checks my eyes and chest, has no objections, sends me on my way.

At a card table in the middle of the long room sits a young man in a white uniform, the fighters' books heaped in front of him. Shouting trainers swarm about the official as if they're begging for political asylum.

My fighter has . . . *no* fights! And we want somebody who has . . . *no* fights! demands a graybeard with a crumpled torso and drunk's face, cherry and spreading.

Milton is in his element, tall in the crowd, glad-handing friends, cracking jokes, mouth curled in its usual wry grimace.

Yo, yo, we want to fight first! he shouts. We want to fight first! Shouting just for the hell of it, acknowledging and extending the chaos. Then he looks over at me.

Now you can see what a bunch of bullshit this is, he says.

These setups are mad corny, adds Will.

From the heap of books, the official must winnow the most evenly matched. You don't want to put a seventeen-year-old with two fights against a seventeen-year-old with two hundred junior fights. His task is complicated by the fact that the books are only nominally accurate. Fighters move from other states, other countries, "lose" their books, rise out of the junior ranks with hundreds of unregistered bouts. The book of the seventeen-year-old with two hundred junior bouts will show only those fights he's had since leaving the junior ranks.* The trainers offer unsolicited advice on possible matches; they will tell any lie to find a soft mark for their protégés. In this, Milton is somewhat refreshing, if cavalier. "We'll fight anyone," he likes to say.

Scanning the book covers on the table, I see a 127, I see a 133. I have a sudden fear that Milton will put me in with a heavier opponent. If he asked me, "Do you want to fight this 'thirty-three?" I would have to say yes. And if Milton said, "Well, he's one forty-five, but you can handle him," I would still say yes. And if Milton said, "Well, he'll be carrying a gun, but it's only a rifle . . ." I would say yes, again, trapped into a yes by the boxer's code.

Back in street clothes, I walk out to the main space of the gym, converted by rows of plastic chairs into an auditorium. Out of the entire metropolitan area, Yonkers seems to have the most shows and the best-organized amateur boxing infrastructure, although the majority of fighters come from the city itself. As far as I can tell, the local boxing people, organizers and officials, are all white. At one table beside the ring sit a half dozen old Italian-American officials, wrinkled eagles in a row. The table before them supports a jeweled cargo of trophies, each crowned by a stylized boxer in stance.

My teammates sit together, and I join them. All the boxing crews sit in tight groups through the half-empty room, the groups brushing one another at the fringes. Julian knows many of the other coaches and fighters and greets them. After handshakes, they stand talking shop: national rankings, fights they've seen. Julian is the Supreme Team's goodwill ambassador to the boxing UN (Milton is our Fidel Castro). Julian has a place here, a reputation. I feel invisible, *am* invisible; I

---

*The shows are invaluable for novice fighters trying to get experience. At a show, a fighter with no fights in his book might actually have no fights, whereas in the Gloves, he's almost certainly lying (only the most foolhardy boxer would go into the Gloves with no experience). Also, trainers at a show are allowed to examine the books and persons of prospective opponents.

haven't won any tournaments or done anything else to prove myself in boxing. With nothing to say to my teammates after three hours in a van, I can find no way to occupy myself. With the patience of experience, Will and Victor sit with Walkmans to shield them from the tension of the wait. Too edgy to sit, I walk back down to the dressing room.

The bedlam around the card table continues. I lean against a wall, waiting to see if they match me. Two white trainers converse beside me in that rough working-class dialect of the outer boroughs.

So I ask him, says Trainer No. 1, "Are you nervous?" Now, I always used to say no, but I was lying. Of course you're nervous. So I ask him, and he says no. And I say, "You gotta be a *little* nervous." And he says, "Yeah, I'm a little nervous." Hey, if you don't have butterflies in your stomach, there's got to be something wrong with you. I don't care if you're George Foreman.

I don't care if you're King Fucking Kong, says Trainer No. 2, and they laugh.

Across the room, I notice a slim, dark-haired man and his obese partner fingering my book. They look at the photo, then at me. They nod to each other and lean over to talk to the young matchmaker. All of a sudden I'm balancing on a surge of adrenaline, six stories high.

The crumpled, red-faced trainer walks away from the table in rageful despair.

My guy has . . . *no* fights. *No* fights. No! No! I don't trust this whole fucking setup. Every fucking time I come here it's the same . . . goddamn . . .

His voice trails off as he leaves the room.

I recognize some of the officials from my last fight, in Bed-Stuy, more than four years earlier. A frail old man carrying a doctor's black bag and a U.S. Boxing Rulebook walks to the card table.

The scale is closed, he says in a musical brogue.

At my last fight four years ago, I heard him make the same announcement, carrying the same kip. The man who refereed my first New York fight, now five years gone, follows him. He wears a knit white skullcap and white robes and looks like a hologram of Gandhi.

A stout black trainer begins screaming at the young matchmaker.

You promised me that fight, what happened?

I had to—

I can't believe this shit.

I didn't have the book.

I got his book right here, the man bellows, waving a book before the matchmaker's face.

The matchmaker points to the table. Well, it should have been right there.

The ancient official grips the matchmaker's shoulder.

Only let the coaches in *after* the bouts are made, he says, or this nonsense is gonna happen every time.

From across the room, Milton glides toward me, finger pointed at my chest.

I think we have a winner, he says.

You got somebody for me? I say, trying to come off nonchalant.

Milton nods.

How many fights does he have?

Milton waves a finger in the air.

One, he mouths in delight.

I feel a certain relief.

Yo, Bob, you should have seen them, Milton says, after they told the official they wanted the match. I'm standing there, and they ask me if I have anybody fighting. I say I got a few guys, including one 'twenty-five pounder. And they say, "Oh, really, who?" And I point to your book. You should have seen their faces. So, they're like, "Really? He's with you?"

Milton mimics them, using his Surprised Idiot voice, complete with facial expression.

So I say yeah, and they pick up the book again, and they're looking at it. "So, how many fights does he have?" I say, "It's right there in the book." And the fat one says, "Yeah, but he could be a ringer." So I say, "Look at him. He looks like fucking Elvis Presley. Do you want the fight, or don't you?"

Milton is delighted by this sequence of events. He breezes away again, laughing.

Out in the main hall, the room percolates. As more of an audience has arrived, the distinct boxing groups have blended into the crowd. A woman leans over a steam table in one corner, tending to hot dogs, her hands wrapped in plastic. So far I am the only Supreme Team fighter with a match.

Milton gestures toward another crew sitting a few rows ahead of us. I recognize the chunky assistant. Milton points out a Puerto Rican boy with an angel's face, a boy young enough to be my son.

That's him, Bob.

The boxers of the other team swivel their heads back for eyefuls of me. I make a mask of my face as they chortle among themselves.

Bob, Milton says, grin flickering around his mouth, they think you're an *ordinary* white guy.

I laugh too and lean back in my chair, trying to look hard. The rush has me trembling, a great bolt of energy, but I'm ready. My fate is clear. With the fight before me, my team has a reason to speak. It draws us together.

Milton stands.

I'm going back there to see if I can find any more victims.

They think you're a pushover, Vic says to me, grinning. Those guys are dogging you.

That's a kid over there, Julian says. You're a man. You just have to take it through willpower. You have to control him.

Exactly, says Vic, nodding. Refuse to lose.

I want to fight immediately, to shuck my jeans for my satin boxing shorts in blue and gold. Instead I'll jump rope in the dressing room for a few rounds and then shadowbox. When the bell rings, I want to start fast. As I walk down the hall to change, Milton emerges from the dressing room.

Milt, I say, I'm going to get warm.

Wait a second, he says. The show might be canceled. They fucked up.

The show might be canceled? I repeat. What happened?

A rumor of disaster winds through the rooms: a problem with the books, first statements ignored, it doesn't go away . . . The officials run back and forth in their white uniforms like TV surgeons . . . I slump back into a chair. There goes my will to fight. I was so ready, so forward, so eager.

Of the forty-odd fighters in the room, only a handful have Year 2000 validation stickers in their books, although there we are, two weeks into the millennium. Without a current sticker, no one is allowed to fight under the aegis of U.S. Boxing. The young official says he expected the arrival of another official, with the stickers.

You mean he didn't give them to you? Gandhi asks. Well, he's at a meeting in Colorado now.

The young official shakes his head.

As the certainty of cancellation grows, the officials desperately try to arrange matches between fighters with valid books. Only a single match can be made: Angel Face and I. And nobody is going to pay ten dollars with us as the main, the only event. The show will not go on.

A man steps into the ring and shouts for our attention.

I'm very sorry to announce this to you, says the owner, a lean figure with drooping mustaches who looks like an unsuccessful pimp. It's not the fault of Boxing Connection. We planned this event months in advance.

No one is listening, the teams already at the doors. There is consternation at the steam tables: all those hot dogs. It's one of the ironies of the sport that as popular as it is in the upscale health clubs, on the grassroots level, in the neighborhoods, it's dying. This sort of neighborhood show, once a weekly occurrence in the New York area, has become ever more difficult to find. In turn, it becomes difficult for fighters to develop. You can't learn the game if you never have a chance to play it. Several times a year Milton drives to New Jersey and upstate New York for matches, and he has even ranged as far as Kentucky, North Carolina and D.C. for guaranteed fights.

This is the last show before the Gloves. I have another reprieve, but what I desperately need is a fight.

· 1 1 ·

J A N U A R Y

Zeal is always at its height at the commencement of an undertaking;
and on this particular occasion the Peloponnesus and Athens were full
of young men whose inexperience made them eager to take up arms.
—Thucydides, *The Peloponnesian War*

The first Golden Gloves tournament took place in Chicago in 1923;
sponsored by the *Chicago Tribune*, the event was conceived as a test
to the Illinois law that outlawed boxing. The first New York City
Golden Gloves, organized by the *Daily News*, followed four years later
and has been held annually ever since. Legendary fighters who have won
New York Gloves titles over the years include Sugar Ray Robinson, Joe
Louis, Floyd Patterson and Riddick Bowe. While the Gloves finals are
held in the Theater at Madison Square Garden, preliminary rounds make
do with community centers, schools, church halls in the city and Nassau County. In the city, the shows are set in Italian-American enclaves,
and in Nassau in working-class townships. The churches are Catholic,
the audiences mostly white. The *Daily News* runs the Gloves as a char-
ity, and the venues receive the money, which, at fifteen to twenty dollars
a head, can be a considerable sum. Audiences at the bouts consist of the
people who once made the *Daily News* the highest-circulation daily in
the city, an audience that recalls a time when there were still plenty of
white fighters with last names like O'Leary and D'Angelo, names still
common in the aging hierarchy of amateur boxing.

Do you remember, Milt, Victor said, what they told me about you, when I was over at the Bed-Stuy gym?

Yeah, Milton said.

Victor leaned back against the ring ropes, the elastic almost a hammock.

I told them I was coming to work with you, and this trainer said, "Milton's a thug! Don't go over with that Supreme Team. They're all a bunch of hoodlums!"

Vic chuckled in delight. As if that weren't a reason to make him *want* to train with the Supreme Team. Still, both Vernon and Milton had spoken to Vic about his trouble, in the only way that might have an impact. "I told him, 'Look what happened,'" Milton said. "It affected your training and made you miss the Metros." Besides Milton, Vernon was the only person in the gym to whom Victor showed a certain deference. I saw him approach Vernon and proudly tell him about a fight he'd won in Atlantic City. Together, the two older men had brought Vic to agree to stay away from gang trouble.

Yet thug life remained attractive to Victor. One day he enthusiastically recounted the story of a kidnapping in the city. Bloods had abducted the mother of a rival to intimidate him.

You think that's all right, Milton asked, snatching someone's mother?

We don't do that, Victor said. That was Bloods. We're the good guys.

Vic's half smile softened his face.

So you're still running with those guys? Vernon said.

I told you [Victor's expression turned sullen] I'm not involved anymore. I just do boxing.

So you just make the call, Milton said, and have other people take care of it?

No, Vic insisted, I'm out of it.

You got to take Bob up there and show him the gangster's life, Milton said.

That's right, I added. I want to see the dark side.

Will, Milton said, Bob wants to see the dark side. Drop your pants.

Will turned his back toward us and loosened his belt.

No, Will, Milton said, that's not the dark side. That's the black hole.

Through January, the gym life swarmed and spread in the pressure of the approaching Gloves: a month, two weeks, a few days away. Boxers who had not bitten mouthpieces for months or years appeared late and fat to beat themselves into shape for one more shot. Chief among returnees in our gym was Efrain, a title winner for Milton in '96 and a childhood friend of Joey's. He was a squat, powerful Puerto Rican with copious tattoos and legendary power; Milton boasted of his feats from the moment he appeared among us.

Once Efrain was working as a bouncer in a nightclub. This guy started giving him shit, and Efrain clocked him, bang! One punch, laid him out. Then the guy's friend runs out and has something to say, so, bang! Efrain drops him too. Then another one of the friends comes out of the bar and says, "What happened to my friends?" Efrain said, "Oh, they're friends of yours!" Wham! He's on the pavement too. Now you've got these three guys sitting on the curb, not knowing what planet they're on, and the owner walks up. "What the hell's going on?" he says to Efrain. "You can't be doing this to my customers."

Yet Efrain's title was years past. After winning, he had immediately been forced to serve a year in prison for an assault conviction (unrelated to his stint as a bouncer). Since then he had settled down with a girlfriend in Queens and worked steadily in construction. At twenty-five, with two children, Efrain discovered the difficulty of dragging himself into the gym after work. He would do the vanishing act for weeks at a time, even with Milton's constant encouragement and prodding. Because of his long layoff, Efrain's timing was off, although his power remained. He needed time, just what he didn't have. After he failed his drug test for the tournament, I thought we had seen the last of him. Milton was anguished. He had envisioned a pro career for Efrain, with himself in the role of manager.

I can't believe we lost one of our best guys without a fight, he said.

Miraculously, Efrain passed the drug test retake (allegedly with the help of someone else's urine) and was back among us in his plaster-spattered jeans. On many nights his babymoms and their two children would come to the gym to watch him sweat.

When Busdriver's kidney stone ceased to ail him, I had another sparring partner. He wore an unusual headgear when in the ring; it looked more like a Crusader's helmet than the cushioned rigs that everybody else wore.

What the hell is that? I asked the first time I saw it.

It's called a facesaver, he said, fiercely.

Can you see?

Yeah, I can see. Don't tell me. Ray Leonard used to wear the same thing when he sparred. Guys always make fun of it, but I've had my nose broken once. Not again. I'll tell you who knows what's best for Joe Penna. Joe Penna knows what's best for Joe Penna.

This was my first facesaver. He pulled the casque over his head, and all that could be seen were his vivid green eyes over the bar.

With Busdriver, I quickly learned the need to control my anger. You had to smack Giuseppe a few times to wake him up; then he would press forward, windmilling punches. The first time I made the mistake of trying to meet his rush, I took a fist in the throat.

Don't be stupid, Bob, Milton said. When you stand in front of a guy trading, someone's going to get hit with a lucky punch. You don't want it to be you. This is what it's going to be like in the Gloves. Guys are going to try to steamroll you. You've got to be tricky about it.

It was a difficult lesson for me. I'd always believed I needed to stand and slug. I associated retreat with cowardice.

The next time I stung Busdriver and he bulled after me, I slipped toward him, under his punch. I let his weight slide from my shoulder and, using his own momentum, spun him around so that our positions were reversed. Then I landed two body blows and danced away before he could counter. Milton jumped up from the chair.

That was a black thing! That was a black thing you just did, Bob! That's how you're gonna handle those wild men in the Gloves!

I called Julian to cement our plan to meet and watch the fights at Stars Café in Times Square (it was Julian's idea, as I dreaded the idea of the crowds in touristland on a Friday night). My call reached an answering machine, a woman's voice saying that nobody was available, then, curtly: "And if you're calling for Julian, don't leave a message here." Julian's cell phone number was disconnected.

The next time I saw Julian, I mentioned the message.

I told her not to do that, he said. It doesn't have to be like that. I'm trying to keep it cool. But if you need to get ahold of me, probably the best thing is to call the gym.

The dancer attempted to help me. She began with my feet. My flat feet were a disaster, knots of gristle and pain. She felt sorry for my flat feet; they had suffered in silence for so long. "Let me try something," she said, and ground her knuckles into the heel and sole. I went stiff with agony. Who knew feet could store so much hurt? My calves were another calamity, an epic of maladjustment and slovenly care. My calves, the muscles clotted, singing in agony to the touch of her fingers.

You're always going to have trouble with your calves, she said.

Why is that? I asked.

Because you're, um, somewhat bowlegged.

Oh.

The dancer's trained eyes discovered the turnout to my right foot, tibial torsion, a minor birth defect that had never been surgically corrected.

That's why you have such an . . . unusual gait.

Oh.

But I like it. On you, it's very charming.

Thanks, I said, understanding that it was a miracle that I could, not box, but walk at all.

Over the months I discovered that beneath Revolution's buff façade, disease cankered and spread. The equipment I had believed state-of-the art was actually obsolete and crumbling. The staff hadn't been paid in months. The classes in dozens of disciplines, classes that packed the wall calendars, drew only a few clients. Trainers were fired for incompetence, minor infractions, arguments over money; trainers quit from rancid frustration.

Revolution was in trouble, promotional brochures and sprung-floor studios aside. Clients paying sixty dollars an hour didn't want to walk up four steep flights of stairs for a class and loiter in queues for the single shower, not when the top fitness clubs had escalators and elevators to usher them toward their treadmills, not when they could loll in saunas and whirlpools.

In an effort to gain exposure, the Fitness Diva scheduled a workout demo to coincide with an annual cancer walk in Central Park. She developed a calisthenics routine the trainers would perform in unison on a park stage, a routine that would get the walkers *pumped*, *psyched* and *moving*. Unfortunately, the trainers arrived in the park at 6:00 A.M. on a Saturday only to discover that the Fitness Diva had gotten the day wrong, and there were no cancer walkers there to exhort.

Her desperation explained the Supreme Team. The only reason we were tolerated was that she needed the pitiful thousand dollars Milton paid every month for our little boxing studio. I almost felt bad for the Fitness Diva; anyone who looked to Milton for help on a sinking ship was doomed to go under. He was already in the lifeboat, scanning the horizon for land.

Hanson (or so Milton called him) was the whitest flake to drop in the Supreme Team shaker to date. Just fourteen, he stood six feet tall, with green eyes and blond hair kept long for modeling. I had no problem understanding why he wanted to box, a skinny, pretty white kid in a New York P.S. Milton adopted him, calling him Gumby, gave him hours of pad work and cuffed him when he made mistakes. I played a part in his education as well, weaving inside his long arms to thump his bony chest.

Fighters cheat on their roadwork. Boxing history is filled with anecdotes of the radical efforts fighters make to escape their miles; Liebling writes of a fighter who would take a warm shower with his clothes on to deceive his trainer into thinking he'd run and sweat, while in *The Fight*, his book on the Ali/Frazier "Rumble in the Jungle," Norman Mailer relates how he went running with Ali in the Congo and found that Ali took such a leisurely pace that fat old Norman with a bellyful of steak and booze could almost keep up.

"Are you doing your roadwork?" the trainer barks, suspicious.

"Sure," say the fighters, but who knows? There are so many reasons not to: It's cold, hot, early, late, you're tired, sick, bored, busy, you'll go tomorrow, it's only one day off. The fact that wind can't easily be measured makes procrastination easier. The trainers ask, but fighters cheat, believing speed and skill will conceal conditioning flaws ("I can't do their roadwork for them," Ollie Kreuger told me with a shrug). But the ring is an awfully small place to hide anything. I've watched Julian destroy an opponent for two rounds, then hug him like a life buoy for the next two because he had run out of oxygen.

Into the cold months the track emptied. At one A.M. I'd be the only person there. On the coldest nights a wind from the river would sweep across the field, grating my exposed face, burrowing through to skin. I'd squint into the wind, encouraging myself with the thought that my opponent wouldn't be out doing his roadwork on a night like this (I considered treadmills a decadent innovation. Victor agreed and also ground out his miles on the streets. Of course, that we weren't allowed to use the Revolution treadmills helped make virtue of necessity). Yet the run eased after the first mile, core temperature rising, endorphin Zen soothing the chill, and all that mattered was the movement, one foot over the next.

One night I saw a cluster of Spanish teens on the track and heard the high buzz of a small motor. Halfway into my first lap, the engine whined toward me and whizzed by, a teen body draped over the tiny frame of a midget motorcycle. They continued their racing as I ran, switching drivers at every lap and shouting encouragement as if qualifying for a pro-am.

Other nights I saw lovers in murmuring embrace, old Polish bachelors with soft hats and canes measuring out their last miles, around and around. Small birds warbled and dashed across the broken field in a flash of white, white underside of gray wings flashing. One night late, a woman leaped into my path and grabbed my arm.

Walk me home please, she shouted. I'm so scared out here, please, please. This neighborhood is very dangerous.

Another night a car struck a lamp on the street bordering the park. Metal crunch, glass shatter and the lamp hood slowly falling to shatter itself in echo. The driver opened his door and stepped out. Crew-cut Spanish, stout and young.

Are you okay? I asked.

Yeah, he said, then started kicking the crumpled fender.

You fucking stupid car! he shouted, kicked again.

I continued to run as young men tumbled from the car like roaches from a hot stove. Each lap brought me a different image:

Men standing around the car in silent amazement.

Men remarking in loud wonder, "I was trying to warn you, but you didn't listen."

Men shoving the car off the post.

And by the time I'm on my last lap they're laughing.

Yo, son, you hit that shit hard!

Busdriver, who had a large family and worked fifty hours a week, was in especially poor condition. If I stayed elusive for the first two rounds, he would become dead-legged and I could hit him quickly and escape before he countered (I also was careful not to hit the facesaver too hard. "Joe," I said, "they should call that thing the knucklebuster"). At first this knowledge wasn't conscious—I just took what was there—but over the weeks I saw the pattern and acted on it. What I didn't understand was that in taking advantage of Busdriver, I was cheating myself. It would have been better work to press him when he was fresh. Milton teased Joe because I was improving more quickly than he was.

Busdriver, you're still punching retarded. Look at Bob. When he came here, he was quadriplegic. Then he got paraplegic. Now he's just plegic. If he stays here a few more months, he'll be normal.

I knew I wasn't getting enough sparring at Revolution, so I called Laura to see if she would come down.

Why don't you come over to Gleason's and spar with us? Laura asked. We could use the work, and it will give you some perspective.

Laura's promoter had made fights for both Joey and her in Pennsylvania in February, and their training had intensified. When I asked Milton, however, he forbade it.

What happened to all the work she was supposed to get over there? he said sourly. It's not what she expected, is it? And now she wants to get more of my guys with her. No way.

I couldn't disobey Milton in this. He had brought me a long way in four months, and I felt loyal.

Hey, all right, Julian said to Stella, I can see you got good taste.

What do you mean? she asked.

He pointed to the McDonald's supersize cup she held, a waxed cardboard tub that could hold at least a quart of carbonated sugar.

Oh, this? Stella said. It's filled with water.

Damn, Julian said, I thought you were down with me. Because I eat a lot of McDonald's.

Julian, I said, you're an athlete. How can you put that shit in your body? McDonald's. You might as well be eating out of a Dumpster.

Julian took offense.

Yo, the Olympic Team book said a boxer can eat whatever makes him feel comfortable.

Uh, Julian, I said, I don't think the book meant a Big Mac and fries.

Along with roadwork, diet is where fighters are most apt to break discipline. After you train hard, you want to eat, naturally. Ali was a late-night habitué of the ice-cream parlors around his Deer Lake camp, while Roberto Duran, with a frame small enough to have been one of the great lightweights of all time, ate like the starving street kid from Panama City he had been, regularly gaining fifty pounds between fights and ending his career as a super middleweight (168 pounds). In a poorly regulated sport, in which most athletes struggle to make the lowest weight physically possible, the temptation is always to cheat and eat. Boxers learn that they can excise six or eight or more pounds of water in sweat immediately before a weigh-in by jumping rope in the steam room with the garbage bags, the rubber suit, the Albolene. The former junior middleweight contender, Curtis Summit, told me he had lost ten pounds the day before a fight by this method. Besides the risk of weakening himself, the fighter also may deplete the fluid in his skull, increasing the danger of brain injuries (one reason why amateurs are allowed to lose only two pounds after a weigh-in; any more, and they are disqualified or moved to a higher weight class). When water loss is not enough, boxers turn to laxatives, diet pills and even the veterinary medication Lasix (a diuretic).

In professional boxing, promoters began to schedule weigh-ins the day before major bouts when the media proved willing to present them as a spectacle. Fighters immediately realized that with a day to recover, they could undergo even more radical purges. The volatile James Toney gained 15 pounds after the weigh-in for his title fight with Roy Jones, Jr.; Iran Barkley went from 160 to 180 pounds in the twenty-four hours before a fight with Nigel Benn. Recent scandals, however, have served to reverse the ante-post weigh-in trend.*

Crackpot diet asides, nutrition these days approaches science. Yet it is a science few boxers take advantage of (some champions have begun to include nutritionists on their staffs). At Revolution, I would walk into our studio and kick the fast-food cartons aside.

Julian assures me that his diet *does* change in the weeks before a fight (since his weight ticks toward 170 when he's not training hard). Starting a couple of weeks before a fight, he says, for breakfast, I'll have oatmeal or grits, something like that. Then something light at lunch, maybe a tuna fish sandwich, not too much bread, though. For dinner, chicken without the skin or beefsteak. If I eat anything fried, I'll only have a small portion. Mostly boiled or steamed. Rice, vegetables . . .

And, in a pinch, he recommends essence of magnesia.

The dancer helped me stretch. She laid me out on the floor and plied my legs in unusual contortions.

It would help, she said, if you moved from your center.

My center?

---

*On February 26, 2000, Arturo Gatti weighed 19 pounds more for his fight with Joey Gamache than he had at the weigh-in. In the fight, Gatti, looking twice as large as Gamache, knocked him out in the first round, inflicting brain damage that forced Gamache's retirement. Questions arose whether Gatti had ever actually weighed 141 pounds (there had been a dispute between camps at the weigh-in when Gatti leaped rapidly on and off the scale without the measures' being balanced). Gatti was unable to make weight for his next fight, at *148* pounds.

The center, as I gleaned from her explanation, was as much a philosophical concept as an actual location. You see, she said, you tend to stick your chest out and arch your back. That restricts your movement in your arms and shoulders. If you try to move more from your base [she pointed toward my stomach], then you'll have more flexibility in your arms. You'll be looser.

I suddenly understood that Milton had been trying to explain this same thing to me for months, that my posture hindered my progress as a fighter. He would grab me as I trained and try to force me into the right position. "Stop sticking your chest out so much. Relax your shoulders." The dancer's explanation helped me to appreciate the refinement of Milton's gaze and the subtlety of his technique.

Milton had sharp eyes and fast hands. He would sit on the bench and show us card tricks or take away nickels and dimes from the fighters at rummy 500. "You want me to write you an IOU? How about a UOMe?" One day A.J. brought in a boxful of mechanical puzzles from a trade show, only to have Milton shuck their wiles in a matter of minutes.

Bring something a little tougher next time, he said. Remember, I'm Puerto Rican.

Through January, rivals appear at Revolution in search of combat sims, the closest thing to a real fight without a referee. Today an old Rastafarian and his five sons, the Joseph family, have invaded the room.

The sparring is already under way when I enter: shouts and sounds of blows . . . boxers lined up for their turn, girt, chin straps dangling . . . opponents measured from eye corners . . . arms swung before the wall mirrors. The old man—dreadlocks gray, mouth short incisors—exhorts his sons in a thick island patois. Five brothers in descending order of experience and size, from the oldest, a light heavyweight and pro, through middleweights and welterweights down to the youngest, smallest baby bear, for me.

Bob, get ready, Milton says.

As I dress, I watch the youngest brother drill, his hands in swift flurries I can only clumsily ape. Every movement precise and smooth, each duplicating the last to the micrometer, the boy a flesh robot, a killing machine. When he snaps jabs and describes a circle, each footfall behind his pivot foot falls equidistant, a perfectly delineated circle around a center point sectioned evenly by steps. His lightness impresses me. He is handsome too, smooth in the way young men sometimes are, skin a creamy brown and clear. He is sixteen years old.

Our turn comes. We rush forward and clash. I slip under his two, landing a two to his body and then score to his jaw with a wild hook. After that punch, our rounds fall into a pattern, his retreat and my pursuit. He moves backward behind a jab until he reaches the ropes, then darts left or right as I push after him. Once I make the mistake of walking after him without moving my head. Crack, his right hand shoots out to explode against my chin.

It is a mistake to think that the punches of different boxers differ only in grades of intensity. I'd come to believe that punches have a personality, deriving from the puncher. Joey's hook, for example, was not particularly fast but carried an enormous weight and felt like a full can of beer crumpling on the side of my head. The right hand of this West Indian kid is the bullet from a low-caliber rifle, eighteen hundred feet per second toward impact with bone.

My knees buckle, and I lunge backward automatically to maintain balance, entire body in a heaving jerk. I have never been hit in just that way before. While I feel no danger of being knocked unconscious, the strings that support me have nearly been severed. He does not follow, and I settle myself and continue to press, remembering to move my head. I very much want to hurt him. Yet I can never finally catch him as he scuttles around the ropes. Occasionally he waits for me with another counter right following my jab, or he slips under my first punch and holds, clinging to one arm and rolling as I try to hit him with the other, until Milton shouts, "Break!"

Between rounds, Milton tells me to press. Feint when you have him in the corner; then come hard to the body. He's tired, stay on top of him.

I try to conceal my fear of chasing him too closely.

And so we go, four rounds and out. Afterward, to the oldest brother, Milton says, It's funny. The kid was the only one of your guys who got tired.

Well, you know what they say about pressure, says the light heavy.

After the patriarch and his progeny leave, Milton encourages me.

That was some of the best work you've done, Bob. You slipped and you dipped and you bobbed and you weaved. You had him missing all over the place. But you got to punch *to* him. You're the one holding yourself back now. You made him miss; now make him pay. The first hook you landed scared him. One punch can do it. You've got to learn to read their eyes. He was scared of you. He was running for his life.

Two days later I look at the log at the front desk of Revolution and find that the Joseph brothers have preceded me. I trace the column, Livingstone and Quincy and Mitchell, Anglo-Caribbean names. Milton has warned me that they would be coming. I remain sore from our last encounter. Fear made me superstitious on the way from my apartment. I rode the train one stop too far: a sign not to spar. The door to the building stood open: a sign that I should spar. On the log, I check the time beside the names to see if I arrived too late, but no. Upstairs the little assassin lies in wait, as in the ring Efrain trades with the largest brother, who yells nonstop, "Whooo! Whooo!" in time to the hip-hop from our stereo.

Is this the guy you were talking about, Milton? he shouts. I'm asking you. Is this the guy?

I'm Sugar Ray! he bellows at Efrain. I'm Sugar Ray!

When the bell rings for rest, he leans over the ropes, hawks and squirts bloody spittle into a bucket. The next round, the talking continues:

What's my name? What's my name? I'm Sugar Ray!

Efrain says nothing, focused, as they stand in front of each other, trading bombs. I wince at the punishment Efrain takes, but he doesn't fade, doesn't bend, keeps banging.

That's all you got? the light heavy shouts. I'm not even hitting you hard.

When it ends, Efrain leaves the ring first.

Nice work, Sugar Ray, he says over his shoulder, a half smile on his face.

Yeah, you're not bad, the Joseph brother responds. Not *too* bad.

Then it's my turn again. This time the boy confronts me in the center of the ring, and I have a feeling that he's received a stern lecture on his last performance. This time he doesn't run or slide around the ropes. In the first minute he tries to draw me in with a fake: He feints a jab and then slips right to position himself perfectly for a right counter if I counter his jab. It's a move Milton has tried to teach me, and I'm once again awed by his grace. He's so artful that fighting him is like taking a crowbar to the Venus de Milo. He gives me a lot of lateral movement as I push forward, on both sides of my advance.

Just touch him, Bob, Milton shouts. Make contact. Then follow with something.

I'm tentative and stay low. I slide under a right but drop too low and don't have space to go under the following hook. The rimfire .22 shell drives through my temple, making me blink. He hits so very fast. Milton yells for me to stand tall and wait for his punches to slip.

Touch him, Bob, he shouts. Tap him, head, shoulders, arm, it doesn't matter. Make contact.

Rounds 2, 3, 4, the boxers crowding around the ring. Julian shouts, "Double jab, two." I begin to listen and score. "Do it again, Bob," Julian shouts. "Do it again. It's there every time." My aggression begins to wear the Joseph boy down. He backs into a corner, losing concentration, becoming easier to hit. At the end of the fourth round, I've had enough, my T-shirt translucent with sweat.

One more, Bob? Milton asks.

I nod yes; I can't show weakness before the competition.

As I walk back to my corner, I hear the boy protest.

No, Daddy, he says. I can't. I'm injured. My elbow hurts, bad, and my knee.

Get back and go one more round, his father insists.

Daddy, I can't, his face that of a suffering saint. The complaint transforms him, from executioner to child. Both their accents are so thick I can barely interpret the words.

All right, Bob, that's it, Milton says, and holds the ropes for me.

I step out in absolute relief.

How do you like my White Lightning? Milton exults as we shuck our gear. Don't have bad dreams about him tonight. No, no, he's all right. That was good work.

Later I sit and talk with the boy and his oldest brother. The family is from the Virgin Islands. Unsolicited, the older brother gives me his record: I'm ten and three, he says, with five knockouts [pros rattle off their records like a résumé]. And two of those losses, well . . .

The younger brother tells me has won the Silver Gloves and the Junior Metros. In a year or two, I will be unable to match him in any way. Tonight I have succeeded simply through strength of will, by being more persistent than a boy.

Afterward Milton says, That kid has a mean little punch. But, then, so do you. In the Gloves, people are gonna be scratching their heads saying, "What happened?"

Every new boxer had to suffer through an initiation rite particular to the Supreme Team. Hanson's turn came on a night in early January.

Hey, Milton, Victor says, tell Hanson about the box.

The box? Milton says. I haven't told you about the box yet, Hanson?

Hanson shakes his long blond hair. Knowing what is to come, the other boxers draw closer.

Well, we were in Puerto Rico, me and Rudy and Victor, Milton continues, and we're driving back from the beach with these two girls Rudy knows. So, we're driving along when we pass this guy and the girls say, "Hey, we know him. Pull over." Okay. We stop, and the guy comes running up. Me and Vic and Rudy look at each other 'cause this guy is a freak. He's got long, greasy hair and a straggly beard, and his clothes are all raggedy. But the strangest thing about him is, he's holding this box, this beat-up metal box, almost completely wrapped in duct tape.

Hanson stares at Milton. The other boxers are silent.

So he gets in, and we're driving for a while. The girls are talking to this guy, you know, "*¿Que pasa?*," "*¿Como 'ta?*," "*Todo bien,*" you know, "How are you?," "What's going on?" Then one of the girls asks this guy, "*¿Qu'está in la caja?*" You know, "What's in the box?" So all of a sudden, the guy goes crazy. He's like, "*¡No demandes! Puta, callate la trompa, no demandes, puta!*" Crazy, screaming, "Don't ask. Just shut the fuck up, you fucking bitch. Don't fucking ask." So we're all looking at them, and the other girl tries to talk to him, she says, you know, "*Calmate, amigo,*" "Chill." So he's quiet for a while, and we keep driving. Then the girl asks him, "By the way, what's in the box?" So here we go again: "*¡Puta, pendejo, chingate!*" You know, "Shut the fuck up! Don't you fucking ask!" Well, by this time, Rudy's starting to get really mad.

He shouts, "Milt, stop the car!" So I hit the brakes. And Rudy jumps out, opens the door, grabs this guy and just starts *beating* him. I mean, he's slamming this guy in the head, hitting him with elbows, everything, but the guy doesn't fight back, just hugs the box with both hands. Finally, he falls down, still clinging to the box, and Rudy starts to kick him. Then Rudy makes to grab the box, and they're fighting over it. Rudy knocks him one more time in the head, bam! So the guy drops it and Rudy throws it into the car and we drive off.

Milton falls silent. Hanson looks at him.

So what was in the box? he asks.

The boxers erupt in a gratified shout. Don't fucking ask!

Milton would ask me, "Do you want to move with so-and-so?" and I would find myself playing backstop for a 135-pound nurse or a wild boy or a stockbroker learning to throw his twos. It was good to stand in front of them and learn how to slip, good to bob, duck and let the punches fly by, soak into my arms, spend themselves on my gloves. Defense is referred to as a lost art in boxing, but I learned defense in those long sessions where the mismatches constrained me from punching. It changed my strategy: Where I had always been waiting for my next opportunity to strike, I learned that to make someone miss was also an art. You could dishearten an opponent simply by getting out of the way.

Milton loved defense.

Everybody can power punch, he would say, but I tell my guys, "You can't hurt everybody you hit. You can beat guys just by frustrating them."

He would have me step toward an incoming punch and slide beneath it. He taught me to use my elbow to spin around an opponent.

You're getting hit less with your hands down, Milton would say. It's incredible, isn't it? None of these stupid idiots understand. All they see is one thing, in one dimension. Their dimension is, "Keep your hands up. Go straight ahead."

No doubt I was getting hit less with my hands down. But why? No book explained it; no trainer accepted it; everyone told you not to do it; you heard them shouting from around the ring, *"Keep . . . your . . . hands . . . up!"* You'll get killed with them down, they said. Sure, Ali did it, hands down, leaning away from punches, but you're no Ali. Ali was cheetah quick, a sport, a freak, a boxing mutant, the heavyweight with a lightweight's speed. He had supernatural powers. You, you keep your hands up, up, up, welded to the sides of your head. Fight Milton's way, and you'll get *hurt*.

In an effort to understand, I studied tape of old bouts. The truth of Milton's claim was there: Many, if not most, of the great champions fought with their hands down, first jab flicking from some point around the navel. I watched Archie Moore, the Mongoose, beloved of Liebling, throw his jab in black and white, throw it like Ali, like Ray Robinson. I watched him turn his shoulder to deflect punches; I watched him lean away from impact and drop his hands to his sides as he shaked and baked (the young Ali trained in Moore's camp while turning pro). But it wasn't just Moore and Ali; it was Ray Leonard, "Lightning" Lonnie Smith, Tommy Hearns, Prince Naseem and Pernell "Sweetpea" Whitaker, whose trainer, Lou Duva, said, "You couldn't hit him with a handful of rice." All the boxers considered slick, slippery, nice, smooth. Why, then, did the trainers always shout for us to *"Keep your hands up"*?

From what I've seen, most boxers fought with their hands down from the twenties through the forties. Yet the slippery style Milton promotes is, as he would say, "a black thing" and seems to have been utilized by African-American boxers (such as Archie Moore) as far back as the thirties, to reach its widest currency into the seventies.

It's definitely a black thing, Milton says. My boxing style is—it's not strange, really, because it's been done through history. Like that Ali pullback. When you do pull back, you've got all kinds of options. You can pull-slip, pull-duck, pull-catch or pull and knock the punch down. There's so many different ways, more than just standing there. I decided, "Hey, this is a lot more fun when you don't get hit." Being a human punching bag is no damn fun.

In recent decades this style seems to have lost ground to both the orthodox school and the body banging favored by Mexican fighters. Perhaps it is difficult to teach, easier to heed "Keep your hands up," and cruise forward like a battleship.*

---

*Julian makes the point that our style suits pros better than amateurs, since we rely on shoulder blocks, which an amateur judge may record as a scoring blow, even though the punch has been deflected.

Why a boxer is harder to hit with his hands down might be related to the center. When a fighter pulls his hands up, he also leans slightly forward; this draws his center forward as well. It has the effect of restricting the fighter's range of motion (the fighter is already committed forward) and shortening the fighter's punching range; he needs to be just slightly closer to strike, meaning he is also a little closer to being struck. Milton's approach seems to give a fighter more options, makes it easier to move backward and laterally.

While I originally thought that Milton's style would favor the tall, I came to realize that it worked for short fighters by extending their range and making them "fight taller" (Dave Marrero referred to Milton's style as "punching long"). It also gives a fighter an instant more to react to the incoming punch. That's what I told myself, anyway, to explain how, after years of boxing, I finally wasn't getting hit.

Salads, sprouts, protein bars, pickles, low fat and no fat, sugarless candy and uncreamed coffee, a few spoonfuls of peanut butter (all natural) to fool the body into thinking it had eaten. At parties, buffet tables beckoned me. My hand would stretch out, return to mouth, stretch out, return, repeat until I sat licking nut fragments and salt crystals from the bottom of the bowl. I was addicted to food. In a fitness book, I read that a well-trained athlete's body will immediately convert sugar to energy following an intense workout; I took this to mean that every night after the gym I could drift toward the candy rack in the local bodegas: gummy jellies, spearmint leaves, orange slices, coconut clusters, licorice. I found myself spending unseemly amounts of time pondering whether to eat "just one more" cracker from my cupboard. The dancer always overordered in restaurants, never finishing more than half her entrée. I would hover above her plate. I understand why boxers cheated, now, why they fell. After bottoming out at '23, I slowly began to drift upward. By the middle of the month, I realized 119 was impossible.

Milton, I said, I'm afraid I have some bad news. I can't make one nineteen.

You can't? he said, disappointed. You would have been killing those crazy little midgets.

Three weeks into the tournament, I still hadn't received my fight date from the *Daily News*. I asked Giuseppe when he had received his as a novice.

You got plenty of time, he said, rubbing his stubble. 'Twenty-five novice, they don't call them until late. I think my first year, I fought February tenth. Around the middle of February. You won't get your card until a week, ten days before. 'Twenty-five is always called late. There just aren't that many guys. I'll probably go about the same time. But listen, you and me need more different sparring. It's okay to keep going with each other, but we need some other people.

Let me talk to Laura, I said, see if she wants to come in.

On the phone Laura told me she needs work also.

I'll call Milton, she said. I don't want to, but . . . Joey's complaining about not getting any sparring here.

He has no one to spar with at Gleason's?

Well, he comes in late . . . I don't know.

Is he doing his roadwork?

He says he is.

What about the match your manager made for him?

Well, I asked him again. I said, "Joey's a great kid. Please don't put him in against the wrong guy." And my manager said, "Okay, the guy he was going to fight would have beat him. But I'll get him someone else." I mean, Joey was talking about moving to Pennsylvania. It's huge for him. Joey's no young kid, you know; he doesn't have many chances left.

A few days later Laura called me again.

I haven't called Milton and I don't intend to, she said. I just wouldn't feel comfortable there.

I told her I understood.

On occasion, the storyteller in Milton would overcome the secret agent, and he would regale the boxers with some colorful episode from his past.

One time my brother stole a city bus, Milton said, and he was so stupid he parked it on Eighth Street over in the East Village. So a cop comes up, and he's looking at the bus, like, "What the hell is this doing here?" My brother runs over to him. "Don't worry," he says. "That belongs to me." "Oh, really?" the cop says. "Then you're just the man I want to talk to."

Once he waved an old passport before us, filled with stamps from places like Kuwait, Australia, Dubai, the Fiji Islands. The Milton in the passport photo was younger, darker, and wore an enormous Afro.

Generally, though, he dropped questions into darkness or dodged them with lame-ass humor.

So, Milton, I asked, did you ever box?

Sure I boxed, Milton said, in Philadelphia.

My attention widened. Philadelphia was famous for boxing; I was about to learn something interesting.

I used to work in a factory, he went on, boxing cheese.

Boxing cheese?

Yeah, boxing cheese. I hit it so hard I creamed it. You've heard of Philadelphia cream cheese, haven't you?

THE STRANGE CASE
OF THE PROFESSOR

In the gym, another white boxer materialized. From time to time, other white men appeared in the studio. Inevitably they seemed uneasy among us, or so we heard from their trainers. I know how they felt. Having to watch fighters, being watched by fighters in your inexpert fondling of the bag. Trying too hard because you had something to prove.

When I saw this new guy, stiff on the bag or the mitts, when I heard him complain to Milton that he wasn't getting it, I knew he was with us. Is this work for me? I thought. Competition? Not much taller than I was, the new fighter, but thickset, with cropped blond hair and an accent from some point between Midwest and South. I asked Milton who he was.

You know, that white guy you were working with today?

Oh, you mean the Professor?

I guess. Is he new?

No, he's been around for a while. But he's not getting it yet.

He was the Professor, or simply Professor, on account of being a graduate student in anthropology at CUNY and an adjunct professor at one of the city colleges. He was also a head trainer at one of the franchise health clubs. He had that former bodybuilder look, the wide torso padded a little with fat. He spoke little, at least to me, although I saw that he was on fairly good terms with Julian and Will. Soon the Professor was in the van, accompanying us to shows, carrying equipment, saturating himself in boxing life. Yet every time I spoke to him, I would elicit only a monosyllable.

So you speak Spanish?

Yes.

You ever been outside the country?

Yes.

I wondered if he bore rancor toward me, the other white regular with the Supremes. I wondered why he was hanging around so much.

One evening, Milton asked me if I wanted to spar the Professor.

I looked over at him.

How much does he weigh?

One sixty, one sixty-five, something like that. Milton shrugged. But he won't be able to hit you.

Okay, I said doubtfully.

In the ring, Professor was a catastrophe, scuttling forward in a jerky rush and standing square before me. His weak jab flippered air. With every punch I landed, confidence surged; I could control this middleweight. Then it happened: when my left cross cleft his guard and smacked him in the face, he swayed and staggered halfway across the ring.

I stopped and stared.

Are you all right, Professor? Milton asked.

I'm fine, he said, and rushed forward.

The same thing happened again. And again. He would wobble backward after a head shot, then hurry forward. This sequence made me extremely uncomfortable. When the second round ended, I wanted no more.

C'mon, Bob, one more round, the Professor said, martial in the ring center.

No, I'm finished, I said, stepping through the ropes.

Later, after the Professor left the studio, Vernon began to laugh.

Did you see that? I'm asking you, did you see that? Vernon demanded in his resonant voice.

You're getting more power behind your two, Milton said.

Professor was *out*! Vernon shouted. If you hit him two more times, they would have had to call nine-one-one.

But we're supposed to be on the same team, Vern, I said.

I don't care, he boomed. You should have taken him *out*. Listen to what I'm saying, you *should* have laid that cracker *out*!

When I sparred Professor again a few days later, Milton wasn't there. Instead Will supervised the proceedings. Again came the phenomenon of my left knocking Professor back and his scuttling forward like a horror film zombie stabbed, shot, eviscerated but still crawling.

After the second or third stumble, Will cautioned him.

The next time that happens, Professor, Will said, I'm going to have to pull you out of there.

Will said this as if Professor had chosen to meander crazy-legged across the ring (but that was the suspicion, his wobbling florid, almost theatrical).

At the break, Will summoned me into my corner.

Bob, follow your jab with an uppercut, he whispered. He's open for the five every time.

The uppercut (slowest of punches) was a favorite of Will's because of his intercontinental reach. The next round, I backed the Professor into a corner and double jabbed. When he leaned away and down to my left, I released the five. I directed it to the body, but I was short and his head so far forward that the punch struck his extended chin. Professor dropped. Will and I watched him struggle to his feet.

That's it, Will said, and slapped my gloves. I *told* you the five was there.

C'mon, Bob, Professor said, primed, hands lifted, I want to spar more.

No more for me, I said, hurrying through the ropes.

Will agreed. You need to give it a rest, Professor.

The next day Milton greeted me as I walked into the gym.

Bob, I go away for a few days, and you start killing my white guys.

Bob almost knocked out Professor three times, Will said like a proud parent.

Every few minutes for the rest of the night, Milton would giggle and say, Bob, leave my white guys alone.

The more I hurt the Professor, the more afraid I was of being hurt by him. What I was doing to him demanded retribution. The fact that he was the larger man contributed to my unease. He wasn't someone who could never hurt me; he was someone who hadn't hurt me yet.

C'mon Bob, let's go a couple of rounds, he would say.

I tried to duck him, but Milton wouldn't let me run away. He told me how to proceed as I sparred the Professor one night.

Listen, Bob, this is good work for you, he whispered between rounds. Just stay away from his face, 'cause you know he can't take that. You don't want to lose your sparring partner. Throw the two, just keep it down. Hit the body. Use him as a body bag. You need to work downstairs more anyway.

Across the ring, I noticed the Professor craning to overhear. When the bell rang to start the round, he had a question.

Milton told you to take it easy on me, didn't he? the Professor said as we circled. Don't worry, you can go as hard as you want.

No, it's not that, I said lamely. This is good work for me.

So I refrained from administering my left to Professor's head. The fact that he didn't punch correctly meant I could land straight twos and uppercuts to his body without fear of a right-hand counter. Still, without head shots, I began to have trouble. The Professor was a solid man; he had taught abdominal classes, and beneath the fat on his gut stood a solid backboard of muscle. I could hit him in the belly all day with little effect. He also began to understand the principle of Milton's hooks and would cast them with a mechanical regularity. When I attempted combinations, the Professor, aware that I wouldn't go for his chin, would counter with a long hook. The first one that hit me spun my head around. Another drove my upper body through the ropes. His long arms and squat body provided him great leverage. The Professor was not in control of himself, and I was too small to control him easily. The only way I could hold him at bay was with head punches that hurt and enraged him. His lack of control took him outside the boundaries of sparring; Professor was a bear on the end of a leash, a danger to himself and the other boxers.

Watching him spar with others, I tried to discern the reasons for his failure. It could have been that years of weight work had restricted his range of motion, made him even stiffer than he would have been. Old essays on boxing state that weight lifting causes the muscles to "set." Another obstacle was simply lack of training. He moved awkwardly, scuttling like a crab. His defense was nonexistent; at one point, he started gluing his right glove to his lips for protection and would paw forward with the other hand. This made him appear feebleminded.

At least he's not getting hit with crosses. Milton grinned.

More than anything technical, however, the Professor's difficulties were born in frustration. As soon as he became frustrated, he went blind.

Milton showed no mercy. When Professor mentioned that he'd been a trainer at a New York health club, Milton asked, Oh, what did you teach there, boxing?

But I'm confused, the Professor said during sparring sessions.

Confucius says, "Box!" Milton replied.

I tried to show the Professor the drills that I had learned from Milton and Laura. As we circled, I threw single punches and had him use simple counters. I told the Professor that he should spar less and focus on his skills.

This is what you need to do, I said, keep working on your defense and your footwork.

Didn't I know? I had been through the same misery, the bloody noses and self-hatred. The drills had converted me, convinced me that boxing was scientific, that cause followed effect: If A, then B; if C, then D. They had made me believe what I had doubted: that I could learn how to box.

Yet the Professor wouldn't stay with the drills. He never worked the floor, and whenever I walked into the gym, he would be sitting at ringside waiting for an opponent. Milton washed his hands of him, never mind that the Professor was paying him $250 a month (Milton charged whatever he thought he could get away with). Professor was the body bag for anyone who had the stomach to hit him.

Our uneasy sparring continued. If I hesitated or declined, he would bluster. C'mon, Bob, what's the problem? Let's go. I'll take it easy on you. Why don't you want to spar me, Bob? What's wrong with you?

It disturbed me that someone who was nearly knocked unconscious each time he was hit on the chin seemed so eager for a rematch, but his weakness was exactly the reason why he was so eager. Professor was caught in a savage test of his masculinity, believing that he could make boxing succumb to the force of his blind will.

Bob, you want to work today?

I don't think so, Professor. I'm not up for it.

Why not?

I just don't want to.

How come no one wants to spar me? he would wail.

And it was true, no one wanted to spar with him: heavier, lighter, bigger, smaller, man or woman. The Professor exposed himself every time he entered the ring, and we cringed away.

I don't like sparring guys like that, Efrain said. He's too wild. The last time I went in with him, he scratched my eyes with his fucking laces.

The Professor's retarded, Milton said with a grimace. You guys just got to beat the hell out of him until he figures it out.

When Milton attempted to teach him defense by sending him in with the women, the Professor would savage them. "Just tap the top of her headgear with your jab, Professor," Milton would command, but after being hit, he would begin arcing tremendous hooks out of his shame. One afternoon, a woman sparring him fled the ring. I found her trembling, eyes wet, beside the watercooler in the weight room.

I can't believe Milton lets him go at me like that. It's a spectacle. I feel like there's this great big animal attacking me.

Professor walked in, concerned and bewildered.

What's wrong? he asked. What happened?

The woman looked away.

You've got to go lighter with her, I said. She's much smaller than you. You can't hit her with those hooks.

I'm sorry, he said. I thought I was going light.

He touched her shoulder. From now on, he said, you just throw punches at me. I won't hit back.

His face was strained below his crew cut. That hook was all the protection that he had in the coliseum. He couldn't understand.

Julian and Will struggled to stay positive about their friend.

The Professor, that's my man, Julian said. I can't say nothing bad to him, but —

Yeah, Will said, he's having a tough time now, but he'll figure it out. He laughed.

The Professor only understands *e* equals *mc* squared.

Yet for all their sympathy, they would not spar with him either.

When I learned that Professor had recommended them both for positions at his sports club, it reinforced what I'd already determined: that the Professor was a decent man. He was always helping Milton with the equipment, loaning people small sums, distributing fast food. He had led an adventurous life that included fieldwork among sex workers in Latin America. Yet in the domain of boxing, he was lost. His behavior in the ring violated the code of conduct: Show no weakness. I had always sensed this code, but it became fully visible only in the Professor's breach of it, which caused me, I realized, to despise him a little.

One day soon after, I entered the studio.

Hey, Bob, you want to spar?

Professor was on me before I dropped my gym bag from my shoulder.

I'm not sparring today, I said, fending him off as I began to dress for my workout.

Why not? What's your excuse this time?

Because I'm not up for it.

Why are you scared? I'll go easy on you, Bob.

I went up in a flash of rage.

You want to fight, Professor? I shouted. I'll take one of those dumbbells off the floor and beat your fucking head in. You want to fight so bad? I'll fucking kill you.

Milton looked at me, eyebrows lifted. I had managed to surprise him and the few other people in the room. I continued to change with my back to the gym, and in a few minutes, Professor left. I felt I owed the gym an explanation.

I'm just tired of him always pushing me, I said to no one in particular.

Repentance followed swiftly.

I feel bad for yelling at him like that.

Just tell him you were on your period, Milton suggested.

———

A week later I walked into the gym to find him goading a stranger to get into the ring with him.

C'mon, let's go, I heard Professor say to the newcomer, a Puerto Rican middleweight in his late twenties. The man, who told me he was looking for Milton, seemed puzzled. Vernon entered the gym and shared my amazement.

Step up, Professor said, tugging on the ropes. Get dressed, and we can do some work.

I tried to make myself believe I wasn't seeing what I was seeing. It was as if I'd walked in on him copulating on the gym floor. This was not done. For all Professor knew, this man was a world champion or a baby who had never worn gloves in his life.

The stranger left. Although I had apologized for my outburst, after our troubles I felt constrained from saying anything. But I had to say something.

Professor, I said, did you know that guy?

No, I've never seen him before. But he was looking for Milton. He said he was going to start training here.

Professor, you shouldn't be asking guys to spar who you don't even know.

Why not? Professor said. I was just being friendly.

But, Professor, guys will think you're calling them out. You have to leave that up to Milton to decide.

Soon after, as he sparred, a woman boxer sitting beside me made a joke. We laughed, then looked up to find the Professor glaring at us. He thought we were laughing at him.

Milton had a story for the gym one evening.

Professor was in here today, Milton said, eating a candy bar. I had him work with Rob [a genial stockbroker]. I told the Professor to go light. I mean, Rob isn't in shape; about all he can do is jab. So the Professor went wild out there and tried to kill the poor guy. I kept shouting at him to take it easy, but he was trying to tear Rob's head off. So I said, "Fine, you want to fight?" And I sent Victor in to give him a beating. I don't know what that guy is thinking.

On the bench in street clothes, Victor delivered his half smile.

$\mathbf{T}$o my relief, Milton began to partner Professor regularly with a rangy light heavyweight, also a physical trainer, but one who had the instinct for boxing that Professor lacked. Sparring, he stayed relaxed enough to listen, and his punches came smoothly; within a month he almost looked like a fighter. His height and reach gave him an advantage over the Professor, who rushed forward in his frustrated rage, awkward and dangerous. His fixation on protecting his face left his body open. As they sparred, I saw an opening for the taller man.

Throw the four, I said, four to the body.

One of the most difficult things in boxing is to be able to apply advice while you are fighting. This punch was perfect; it landed with the sound of an ax halving a cantaloupe. Everyone at ringside winced. At the end of the round the Professor collapsed on the canvas. He was gasping and blood shone on his face. He lay there inert as we watched; I wondered if he was having a heart attack.

When we saw that he wasn't in immediate danger of death, Milton gave me his clownish sprawl-eyed gaze. We removed Professor's headgear and doused his head with water. He still lay motionless, the canvas dull gray where the water had splashed around him.

Just leave me alone, he said. Leave me alone. Over the next few minutes his breathing slowly returned to normal.

A few days later I heard that the Professor had broken ribs and would be out for six weeks.

I saw him once more at the gym. He told me that he couldn't wait to heal and come back. I suggested he take the opportunity to develop his footwork, that if I could have started over, I would have nailed my footwork early. He nodded and smiled distantly.

Two months later Milton told me that he'd gotten a call from the Professor saying he wanted to fight in the next show we entered. Milton shook his head.

·13·

RESPECT

It is thought by many that a knowledge of boxing tends to render the temper petulant and quarrelsome, and to make people fond of seeking opportunities of displaying their skill and ability.
—*Art of Manual Defence* (1789)

I walked into the front office at Revolution to find Milton bullshitting with a group of boxer types. As the men filed into the stairwell, Milton grabbed my shoulder.

Do you know who that is? he mouthed, pointing at a spindly black man wearing a leather jacket.

I mimed ignorance.

That's Mark Breland, Milton whispered.

This made sense, as the jacket back bore a U.S. Olympic Team logo. Breland had won a gold medal in the 1984 games and later been a welterweight world champion. He made Will look chubby.

Milton followed the men downstairs and I signed in.

Upstairs, I found Julian on the bench and, hitting a heavy bag, a shirtless boxer I vaguely recognized. He was around twenty-five and extremely handsome, with golden tones to his brown skin. His torso was heroic, and he had even features on his small head. As he struck the bag, he seemed agitated.

That's good, Julian said. Now double jab and follow with—

No, no. The man shook his head. Just let me work. You're Miltonizing me. You got a good amateur style. But I'm picking up a pro style now. That's what Vito got me doing.

I had seen Vito Antuofermo, the former middleweight champion, in our studio twice that week. Now I knew why.

Julian seemed offended. It's not just an amateur style. What I'm telling you is good for everyone. I—

I've won three titles, so I don't need anyone to tell me anything.

I've won titles too, and—

Well, I won the Gloves twice, okay, so I know what I'm doing here. Let me work.

This, I understood, was a dig at Julian, who for all his success had never won the Gloves. As the man punched, he was awkward, yet every awkward right hand crumpled the middle of the bag.

Even if you won the Gloves . . . Julian said.

I can't listen to this shit anymore! the man yelled, spinning away from the bag and yanking off his gloves. I can't get any work here with you motherfuckers distracting me! I wasted my whole day to come here, and now I can't even work out!

Shouting, he paced from his heaped clothes in one corner to the heavy bag and back.

I was supposed to spar here today, and there was nobody for me to spar. Mark Breland came down here to watch me, and fucking Milton fucked that shit up!

He stalked the lacquered floor. Milton walked into the room with a grin slathered across his face and immediately fell into the golden-skinned man's rage.

Milton, what the fuck were you doing, telling Mark Breland I didn't want to spar?

Milton's smile vaporized.

I thought you—

You thought? You didn't think shit! They came all the way down here to see me, and you stepped in! You told them I didn't want to spar! You fucking made me look bad in front of them! I couldn't believe you were doing that shit to me!

Yeah, but you said—

Fuck that! I didn't say anything! You're cock-blocking, Milton! They came here to see me. When you were downstairs telling them I didn't want to spar, I almost walked over and punched you in your fucking face right there! But I kept it chill.

You said you—

He swelled and started at Milton. I didn't say anything! Your man said he couldn't spar! I *never* complain!

Vito told me you had air in your back or something.

Vito nothing! I was here. I'm a man. I'm almost thirty years old! I'm thirty years old, and I make my own decisions! I was ready to spar and you fucked it up. Breland and those guys came down to see me, and they didn't get to see shit.

I didn't know Mark came here to see you, Milton protested.

Why the *fuck* else would he come here?

Sometimes he comes down here to watch the guys work.

Fuck that, Milton! You're cock-blocking! Then you turn around and go behind my back, telling Vito that I'm walking around without a shirt. I'm getting out of this *faggot* gym and moving over to Gleason's. You know, Milton, I thought we settled that up, man to man. Then you go and tell Vito, "Oh, your guy's got to chill out." Well, you know how these Italian guys are, when you're talking to them they just nod their heads, but they don't forget a single word. So Vito came to me and said, "Your man there is talking shit about you." It was my idea to come here and use you as second trainer. Vito doesn't even know you, man. He might have heard of you, but I'm the one who brought him up here. And then you go around and stab me in the back.

Nothing Milton said could quell the man, who continued his angry pacing. I feared he would attack Milton and was glad to have Julian there.

I thought you were my assistant trainer. But when I asked you to work the pads with me, you said no. What kind of fucking trainer is that? I'm getting away from these *faggots* and going to Gleason's, where you can walk around without a shirt.

Well, go to Gleason's then, Milton said softly.

And you know what? Now all these guys down on Carmine Street are gonna think that I didn't want to spar. You fucked me up good, Milton. All you got to do is apologize, but you're still talking, trying to get out of it. You can't apologize. You can't even do that. You're never wrong, Milton. That's why everyone fucking hates you. But I don't back down. These other guys back down, not me. I'm sick! You know that, Milton. I'm a *sick pup*.

He lunged toward Milton, then held himself, fists tight.

I'm close to— I'm about to— This city is *full* of fucking guys I beat down and later we could sit and have a beer and be friends. I don't *care* how old you are, Milton. I'll fucking do it!

He grabbed his gear and stomped from the room, leaving us in the scalded air.

The room was silent. I started to jump rope, and Milton soon walked out.

Hey, Julian, I asked, who was that?

That was Born Crazy.

Oh, *that* was Born Crazy. I had heard a great deal about the man.

Yeah. Can you believe that guy saying I got an amateur style? Julian shook his head in disgust.

So what happened?

Well, Born's getting ready to turn pro, so . . . he's pretty sensitive.

Talking with Julian, I managed to trace the main lines of the story. Born was being managed by a consortium fronted by Antuofermo, who also served as Born's manager (Vito's scarred brow and crushed once-Roman profile were memorials to his brawling style). Born had suggested that they begin working at Milton's space. On this particular day, Mark Breland had come to Revolution at the behest of the consortium to watch Born work. Milton hadn't known this, and, as soon as Mark arrived at the gym, Milton had monopolized his attention.

The quarrel between Milton and Born wasn't about sparring; it was about respect. Julian put it well: "Born thinks Milton pushed him to the side, you know? Disrespected him. Hey, I'm not frontin'. Sometime Milton do that." For young men in the gym, especially those from inner-city neighborhoods, respect serves as a form of social capital. And although boxing can draw fighters out of the matrix of street life, the street impinges on the ring. At the 12th Street gym, I once saw a boxer, outclassed in a sparring session, tell his opponent he wanted to fight on the street. The opponent declared that if the other man were to attack him outside, he would shoot him. After winning my first bout at a Gleason's show, I was stunned when Darryl told me that I should sneak out of the room before the show ended so I didn't get jumped on the street by the teammates of the kid I'd beaten. In beating him, I had disrespected him, and justice called to be served.

Respect was as important to Milton as any of his fighters. His feud with Julio, the proprietor of 12th Street, had gone on for years, long after Julio lost the space. When Milton discovered that the owner of the gym Julio had moved to was slandering him, retribution followed.

This guy doesn't even know me, Milton said. He's never seen me train. I've never even met him. Yet here he is, talking shit about me.

Milton's first act was to send a few of his young fighters to the gym, where, posing as prospective customers, they asked the owner for his opinion of a certain trainer named . . . Milton. The owner responded with the usual claims that Milton was a thug and hustler. Soon afterward someone pointed out the owner to Milton on the street, and Milton went running after him.

Are you————? Milton asked.

Yeah, the owner said.

Do you know me?

No, the man said.

Well, I'm Milton LaCroix, the coach of the Supreme Team. And if you don't know me, how come you're talking all this shit about me?

They fought. Three years later the feud continued. When Milton appeared at an amateur boxing show in the owner's gym during October, the owner promptly called the police and had Milton ejected. Milton in turn launched an effort to have the owner sanctioned by U.S. Boxing for restricting access to his shows.

To protect the honor of his Supreme Team, Milton would take extraordinary measures. When one of his boxers walked into a public gym in Queens, wearing a Supreme Team jacket, a security guard told him he had to leave. Asked why, the guard said that the Supreme Team was disruptive and caused trouble. One of the fighters present shouted, "Fuck Milton! Fuck the Supreme Team!" Milton's fighter asked for the man's name and left.

Upon hearing the story, Milton launched into cell phone hyperdrive. He called U.S. Boxing and the Parks Department, registering complaints with both. Then he accosted the trainer of the boxing team that worked out of the Queens gym, who just happened to have the name that Milton's fighter had been given. The trainer was apologetic and evasive. Milton kept cool: No, he didn't think his fighter had started the problem; he was a good man, a workingman, a family man. No, he didn't think the security guard knew anything about the Supreme Team. What did "Supreme Team" mean to anyone outside boxing? Well, of course, the trainer had to know that this sort of thing would get back to Milton. It was a public facility, open to all. No, of course, Milton understood that it wasn't the trainer who had instigated the incident. So who, then, was the culprit? It had to be a boxer, Milton said, someone on the inside. His fighter had identified the other man as a white. "You don't want a problem," Milton said, "but here we have a problem. My fighter, offering trouble to no one, has been insulted and thrown out of a public facility. Of course we have a problem." The Parks Department had already been contacted. Whoever had provoked the incident would have to identify himself and apologize. Milton traced the origin of this incident to the Metros, where Will had defeated one of the other team's fighters. The fighter had challenged Will in the dressing room afterward, and only the intervention of Julian and Milton had stopped them from brawling there.

Milton, I said after he disconnected, have you ever considered a legal career?

I'm going to find out who this guy is, Milton said, that's for sure.

Remind me not to get on your bad side, I said.

Throughout boxing history, a debate has persisted over whether boxing stabilizes the lives of the poor kids who practice it. The consensus is that "Yes, boxing gets them off the streets." Through boxing, the thinking goes, for the first time in their lives, many of them have a goal that demands such middle-class virtues as hard work, self-denial, delay of gratification and temperance, virtues that could be turned to other pursuits when the time for boxing has passed.

Yet this view goes only so far. Horst, my German trainer, put it well one day when speaking of Tony Ayala. Ayala was a ferocious fighter who would spit on felled opponents. He turned pro at seventeen and won nineteen of his first twenty-two fights by KO. Ranked first in the world, with a title bout scheduled, Ayala, drunk and on heroin, left his sleeping wife, forced his way into a neighbor's house and raped her repeatedly.*

They take these kids like Ayala, Horst said, who don't know anything, and they turn them into killing machines, right? They tell them, "Good, kill, destroy, the worse the better." That's everything for them. Then people can't understand when they get into trouble.

Boxing blurs the distinction between acceptable behavior and wanton violence. In American society, fist-to-fist violence has generally disappeared. For the man on the street, the shift to violence is a radical one, one that takes a certain resolve, even under the influence of alcohol, and most encounters descend into harmless shouting matches. For the boxer, however, the shift to violence is almost imperceptible. There simply isn't that much difference between someone hitting you in the gym and someone hitting you outside it (except that in the gym you're probably going to get hit harder). Shove a boxer, and his automatic reaction will be not to shove you back but to hit you with a three-punch combination.

From eighteen to twenty-seven, I had perhaps two fistfights. In the years since, my main boxing years, I've had six. Always with larger men, often under the influence of alcohol. I can't fully understand why. My brother, a serious bodybuilder, fought often in college and the years afterward and sometimes ended up unconscious or in jail. Yet at some point he made a decision and stopped placing himself in situations in which he would end up with his elbow clamped around another man's neck. He remains a large, angry man, but he has learned to control the wildness that led him into violence. I have yet to follow his example.

I'm not sure why I can't make myself stop. In the abstract, I know it isn't worth it. But anger sweeps away my mind. There will always be someone bigger, stronger, luckier, someone with a knife or a gun, and I will be left badly injured, for nothing. For respect, the force field that dresses a man from head to toe, that can spread across a continent. Respect, a tender thing, so easily injured, so difficult to soothe, con-

---

*Released from prison after sixteen years, Ayala was in the middle of a comeback attempt when, in a bizarre incident, he was shot by a female acquaintance after breaking into her home at 3:45 A.M. He now faces trial.

spired against, reviled, ridiculous and precious and often at risk. Look around you and see it everywhere, locked down behind male faces, the tick-tick-tick of time bomb respect. If you think it's only testosterone-hopped teens or ethnic toughs who tick like that, think again. My old modernism professor told me he went on mood-stabilizing drugs to control his anger. "I realized that I was going to get into a lot of trouble," he said, "if I kept telling random people to obey traffic laws and not throw garbage in the street." New York City makes it worse; in the city the world hits you like gravel from a gun. You've had five and a half hours of sleep. The train comes, and you lunge into the press of bodies. The train lurches and stops in a tunnel as if it had dropped into a hole and you're already late for a shitty temp job where a lawyer will scream at you because his computer crashed and you will want to bash in his fat face.

O n a night in mid-October, I went for my late run. Although the weather was still warm, the life on the track had faded; goodbye to the Polish girls and the handball games until spring. I ran to the sound of my own footfalls, the night around me quiet and clear. After my laps and sprints, I left the track and crossed the baseball field toward home.

From across the field, a barking dog bolted after me. In moments it tangled itself with my legs and snapped at my calves: a pit bull, with those dense muscles and that shark grin. I slowed and tried to kick the dog away, but it pressed and bit. A man and woman ran toward us on the path, screaming the dog's name.

Don't move! they shouted at me. Stay still!

Stay still? I kicked the bastard dog again. The voices finally drew the animal away and I glanced at the owners. Their voices had identified them as white and educated, and so they seemed. He was a healthy-looking twenty-something a few inches taller than I was with solid legs in khaki shorts. She was a brunette, slender and nondescript. They seemed a little Upper East Side for Williamsburg, and it was late for them to be out, but dog walkers were the whites you were most likely to see after midnight.

I turned and started again toward home.

That thing should be on a leash, I shouted over my shoulder.

Fuck you, asshole, the man replied.

I stopped.

What? I said.

The dog bolted toward me again (perhaps the man had loosened his grip on its collar). This time I braced myself. I kicked it hard in the snout and then punched the side of its head as it leaped. The owner charged. Fear seized me: I had just run four miles and my body was tired. I had also reinjured my right hand sparring the week before and could not strike without pain. But anger overruled fear; I wanted satisfaction.

As Khaki Shorts tried to grab me, I hit him three-times-quick in the face—not strong punches, but he stumbled back. The dog bit my leg and laddered up my back. I flinched, expecting Khaki to counter, but he tried to wrestle with me. I hit him again. Khaki kept coming forward to grabble and scratch; he tried to kick me in the groin, and his foot glanced off my upper thigh. He simply could not fight. The dog was no longer at my back. The next time Khaki clawed me, I hooked him with my injured hand, a red flower of pain blossoming up my arm. He fell heavily on the pavement.

Brian! his girlfriend shrieked.

He rolled away and rose quickly, then rushed again. He tore my sleeveless T from my shoulders, then kicked me, this time almost catching me between the legs. It seemed unsporting, so I kicked him in the same place. Not wanting to brawl, I took a better stance and began to flick jabs at his face (my hand throbbed with every punch). Now he backed away, arms raised, hands open.

I just don't like people messing with my dog, he said.

Your dog attacked me, I reminded him. For him, the fight was over. We had struck each other and the first rush of adrenaline had faded. Now we could be friends. But I was still angry. I wanted an apology.

Well, you were running. He smirked.

I was running? I said in stupid fury. This is America, I can run wherever I want.

Oh, this is America? he said, grin widening.

I took a step forward. He took a step back. I still wanted to hurt him. If he could stand and smirk at me, I had not hurt him enough. I would have to attack him, though, and I couldn't.

You piece of shit, I said, you're just not worth it.

And then I went running off across the park, the rag of my shirt flapping about my hips. I lifted the rag and threw it behind me. I was already thinking about the story I would tell at Revolution.

At my apartment, I examined myself in the mirror. Just under my left shoulder blade were two parallel gashes oozing blood where the dog had bitten me. I cleaned them with alcohol, delighted by the fact that I would carry a scar. Someday I would not be so lucky, but even that thought added to the thrill. If there wasn't danger, it wouldn't feel so good.

As Julian and I discussed the Born/Breland incident, Julian reminisced about another time Born Crazy had clashed with Milton. It had happened at the old gym on East 14th Street. Milton had given Born some advice, and Born had exploded.

We had started talking to him about how his jab was gonna get him disqualified, Julian said. It was more like some kind of backhand. I still don't know how he won the Gloves in Atlanta. Sean Black—

Sean was there too?

Yeah, so Sean jumped up on that top rope like it was the World Wrestling Federation and started shouting at Born. Julian laughed. To tell you the truth, I was a little worried that Sean was going to hit his head, 'cause the ceiling in that old place was so low.

Wait a second, I said. You were there that day? I walked in just as it was happening.

It had been my second day with Milton the year before. I stepped through the door to hear shouts and see Sean perched on the top rope and the rabid Born screaming about how he was from the Bronx and harder than anyone (and a more successful male model). At the time I hadn't known any of the principals except Milton and had forgotten about it.

Yeah, I was there, Julian said. Born kept telling me, "Shut up, kid."

Julian pursed his lips, then smiled. That dude is sick.

I guess there's a reason they call him Born Crazy [a man who had once demanded that Milton clear the gym because he needed complete solitude to train].

Yeah, and Sean is sick. But I'm sick too. I keep it cold in here, though. I don't know how I kept it chill for so long, I just do.

Julian rarely boasted of his wild past and did indeed keep it chill in the gym, letting his fists talk. Yet I know why he insisted that he was sick. As long as Julian boxed, as long as he remained a man, a part of his identity would rest on pride in insanity.

It was important to me too. I was a little sick and forever needed to live up to it.

A week after his eruption, Born was back in the gym, talking to Milton about the two floors Milton planned to rent for a new gym on Park Avenue. The gym would be upstairs, and Milton would tenant the apartment below.

We can share the space, Born said enthusiastically. I'll take one of the bedrooms, and we'll be able to rent out some of the other spaces as studios. It'll be sweet.

Milton agreed that it would. They shook hands and Born went on his way.

Milton, I said, concerned, I hope you're not planning to live with that guy.

Milton looked at me as if my name were Born Crazy.

· 1 4 ·

THE AMATEUR

Six days a week, Giuseppe Penna—aka Busdriver, aka Joe Penna, aka José Peña, aka Slow Joe, aka Joey Bags, aka Six-Depot Joe—rises to the red ringing of an alarm at 3:30 A.M. "I need to give myself at least two hours to get ready in the morning," he says. That is, get ready and make it out of the house for a 6:05 start time driving a bus for the Metropolitan Transit Authority (MTA) of New York. He drives into Brooklyn from his Long Island home in the town of Lynbrook, three or so miles outside Queens and bordering the town of Oceanside, where he was raised. When he leaves the house, his wife and three children are still asleep. Even with the 3:30 alarm, he still arrives late ("It just takes me a long time to do things," he says), and after he parks his car in a lot, he has to run the half mile to the depot ("That's my little workout in the morning"), carrying the bags that gave him one of his nicknames among the other drivers.

Every morning I come in a few minutes late, he says. They hold the ride for me. My boss holds my ride for me. I pull out the bus late every single day.

Giuseppe's daily run is on the B57, local service between downtown Brooklyn and Maspeth, Queens. A circuit from Flushing Avenue in Maspeth to Boerum Place downtown and back again takes one hour and eleven minutes. He makes six circuits daily, then meets his relief driver, Tweety, on Flushing Avenue. Tweety is a pudgy, genial Puerto Rican whose sobriquet derives from his custom of wearing a Tweety Bird earring in his left ear. It is 3:10 when Giuseppe returns to the depot, where

"I turn in my trip sheet, do my paperwork, shoot the breeze with the fellas, look on the bulletin, see what's posting, if there's anything changed." Then it's the half mile back to his car and home for dinner.

In December, however, Giuseppe's routine changes, as it has every December since 1994. Instead of driving home from the depot, he looks for a place to take a nap for a half hour (a bench in the locker room, a padded chair in the office), then drives to and parks at the Myrtle/ Wyckoff subway station. From there, it is twenty minutes on the L train, more or less, into the city to Milton's gym, where Giuseppe begins his training for another Golden Gloves. Less the time of his nap, he has already been awake for sixteen hours by the time he walks through the gym doors.

One day in midwinter, I meet Giuseppe on his bus. He talks and drives, a slender man with bright green eyes and a narrow mustache. I think of him as my boxing döppelgänger, my Long Island twin. We're exactly the same height, with the same pale stalks for legs (I'm a few inches wider through the chest and shoulders, making it a little harder for me to suck down to 125 pounds). Both of us were raised Catholic too. Now I sit across from him in what's known as the rap seat, the seat on the bus closest to the front door where all the lonelies and crazies come and burble at the drivers. The bus lumbers ahead at the guidance of his fingers.

When I boarded, a pretty Haitian girl was sitting where I'm sitting now. Giuseppe gave her directions and asked her about her life. She spoke little English, but that didn't keep him from conducting a one-sided enthusiastic conversation (or extracting her phone number). When he speaks, Giuseppe's vocal rhythm, his dialect, is close to the Brooklynese of old, the white, working class Brooklyn that left for the not-quite-suburban split-level townships around the city a generation ago. Giuseppe could easily be the Brooklyn tough guy from a fifties film, tough and tender in black and white. With him I experience in Brooklyn present a Brooklyn past; a Brooklyn, say, at one remove.

Upon arriving at the gym, Giuseppe invariably disappears into the bathroom for twenty-five minutes; we shake our heads and ask, "What the hell happened to Peña?" Slow Joe is a most particular man. His costume change in the bathroom takes the time it does because everything must be exactly right. The belt has to be on the inside of the shorts. The shoes must be laced to a precise degree of tension (this lacing goes on for at least five minutes). Everyone in the gym must be greeted and spoken to.

Milton shakes his head. Peña, hurry the fuck up. I need you to spar. Tonight would be good.

Giuseppe smilingly ignores him and continues with his routine. Sometimes it seems the only part of him that moves quickly is his mouth or that the motion of his mouth brakes the rest of him. He talks as he stretches, as he shadowboxes, scanning the room. He cares extravagantly about people, the people around him and people in general. He is solicitous, remembers names and birthdays. He visits the ill and the incarcerated. One thinks that he would make a good politician.

Peña, shut up and start training, Milton says. I got your voice in my head. It's driving me fucking crazy.

You hear my voice in your sleep? You dreaming about me, Milton?

No, I don't hear it in my sleep. I hear it now. So shut up.

All Milton's scolding doesn't increase Penna's pace by one step. "I don't pay attention to him," Giuseppe says. "Milton doesn't know what's best for me. You know who knows what's best for Joe Penna? Joe Penna knows what's best for Joe Penna."

His training is as deliberate as his every other action. He strikes the bags in casual fashion—tunks them, one could say, talking as he goes. Does a few halfhearted crunches. Gives a vague impersonation of someone stretching. So that one wonders where this man gets the impetus to box and the arrogance to consider himself a fighter. Milton sighs as he watches Penna work.

Bob, he asks, could you just beat the hell out of him so he doesn't come back here anymore?

By the time he leaves the gym, it might be nine or nine-thirty. He reboards the L, retrieves his car and finally returns home to Lynbrook where his wife has dinner waiting and his children are in bed. He is eating by ten-thirty. "After that, I go and lie down on the couch so I don't pass out sitting at the table and choke on my food. I'm in bed, usually about, close to, eleven-thirty. Then I bounce up in bed about two, two-thirty so I can start thinking about getting up for work again."

On the bus, we cruise down Flushing Avenue in a grim section of East Williamsburg, abandoned factories and drab tenements around us. The bus lurches and rolls.

Look at this road, Giuseppe says. You will never see a road this bad in any other city in the United States. Look at it.

He states this with fervor and absolute conviction. I wonder where he gets his assurance, but the road is bad, tar eroding from old cobblestones.

Look at it. In no other city. See those rails?

He points to a pair of iron rails running down the center of the street.

Those are left over from the cable car days. And they're still there. This road will never get fixed because the people in this neighborhood are poor. They can't get together and make the city change it.

Penna was born and raised in Oceanside, Nassau County, a once-bucolic beach town trampled by the expressways and the bodies they brought in the fifties and sixties. Oceanside stands somewhere between working and middle class; like many Nassau and New Jersey towns, it lay too close to the city to avoid endless subdivision, small houses rising on shrinking lots. Giuseppe's parents emigrated from Calabria, Italy, soon after the Second World War. His father worked as an equipment operator (backhoe, payloader, grader) for the town of Hempstead for twenty-seven years. His mother worked as a tailor, doing piecework from the house. Joe's father ran a landscaping and cleaning business on the side and came to own three houses. Of five children, Giuseppe was the baby. He grew up a playground rat on the streets of his hometown.

I played football, he says. Not high school football. I played for the Oceanside Stallions. It was like Little League. And I was always the skinniest kid on the team, crashing helmets with the big boys. I did four years of that, made it to the all-star team twice. I wrestled in high school. Was division champion at one hundred five pounds my junior year. At ninety-one pounds, my freshman year, I was runner-up in the divisions. I was ranked fifth in Nassau County. I got my picture in the Hall of Fame at Oceanside High School. It says, "Joe Penna, wrestling,

1984." They all know me over there in wrestling. But I always wanted to box. I wanted to become a boxer at the age of nineteen. My brother-in-law talked me out of it. He told me I was too old. I listened to this guy and look what happened to me. I'm getting my head cracked in at thirty-three years old here.

Giuseppe's light blue uniform shirt hangs a little loose on his slender frame. To keep his weight down on his ass-chafing job, he eats only two meals a day. The bus lurches around a corner, and we pass a small diner. Giuseppe slows. He honks and waves.

There's this really cute Dominican waitress who works in there. I always slow down and say hello.

His uniform jacket, a darker blue than the shirt, droops over the back of his driver's seat. Down one sleeve below the MTA logo are six patches, one for each of the depots out of which he's driven. The depots are Flatbush, Walnut, Jackie Gleason, East New York, Ulmer Park and Fresh Pond, five in Brooklyn, one in the South Bronx, each depot with its own buses and routes. Driving the bus got Giuseppe into boxing.

I started getting a belly on the bus, he says. I was twenty-five years old. I came on this job with a thirty-inch waist, and I went up to a thirty-four-inch waist. I was one hundred thirty pounds, I went up to one forty-deuce. Right in the gut. Four inches on the gut. I was married to my first wife. Had a son at the time. I was a wrestler, and I couldn't wrestle no more 'cause after college is the Olympics and there was not really any clinics . . . any outlets for me. Nowhere to really wrestle unless I go like on my days off, go back to my old high school and wrestle but—that wasn't going to cut it on my two days off. I didn't like weights, so . . .

Giuseppe joined Gallagher's Gym in Ozone Park, Queens, where a few of his friends already trained. Like anyone who enters the culture, he began, after a time, to wonder how far he might go. It happens that way: When you start training, you think about sparring; then, once you start sparring, you start to think about fighting. The thought itself becomes a goad as you measure yourself against the fighters around you. Joe believed he could fight. After all, Todd Miranda and Jimmy Spoto from the neighborhood had done the Gloves in '92 (Todd going all the way to the semifinals) and they were no tougher, pound for pound, than Giuseppe Penna. Hadn't he won the divisions in wrestling at

105 pounds? Wasn't his picture in the Oceanside Hall of Fame? Hadn't he survived, even thrived, on Parris Island in the marines? So in 1994, at age twenty-seven, he had his first fight, in the Gloves, representing a gym in the enormous Starrett City housing project in central Brooklyn.

The bus comes to the end of the line in Maspeth, a neighborhood of small apartment buildings and closely packed one- and two-family houses with miniature yards. It is 2:07.

I go off on my lunch break now, Giuseppe says. We have approximately fifty-nine minutes. I do one more run and I'm finished.

He begins to cram objects into the plastic bags beside his seat, including a radio ("You're not supposed to have these. It's a violation, but you can usually get away with it") and a padded cushion for his weary ass.

I got to hurry. We gotta relieve the drivers now. Some of these guys get pissed off 'cause they want to get in the seat and go, and they're like, "Yo, you carry too many things with you." So now I pack up at the end of the line.

At my request, a quick inventory of the bags discloses a baseball cap, a newspaper, gloves, bus schedules ("People leave them on the bus. I'm very conservative, so when I go back to the station, I'll put them in the slots where they go"), dental floss, beeper, beige paper, Tucks medicated pads ("to get a good extra wipe"), money pouch, rubber ball to squeeze, rubber band, small bags filled with candy (including Hot Tamales), sunglasses, transfers, napkins, daily route logs. Condoms were a staple in the bag before his recent marriage. Giuseppe tells me that driving a bus is a fabulous way to meet women though he insists that he has not cheated on his wife.

With this job, you don't have to go to a club. You don't have to go to a bar. You meet women right here. What have I got?

He digs in his pants pocket.

I got one number yesterday and today . . . I got two numbers here today. That Haitian girl, she could be looking for citizenship, who knows? They see that you have a good job, that you're in uniform, you're clean-cut. They like that. Some people are just looking for money. You see that *M* [he points to the MTA patch on his sleeve]? That *M* means money.

The relief driver taps on the glass and we stand to leave. There is a brief conversation about condoms and how much we hate them. The new driver, a stout and pockmarked Puerto Rican, says, "It's safe, though. It's safe. In certain situations, if you're getting a little desperate and you have to have it, you got to use it."

Joe tells him that he just heard on the radio that even with a condom, there is a 30 percent chance of contracting HIV. I tell him this is not true, but he insists.

No, I heard it. Bob, c'mon, tell me, Bob, would you get on an airplane if there was a thirty percent chance of it crashing?

For his first fight, Giuseppe had the good fortune to draw an unattached fighter from Staten Island with the same virgin 0–0 slate. Darryl was his name, and unlike Giuseppe, he lacked the toughness requisite to bolster feeble boxing skills. Darryl kept his head down, grabbed Giuseppe at every opportunity and, after several warnings, was disqualified in the third round. The referee lifted the victor's hand into the air and Giuseppe Penna, bus driver for the city of New York and father of two, was still undefeated. A bye sent him sailing into the quarterfinals, and Giuseppe found himself two victories away from Madison Square Garden, on the verge of a championship after only one fight. He read his name in the *Daily News* sports section and clipped the little blurbs. He began to think that if he had only started a few years earlier, he would have had a chance at a pro career. No matter who the draw put before him, he would be ready. His opponent might have more experience, but he would not be prepared for the ferocity of Giuseppe Penna.

Chance made his semifinal fight his first and unfortunate meeting with Milton, through the medium of Joey Colon ("Peña was lucky that year," Milton says. "We had to fight three times already before we got to him").

Colon had fought in the Gloves already, winning a title in 1992, which should have forced him to fight in the open class rather than the novice one. However, in 1992, the *Daily News*, suffering through strikes, bankruptcy protection proceedings and a sale, did not sponsor the Gloves (for the first time since it was founded in 1927). Joey's title did not count against him. Thus Lucky Joe Penna marched into the ring against a Joey Colon who had been boxing since he could crawl.

Who knows how many fights he had? Giuseppe asks, shaking his head as he steers the bus. His book said one thing, but he fought another way.

The crowd caught on quickly.

Everybody kept saying he was a ringer. A ringer means . . . you have a lot of ring experience and you don't belong in the novice class. They were teasing him a lot and ranking on him in the stands.

The beating commenced immediately and Joey knocked down Giuseppe in the first round.

He caught me with a hook. Flush on the jaw. Perfect punch. I went down, and I got up. I thought I wasn't even going to get up, but I got up. They let me keep fighting. The ref kept asking me, "Do you want to fight? Do you want to fight?" I did a lot of clinching and holding that fight.

In the third round, however, Giuseppe claims, "I hit him with some solid rights and gave him a black eye." This is how a fighter's mind works, slowly rearranging every defeat to illuminate his success within it. This willfulness is what allows Joe to box at age thirty-three, with wife, family and friends pressing him to quit.

It was a painful and dreary six minutes for Giuseppe on his way to defeat against the eventual tournament victor. After the bell and the decision, he sat in the locker room nursing a headache ("I walked around punch-drunk for a week. Literally. A week"). Milton congratulated him, saying that out of the boxers who'd met Joey in the Gloves, he'd given him the best fight. Than he asked Giuseppe if he could train him. "But I told him, 'I can't do that to my coach.' "

At a pizzeria across the street from the bus, Giuseppe strides to the counter. He knows everyone and greets the counterman, waiters, manager, dishwasher. As we wait for our food, he begins a one-sided conversation with the counterman.

You still boxing? Practice boxing? This is my sparring partner, at my gym, you know? Bob, this guy is Brazilian. He boxes too. Hey, this is Bob, he's my sparring partner. What weight are you? What weight?

The man seems confused. This does not faze Giuseppe, who unearths his three phrases in Portuguese. He can talk to anybody, anytime, about anything.

Okay, okay, he says to the counterman, smiling ferociously, you come spar with us sometime, okay?

Over pizza, I ask Joe about the two sons whose names adorn his shorts.

Their mother took them away from me when we split up. She moved to Florida. I haven't seen them in six years. I pay child support too. I'm supporting two families. That's why I work that sixth day every other week. I don't know where I'd be if my parents didn't give us a break on the rent.

At age twenty-three, Giuseppe met his future first wife near Wall Street. He was downtown for a job interview; she was working a temp job in an office. Giuseppe found her striking and followed her into a variety store.

My ex-wife was Puerto Rican, he says. She never met her father. She always said her father was French, but she had to be African because her hair was very kinky, you know? All the brothers and sisters thought she was black. You know, light-skinned. You could tell there was Spanish in her.

While they flirted, Giuseppe handed her his phone number. "But I knew she wasn't going to call me. And she wasn't going to give me her number." This forced Giuseppe to resort to other tactics. "She told me she lived in the Bronx and I said that I didn't believe her. So when she took out her license to prove it to me, I memorized her address."

Still, Giuseppe hesitated at visiting her unannounced. "What if she lived with a boyfriend? What if she didn't want me there and had someone pop me? This was the Bronx, you know." Nine months later, however, he arrived at her door (with a friend for backup), and Denise was delighted to see him. She had thrown out his phone number only two days before.

She was always like a crybaby, Giuseppe says bitterly, an exaggerator. Too . . . I don't know the word to describe her, sensitive? She always felt like, you know, nobody's your friend. Don't trust nobody, you know? Never had much friends.

From the first Joe also had problems with her family.

Her mother was into that witchcraft stuff. You'd see statues and candles. You know, Santería. But denied it. Always denied it. But you see cigars, altars, statues of little dolls and all that around the house, you start to say, you know, is this normal?

The relationship was turbulent: young love 101. They kept fighting and making up, fighting and making up, all the way into Denise's pregnancy. As her due date approached, the friction intensified, until Giuseppe found himself in the worst trouble of his life.

My ex-wife's sister's boyfriend wouldn't let me—wouldn't let me in the apartment. Wasn't even his apartment. She was carrying my kid in her stomach. She was ready to burst. Like any day, she was going to give birth. So I'm there to check up on her and stuff, you know? But he said, "No, man, I can't let you in. You're not coming in." You know, he just came out stupid with me, you know. That's how it started. So I was pissed off, and my big friend, this guy called Hal, lived around the corner. And I got him and came back. Not to do anything. I was just like, "Watch this man." You know, Long Island style. I'm gonna duke it out with this guy, hands up.

Much to Giuseppe's dismay, the fight was conducted in a style that was not Long Island but pure Bronx.

The guy came out with a freaking butcher knife, man. Tried to kill me. And I wanted to slug with him, you know? And he stabbed me, and it was . . . outside a video store. And I was saying my last prayers. I was praying. There was about thirty people watching. And there was a guy standing there. Some construction guy with lightbulbs? You know, like those lightbulbs they put up? All that was running through my mind is, "Grab it and throw it at him." But I was afraid that the guy was gonna grab me and say, "Hey, you gotta pay for this now." You know? "You broke it. This is my material here." So all that was going through my mind. But I ran away. Oh, that was a chance, man, that was a chance. Let's say, Bob, let's say that knife would have came here.

Giuseppe points at his chest.

I'm dead. And the knife is this big. One of those butcher . . . Japanese butcher knives, you know. Oh, God. Life is precious. You get older, you start to think, you know? I pressed charges on the guy. And then the courts was retarded. They were like, "Oh, well, you only had three stitches in your arm, so it's not a felony, it's a misdemeanor." The district attorney in the Bronx said this. I'm like, "Listen, if this was where I come from, Long Island, he'd be doing nine months in the county jail. That's the bottom line." He paid a three-hundred-dollar fine, and six months later he ended up shooting somebody in the stomach and went to jail for like a year.

I was involved with the wrong people. Her family showed no mercy. They didn't even say, "Oh, sorry. Sorry, José, that you got stabbed. I can't believe Frankie did this to you." They showed no mercy. After I got stabbed, I said, "I'm not getting involved with this girl anymore."

But when she was giving birth at the hospital, she wanted me to go see her. I told myself, "That's my son. I'll put down my name on the birth certificate, and I'll support him. I just don't want to be around these people anymore. I'll raise the kid. I'll get visitation rights, whatever." So it stood like that until the baby came. You know, your heart changes and I guess God was leading me. I was in the reserves, and I got called for the Persian Gulf War. Then my brother was like, "Look, you better marry her. If you come back in a body bag, she'll have all the benefits and everything." I was like, "All right. I better do it." You know, you go out and you feel what you have to do. "I gotta do the right thing. Stop sleeping with other girls. There's nothing but AIDS going on. All these other girls you're doing it with, all they want to do is just have sex and have a good time, and that's not what it's about. Here's a chance for you to raise this kid." And she wanted to get married too. So we got married. I told her, "I'm not going Catholic. We're gonna go in a Christian church." And we went for Christian counseling to restore the relationship. And got married, in the Christian church.

Soon enough, though, we stopped going to church. One thing led to another. I cheated on her a lot. She used sex as a weapon. She wasn't having sex with me. I was like, "Yeah, the hell with this. I can get it somewhere else." Maybe that was the excuse that I was using? I don't know. What happened was, things got real bad and she split on me and I never saw my kids again. Maybe that was the punishment, you know? Being that I messed around. But if God's a loving God, why do my kids deserve to be without a father and suffer? I don't know what the whole deal is. The last year we were together was just terrible. We fought all the time. So we got into another argument. Normally, when we'd do that, she'd take the stuff off the wall like she's leaving. The pictures and stuff, she would like, take and go to her mother's. So I figured it was one of those kinds of arguments. This time it was for real. She came back six weeks later with the police to get all her stuff out of there. The kids weren't with her. She lied to me. She said, "Me and you are finished but you can still see the kids, and the meeting place is going to be your mother's house. On the weekends." I've been waiting for that meeting spot for six years already. She did it out of spite, you know? She didn't want me to see them. She probably fed them nonsense. And she broke one of the kid's hearts 'cause the kid was very attached to me. I raised him for three and a half years, my son Giuseppe.

I look up from our paper plates with their rinds and translucent circles from dripping grease. The clock reads 3:04. Our fifty-nine minutes are over. Another bus waits for us outside. Giuseppe shows me how to get the bus doors open from the street (a little switch beneath the driver's side window) and how to start the bus. "That's all there is to it, Bob." He runs down the aisle, picking up trash ("This bus was not cleaned after the last shift. I got to note that in my log"), and pulls open the overhead hatch.

There's a lot of germs going around on these buses, he says, so I try to keep the air moving.

Giuseppe did not enter the Gloves in 1995. It was a difficult year for him, the year he and his wife split up. But he still trained when he could and attended the occasional amateur show.

"Hey, Busdriver!" Milton would call out to him at the shows, adding a nickname to Giuseppe's swelling list of aliases. "When are you coming over to the gym?" To which Giuseppe would reply, "One day, Milton, one day." Then Giuseppe's regular trainer landed a job at Kennedy Airport and no longer had time to work with him. It was the late fall of 1996. Giuseppe, scenting the Gloves, picked up the phone and gave Milton a call (in Milton's version of the story, Joey impressed Giuseppe so much by thrashing him that Giuseppe arrived in Milton's gym one day wanting to learn the style).

Just six weeks before his '96 Gloves match, Busdriver walked into Milton's gym for the first time. He received Milton's deluxe treatment for wannabe fighters: the blows and the curses, the sarcastic asides, the nickname. Naturally, he was converted to southpaw. In the first round of his Gloves fight, Giuseppe grew frustrated with the new style and switched back to orthodox. This infuriated Milton, who sat in the front row.* He began to scream that if Giuseppe didn't switch back to southpaw, he would walk out of the hall.

Milton was yelling, Giuseppe said, "If you don't fight like I told you and switch to southpaw, I'm going home!" Screaming his lungs out in the stands. Everybody's looking at him like, "Who is this maniac?"

So at the start of the second round, Joe came out of his corner as a southpaw again. Almost immediately he caught his opponent with a solid hook, and the other man received a standing eight count. Joe pressed, throwing combinations; his opponent didn't punch back. The hook had drained his will to fight. A few minutes later the referee raised Giuseppe's hand into the air.

For Milton, it was vindication. He had taken a man with two left feet and in six weeks turned him into a knockout machine. No matter that Giuseppe lost his next fight (to the silver medalist). "People came up to me after that fight," Milton says, "and they congratulated me for what I did with this guy. They say they can't believe how far I brought him."

We're heading back down Fillmore through that tough section of East Williamsburg. Encroaching night has brought prostitutes to the corners, sedans loitering beside them. Giuseppe's quick eyes fly to the movement and dealings on the street.

There's a lot of hookers on the backstreets here, he says. They start coming out when it gets dark. And then the cops come by, maybe they're paid off, who knows? I don't know. I've never seen cops arresting anybody. I'm just in and out of here, I don't know. I just see what I see

---

*Milton had turned his banishment to his advantage. Cornermen are not allowed to speak to fighters during rounds of amateur fights, but there is no law against screaming instructions from the seats.

with my eyes. That girl there looks crack-dependent. I don't know how someone . . . It's like you're sticking your hand in the fire to get burnt.

We draw away from the grim streets, Giuseppe talking steadily. A woman passenger takes exception to his chatter.

You're driving real slow, she says, heading for the exit.

Thank you, he replies.

You see the sign. She points. People are not supposed to talk to the driver.

Yes, thank you, he says as she exits. Thank you very much. Have a good night. Good night.

He begins honking his horn after her while we slowly pull away.

Ah, he sighs, she'll probably report me.

Life goes on outside the gym. Giuseppe watched the board, where he has risen to 1,027 out of 2,500 drivers, waiting for the day his number will go farther down and he won't get bumped off the plum assignments, waiting for his solid pension. The word "pension" occurs often in Giuseppe's conversation. His father has one; his uncle in Italy, a former bus driver, has one; his brothers and he are waiting for one at the official retirement age of fifty-five. Twenty-five years and fifty-five. "I'll have the years before I have the age. I started this job too young. I should have started this job when I was thirty."

For Giuseppe, Milton's style had serious consequences. He injured his right hand so badly throwing Milton-style hooks that he missed the Gloves in 1997. He stopped training but stayed around Milton's gym, helping out, working corners, even coaching a little. Amateur boxing is like that, there in the root of the word, Latin for lover. Love keeps people like Joe in that little world; love brings them back, returning to a place little changed from year to year.

As evening becomes night, we approach downtown Brooklyn, the buildings framed against a sky that undulates chocolate and rose.

The bus route I'm driving goes right past the jail where they had Efrain, Joe says. Here, we're going past it now.

The building rolls by on our left, a squat brick structure, tiny windows sheathed in metal grilles.

That's the old Brooklyn navy brig. They used to stick guys in the brig. Efrain was here for a year. He beat up somebody in the building where he lived or something. The guy got stupid with him, ratted him out, peached on him, and Efrain retaliated. Hurt him so bad it was assault charges. Efrain won the Golden Gloves that year. He had a court case going, and the judge gave him a break and said, "When the Gloves are over, you have to go to prison. You have to serve a year."

Giuseppe fought again in the Gloves in 1999. He drew a tough fighter in the first round, a Mexican nicknamed Jalapeño. The Mexican earned "Fighter of the Night," and the *Daily News*'s Gloves reporter could happily write that "Jalapeno peppered Penna." Laura saw the fight and was moved by Giuseppe's valor. She told Milton that Joe was the best fighter he had.

He fought the bravest fight, Laura said. He showed so much heart. And all Milton does is yell at him and make fun of him.

The loss didn't cool Giuseppe's passion for fighting. In his daydream reconstruction of the Jalapeño fight, he came close to winning, never mind that he received two standing eights. He planned to fight in the Empire Games in the summer of '99, but during his first sparring session back in the gym, he damaged his hand throwing Milton's hook and was out until the November day I saw him walk through the gym doors, smile broad and eyes bright.

·15·

FEBRUARY

The law is a big Disneyland of suffering. When a poor man lets himself get caught in it, you'll hear him screaming for centuries.
                                        —Céline, *Death on the Installment Plan*

A little before five A.M. on February 7, I woke to pounding at my
door and front window. A strong light probed the windows and
pierced the curtains, exposing the room. I squirmed a little further
under my blankets and then lay still. Although the room was as cold as
a meat locker, sweat girdled my neck and drenched my T-shirt. I knew
exactly who was banging at my door, which only increased my dread,
for who would help me if I told him that the New York Police Department was trying to get me? I prayed for another chance. I promised to
be good. The banging continued. Then voices and footsteps went down
the stairs, away. Away, but not without a last thirty-second blast on my
doorbell, a final "fuck you" from the men in blue. Rat-tat-tat.

For the next hour I couldn't sleep for twisting with rage and fan-
tasies of shooting cops. I sent fat blue bodies spilling down my stairwell, riddled with holes. I would claim fear of burglars pulled the
trigger. I wondered how it could happen. How could they violate your
home so easily? They hadn't identified themselves. Although in a less
grave form, I thought I had touched what it must be like for the disappeared in Latin America: to be surprised in your bed and be unable to

think of anyone to help you, since the people who are supposed to help you are the ones dragging you away.

I knew why they had come. My buzzer had sounded a few months earlier on a Monday morning to be followed by a similar pounding. A phone call a few minutes later had provided the identity of my visitors.

Rooberrt, my landlady said mournfully in her thick Polish accent, the police came to arrest you this morning. There were six of them. Big men. You must be careful, Rooberrt. I know you are a good boy, so I told them a woman lived there. They ask me if she has a boyfriend, but I say no.

The Friday before the Monday, a cop had ticketed me on a subway platform for carrying an open container (a bottle of beer in a brown paper bag). It was a civil penalty, fine payable by mail. However, to avoid being taken to the station, I had been forced to show identification. The enterprising fellow must have run my name for outstanding warrants and found that I'd never appeared in court after jumping a turnstile almost three years earlier. The summons for that crime lay beneath a magnet on my refrigerator. For my family and friends, these encounters were a source of concern. My mother advised me to contact a lawyer; an older writer who had been involved in radical politics in the sixties warned me that friends of his had been gunned down in such encounters thirty years earlier.

At the gym, my troubles brought only laughter.

Bob, said Vernon, you're the only white guy I know with a black man's problems.

Five o'clock in the morning, I said.

Yes, they *do* come at the most inconvenient times, Vernon said. The warrant squad came after me once on a Saturday afternoon about one-thirty. Now, I had told them on Friday I'd be down at the courthouse on Monday. They said, "Fine," but there they were on Saturday, screwing around on my day off. I had to go out the fire escape.

What did they come after you for, Bob? Vic asked.

This being Vic, I wanted to say, "I killed a couple of guys and robbed an armored car." Instead I was forced to admit that I'd been arrested a few years ago for jumping a turnstile.

Oh, Victor said, and turned away.

You'd better take care of it, Bob, Vernon said, because they *will* come back. And they *will* kick in your door at some point.

They'll kick in my door? For a fare evasion warrant? No.

Oh, yes, they will. Vernon chortled. They don't like it if they think you're hiding from them. I would not stay at my house this weekend if I was you.

On February 12, Joey Colon and Laura Kielczewski fought their fourth pro fights on the same card (Laura 3-0, Joey 0-3) at a Days Inn in Allentown, Pennsylvania. The motel marquee proclaimed the event (and "help wanted" and "cable in every room"). In the snow-buffered lot, the equipment trucks of a local cable company clustered around the back door. Heavy lines ran from the trucks into the building like a life support system.

Inside, a house band played standards from "Rock Around the Clock" to "Knock on Wood," the singer wearing a rhinestone gown that gripped her like leeches. The lobby sported vast bouquets of plastic flowers and a carpet the color of royal blood. Framed by the flowers, boxing celebrities gave photo ops and signed autographs. "Terrible" Tim Witherspoon, briefly heavyweight champion in the 1980s, patted a small boy on the head and proudly announced, "This is little Terrible Tim. He boxes too." Larry Holmes stood there as well, smiling brown burgher in a bespoke suit, his long, narrow arms dangling, unusually long arms that had kept him champion. Holmes was one of the ex-champions who had landed clear-eyed and levelheaded. He was a mogul in nearby Easton and its surroundings (the band announced that they would be playing Wednesday night at Larry Holmes' Ringside Restaurant, and on the drive home we were to pump gas at Larry Holmes self-serve).

In a corner of the room, the matchmaker on his cell phone shouted at a trainer whose fighter had gone AWOL. This guy signed on the dotted line, and now he's not here. You're his trainer, right? Well, he should have called you . . . What? . . . Well, he's the fighter, and he agreed to fight . . . I don't care! If he's not here in twenty minutes, I'll have his ass suspended for as long as I can.

With his battered face and corona of white hair, the matchmaker was from the same blue-collar mold as Ollie Kreuger (right down to the Marlboro rasp).

I shot pool with Joey in the bar/lounge while we waited. He wore an electric blue padded warm-up suit that made him look like an enormous baby. That morning he had comfortably made his contract weight of 135. Across the room Laura sat with her parents and friends. Her father was a grizzled, backslapping man with a card around his neck that read, "Laura K., the Champ!" He had enormous hands and a punishing grip. Her mother had stern features and a grace of carriage, but her face was tight with worry. The conversation rattled and jerked. Laura said that an official at the weigh-in had told Joey, "You're zero and three, so you really need a win tonight," implying he would lose his license if things went badly.

Toward five P.M., Laura and Joey returned to their rooms to rest. I talked to the promoter in the lobby. This is just a sideline, he told me. I'm a lawyer by trade. But I've always loved boxing. I used to be the captain of my college boxing team.

He was a Greek with the dark eyes and the solemn beard of an Assyrian bull god.

In the motel showroom, cameras and klieg lights perched over our heads. Ringside, the commentators wore tuxedos. Families in weekend finery filled the plastic seats. Following three other prelims, Joey fought a mustachioed Mexican, the local favorite. The fight went at a moderate pace, which I thought in Joey's best interest. The Mexican tried to box, not brawl, his mistake, as he wasn't going to outslick Joey Colon. Joey landed more and cleaner punches, clearly winning each of the four rounds. The split decision was a tribute to home court advantage but when the referee lifted his hand, Joey had won his first pro fight.

Between rounds, the ring card girls—certainly strippers from a local club—tottered around the ring on fantastic stiletto heels. The girls changed costumes between fights: miniskirt and halter top down to bikinis, down, down to silver-spangled G-string and cropped pudenda, each costume change unveiling more plucked and shaved flesh. During rounds they sat robed in the front row before the rubes, yawning.

For Laura's fight, the card girls were given a break. At the bell Laura collided with a cousin of Terrible Tim's, a girl released from a halfway house for the contest. She was a brawler with over twenty pro fights (and more losses than wins) who needed the few hundred bucks the night would bring. She had come to the weigh-in a few pounds over, and Laura had forced her to sweat it off ("I'm a professional," Laura said, "and I work hard to get ready. Why should I give her an advantage?"). Although she was only in her early twenties, her mottled brown face seemed a decade older. Over six two-minute rounds, the two women stood in front of each other and slugged, to the crowd's boisterous approval. I couldn't understand why Laura didn't use her mobility and skills. Just before the bell in the sixth, Laura drove the Witherspoon girl into a corner with her best flurry of the night. She won another split decision (and later learned she had fought the entire contest with a fractured wrist).

By the middle of January I'd become a poster boy for Milton's style. When I left the ring after sparring before new eyes, Milton would ask the question: So, Bob, how long have you been with me?

Oh, about four months.

Already, I see it coming. It's the Milton and Elvis dog and pony show.

Look at Bob's T-shirt, he'll say, white as a Klansman's pajamas. Before Bob joined us, he was a punching bag. His white T-shirts would be turned red.

The new clients nod and their eyes widen.

It is Milton's unshakable conviction that before I trained with him, every sparring session was a bloodbath and I had required transfusions.

And look at him now. He's Bob and Weave, moving like a black man. I should have before and after photos up on the walls. Do you save those old T-shirts, Bob? 'Cause I want to frame one.

At times, I wonder if I've really gotten as good as Milton says, since the miracle is that the dog can talk at all.

My fiesta with the police continued. I received two phone messages from an Officer Nazario, who instructed me to call him immediately. A few days later I returned home to find his business card in my lobby. I called. On the phone Nazario told me that if I went down to the court-house myself, I would have to deal with a maze of bureaucracy, that the entire day would be wasted. Instead he recommended that I take advantage of his special offer: have the police come to my apartment in a van (unmarked) and bring me to the courthouse, where matters would be expedited ("You'll be expected," Nazario said). I said I would consider this and call him later.

When I related the story to Milton, his head started to shake before I finished.

Uh, I don't think so, he said, grinning. They take your ass away in an unmarked van, it could be a long time before anyone sees you again.

The early rounds of the Gloves went poorly for the Supreme Team boxers. Will lost first. Then Victor and Julian lost on the same night: Julian in a bizarre disqualification, Victor a close decision. Then, to the vocal disbelief of a large posse of friends and family, Efrain lost to a Russian in a Williamsburg church hall.

Although all our boxers showed flaws, all the decisions could have easily gone in their favor. Will remained passive, waiting for a chance to counterpunch. He had also developed the bad habit of jerking his left shoulder before he threw his two, telegraphing the punch, yet his opponent, a much shorter man, had trouble working inside Will's arms and was awarded the first round without landing a single blow. After winning three rounds easily, Julian was disqualified in the fourth round for pushing his opponent's head down (one of Ali's favorite tactics); although the other man forced the issue by butting Julian's chest, he didn't receive a single warning. Because of his lackluster training, Efrain missed counters, but the Russian ran backward through the fight, retreating behind his jab and wilting every time Efrain did connect. And Victor? He fought as well as I had seen him, stalking his opponent and throwing punches in number. While his opponent had faster hands, Victor certainly landed the harder punches.* After the loss (after all his losses), Victor didn't complain or change expression. He squared his shoulders and went back to training.

---

*A year later a trainer who had no love for Milton remarked on how Victor had been "robbed" in the Gloves.

A greasy cloud of despair filled the gym. We murmured that the Supreme Team couldn't win a close fight, that we needed knockouts to advance. We blamed Milton for this: His flamboyance and disdain had alienated the boxing world. His chickens were coming home to roost on our shoulders.

As for me, by February I was forced to accept that Milton was ignoring me. I appeared in the studio, stretched, worked out, went home without a word of advice from my trainer, so called (what was I paying him for anyway?). He still *used* me as a crash test dummy for the women and the white collars and the new blood rookies. But when I was up in the ring, doing my thing, all of Milton's wise words went . . . to the person trying to kill me. So that I might easily have spoken Laura's phrase "Am I so perfect?"

I didn't understand the how or the why of the change. Three months earlier Milton wouldn't leave me alone. "Use your feet when you slip," "Turn the hand over," "You're still punching handicapped," "retard," "Stevie Wonder," "plod." "You won fights? Who did you beat, Kenny Breathe and Willie Getup?" I had dreaded the summons to the punching mitts, the cuffing and correction, my arms going dead, black spots of nausea before my eyes and Milton saying, "You're tired. Hey, I'm not tired, and I'm forty-four. Keep working!" Now, nothing, and I was far from perfect. I still lacked power in my fours and had a bad habit of backing away from opponents rather than staying put and trusting my skills to slip and counter (I had been hit so often that now, having learned to escape, I was leery of all contact). At first, I had welcomed the obscurity, but I'd come to resent it. I worked hard; I deserved more attention. Here it was, just weeks before my fight; I needed *fine-tuning*, I needed *intensity*.

Preparing for the Olympic Trials, Julian faced the same predicament. Three wins from Sydney and there he was, hitting the bag alone, jumping rope alone, even as Milton crowed over Julian's Regional victories, which played continuously on the Revolution VCR.

You know who's got to get yourself ready? Julian said as we discussed the matter. You do, that's who. Yeah, it would be nice to have my trainer helping me out but—

He glanced at Milton in the ring, where he was explaining the two to a slender Asian woman. "Like stirring a pot. Circle the hand."

—his mind is somewhere else, Julian continued.

Yet Milton did not ignore all his regulars. Several days a week he accompanied Stella to another gym, where she sparred the women's amateur champion at 119 pounds. He worked the mitts with her as well, and when she and I sparred, he shouted instruction . . . for Stella. I could understand Milton's ignoring me—I was a scrub with no future past the Gloves—but Julian? It made little sense. In Julian, Milton had the perfect student, a boxer who would watch tape not only of pro fights (as is common) but also of amateur. He could tell you the how and why of each one of Tommy Hearns's eight amateur losses (to 155 wins).

On February 15, nearly six weeks into the tournament, I finally received my card. I would be fighting on February 29, at St. Catherine's Church in the town of Franklin Square, Long Island.

Hey, Milton, do you have any sodas in the fridge? I asked.

No, he said, but look out on the fire escape.

I did. The fire escape faced the back of the building, one of those gloomy, steep, pigeon-shit-encrusted shaftways between Manhattan blocks.

Are there any out there? he asked.

Yeah, I said, and reached out for one. And cold.

It's a Puerto Rican refrigerator, he said. It only works in the winter.

From an unimpeachable source, I learned that the Fitness Diva was scheming to evict the Supreme Team. The source (let's call him X) divulged that our rent would be raised to a figure the Fitness Diva foresaw Milton would refuse to meet. Rid of us, she planned great things: Walls would be demolished, space reconfigured; a new Revolution would spring from our ashes. X told me that the Fitness Diva had already booked a martial arts group to recover the revenue she would lose with us. In truth, I was surprised we had lasted as long as we had.

When I passed on this information to Milton, he seemed unconcerned.

Oh, really, he said. And who told you this?

Let's just say it was someone in the know.

Milton did not respond, his royal manner of informing me that our audience had come to an end.

From the moment we arrived at Revolution, Milton and Vernon had been searching for a new home, preferably on or near 14th Street. Fourteenth Street serves as a sort of center to Anglo-Manhattan, a median line between Wall Street wampum and Midtown mazuma, and Milton was 14th Street's cowboy king. It was his range to roam; he knew the realtors and merchants, he knew the pedestrian faces and could not cross two avenues without an open-air meeting. Over the months Milton and Vernon sang of the places they were investigating, entire floors empty, stretching across city blocks. They were always on the verge of closing a deal. The owner of one building was a big boxing fan, Milton had done some work for him, the man loved the idea of a gym . . . Another space, on Park Avenue South, was available. "Two full floors," Vernon said with glee, "and cheap." Milton's eyes were open. He searched; he scattered queries and cultivated possible investors. No need to worry, the Supreme Team would land on its feet.

Although Milton showed little concern over my news, his courtship of other trainers at Revolution intensified. He was trying to assemble a solid cabal of trainers to make the move with him. He needed their money; money was his incubus. To lease real estate in Manhattan, you need investment capital, capital to pay the rent, to buy the equipment, to keep the boat afloat through those lean first years. While Milton might have had a decent monthly income (and owned two geriatric Cadillacs), it was irregular and off the books (I asked him if he had an accountant and he said, "An accountant? Why? I have nothing to count. I'm so broke I can't pay attention"). I couldn't see Milton walking into a bank and being found eligible for a loan by a bank officer, at least one who wanted to keep his job. He was almost entirely in the gray economy, and only he knew what credit horrors lay decaying in his past.

———

Every day when I came into the studio, Milton would ask, Bob, did you take care of your warrants yet?

I would shake my head no. No, day after day. The pressure made me stubborn and resentful; the more the police squeezed me, the more I wanted to fight (at least when they weren't pounding on my door). As I told my story around the gym, I heard, in return, from every black and Spanish man, stories of their run-ins with New York cops. Even Hassan, the serene desk clerk at Revolution, had nearly been shot by the police over a ten-dollar bag of marijuana.

At Efrain's fight, his family and friends formed a cheering section in the church hall, the ringleader a tubby young man who hooted and barked through the action.

He's scared of you, dawg! Whoo! Whoo! He's running! Awhoooo!

After the fights, the posse stood on the street before the church, grating against a large police contingent. Staring contests, circled wagons, loud voices. The Amadou Diallo trial was in its second week.

Amadou! the tubby young man said. Amadou! Say Amadou to those cops, and they'll be like, "Can I get you a cab, sir?"

Big laughs. Cop glares.

Amadou, Milton said, I'm-a-Do whatever you say, officer, if you don't shoot me.

The fat kid held up his wallet. Don't shoot! Don't shoot! Does this look like a gun to you?

My troubles transformed the city. I didn't know if transit cops worked the same subway stations regularly, so I went into my station with a hat pulled low and my collar up. Fearing the warrant squad's return, I kept the shades drawn and my lights off. Coming home, I paused at the top of my block to look for police cruisers and had the dancer scout the building to determine if any cops lurked. I asked myself what other crimes I might have committed and forgotten. It reminded me of ducking detention in high school, except all of New York was the school (and the hall monitors carried guns). I assumed that the worst I faced was a night in jail, but a night in jail was not my idea of a holiday. Still, there were more important things to worry about than criminal court; I had a fight coming.

One Saturday, young Hanson, our six-foot-tall blond boxing apprentice, brought his older sister to Revolution. She was fifteen and a half and the theater type, coming out of rehearsals for some oofy Upper West Side high school show. The presence of a roomful of certified men incited her to perform. She pirouetted, recited lines in a loud voice, trotted back and forth. She was a smaller model of her brother and had just discovered the color black; her blond hair bobbed on her shoulders as she twirled on sneaker tips. The boxers in the gym couldn't help but be . . . interested. They moved closer.

So you're doing a play? said Zeus. What's it about?

It's *Troilus and Cressida*, said the sister, extending into an arabesque, William Shakespeare.

Zeus pondered. He was one of the more interesting of Milton's irregulars, a black, bald just-ex con, roughly my height but twenty-five pounds heavier, every ounce of it prison yard bulk. Dark green tattoos sheathed his bulging arms.

Shakespeare? he said.

You know, she said, "All the world's a stage, / And all the men and women merely players."

Damn, Zeus said, how come everybody got to be a player?

On February 7, Julian missed his morning flight to Florida for the Olympic Trials and was forced to take a later plane to Tampa. The other New York boxers having preceded him, Julian met no welcome, and it was hours before he reached the training center. The eliminations were to commence the next day; eight fighters in each division, three wins to qualify for Sydney.

In New York we waited for the news. I was out of the gym for two days and walked in on a Saturday to see, to my surprise, Julian seated on the bench.

Julian, what happened? I said.

He lifted his right arm to display a small cast on his hand.

The first hard punch that I threw, that was it, he said, shaking his head. I felt the pain like a lightning shot went up my whole arm to my neck. And from that point, being that it was so early in the bout, I started thinking, "All right, defense." And then when I did think offense and attack, it was hurting more than I thought. I started thinking more about the pain than concentrating on the fight.

So did you tell your corner? I asked.

After the second round, my corner asked me how was my hand doing, and I told them it was hurting. And they called the doctor. But I was trying to tell him, you know, to let them see what it was like after the third round. But he was just like, naw, because if you break your hand, you still won't be able to fight anyway. And so my corner retired me, and then we got an X ray, and we found out that it was a stress fracture, a chipped bone or whatever.

Julian's Olympic dream had ended in less than four minutes.

Well, he said, looking at his hand, out of all the time I would have picked for the hand to go, that wouldn't have been it. Everything happens for a reason, though. Before my fight, everybody was like, "That kid Julian Townsend." "That kid Julian Townsend. Yeah, you know, I don't want to pick *him* in the first round." I actually heard this with my own two ears. So, that's what made it good. I knew that I was a force to be reckoned with. Two years ago I wasn't even in boxing, and who would have thought that Julian Townsend, in a division loaded with talent, and 'fifty-six is *loaded* with talent, would go all the way to the Olympic Trials? Nobody, that's who.

Every month, I walked the few blocks to my landlady's row house to pay rent. She was a middle-aged Polish woman and North Williamsburg was her village. Our relationship was Old World: a stack of twenties for her, cookies for me, gossip about the neighbors and the sufferings of stray cats. From time to time a Hasidic man was there, which always surprised me, his dangling *payes*, black suit and Abe Lincoln hat a nineteenth-century inkblot in her immigrant kitsch-en. I was surprised because she was a terrible, ingenuous anti-Semite (she saw a picture of my mother and said, "She is maybe, Jew?," and was always talking about the Jewish money), while the local Hasidim disliked just about everyone. There they sat, though, over tea, their relationship going back decades to when my landlady was employed in his sweatshop and he gave her advice on her first real estate purchases. And there I sat, quite fond of both of them, although religious fanatics and anti-Semites are two of my least favorite kinds of humans.

The television chattered before us, Giuliani with his pinched face making some Grinch-like pronouncement.

So what do you think of Giuliani? the Hasidic man asked.

I can't stand him, I said.

Why not? the man asked, surprised. He's a very good mayor.

Not really, I said. Look at how the police are out of control, look at how he treats the homeless and the poor.

But Rooberrt, my landlady said, the police wanted you because you broke the law.

Well, what about your brother? I said. They arrested him for no reason and you had to go get him out of jail.

Do you remember how the city was before? the Hasid asked. Do you remember?

Of course I remember; I had been in New York in the eighties, had seen the filth and the decay. I thought of making a speech about how you couldn't applaud Giuliani for the improvements—the crime rate had declined steeply before he took office, and a decade-long economic boom had lifted the city, but they wouldn't have been interested. They liked Giuliani for the same reason they could be friends: they both owned property, and Giuliani made them feel that their investments were protected. My landlady might lie to the cops to protect me, and mourn the fact that her brother spent the night in jail on a fabricated charge, but she was willing to tolerate those things for stability.

I felt neglected and distracted, and then I found myself without sparring partners. Late in the course of a session with Busdriver, I drilled a straight left into the weird helmet he wore. Over the next hour, the flesh around his eye swelled to monstrous proportions and took on pleasing rainbow hues.

I can't believe you did that, he said, gawking at himself in the mirror. Right through the facesaver. That hasn't happened in the five years I've had the thing.

Ah, little hands. I was delighted with myself: "Mommy, look what I did!" A shiner, a mouse, and I had put it there; it looked like a wedding in the rain. The consequence, however, was that Giuseppe, with his fight just two weeks away, couldn't spar.

And I needed sparring. A few weeks before his fight, Joey Colon had showed up to illustrate just how far I had to go. Milton scowled at his entrance and wouldn't speak to him. Joey's smile parted the gloom.

Bob, you want some work? Joey asked.

Of course, I said yes. In our first round, I did everything right. I beat Joey to the punch and landed clean combinations, my punches flowing one to the next. Milton exulted in my corner after the bell.

Bob, you're going to surprise some folks in the Gloves. [Whispering] This could be your year if you stay focused.

By the second minute of the second round I had stalled, and in the third, I broke down. Joey had weathered my first-round clinic and was ready for his turn. The gap between us began to show; Joey had thousands of rounds behind him, titles, tough losses. I'd seen him spar Will, Julian, Victor; a few good minutes from me were unlikely to discourage him. His right hand swiped out, crumpling the beer cans on the side of my head. I began to tremble, retreat, "bitch out," as Milton would say, my punches having no effect on Joey's forward progress. While I made Joey miss plenty, every solid blow he did land fragmented me even more. When the bell rang, I sprawled back against the ropes.

Are those three-minute rounds? I said. They felt like days.

Only two, Milton answered.

I couldn't believe it. I was used to going six, eight, ten three-minute rounds without tiring. I would clown in the ring, drop my hands, close my eyes. This was a different sort of round.

The fourth round brought more of the same. I left the ring humbled.

Well, how was that? I asked Joey, who hadn't moved with me in months. A little better?

Much better, Bob. Joey smiled approval. You're letting your punches go.

I turned to Milton.

What happened, Milton? I asked. Why did I get so tired?

Some of those rights started to get through to you, Milton said, and you lost concentration.

I had imagined I was perfectly conditioned, but I had forgotten the stress of pain and fear. There was a certain kind of conditioning that only hard sparring could bring. Joey said he would return in a few days but failed to appear. I can't say I minded all that much.

Here's a nice story for you, Milton said. White kid, doesn't start trouble with anybody, and the cops are after him. You could have got shot. This is the same shit they've been doing to us for years, and nobody listened. But now that it's happening to white people, they're starting to listen.

Mayor Giuliani's policy of aggressive policing had led to regular stop and searches of thousands of black and Spanish men, and his nontolerance of "quality of life violations"—everything from open containers to jay-walking—had come to affect whites as well (even Busdriver, friendly with a number of city officers, had nearly been arrested for daring to argue with a cop). The previous year had also seen police kill four unarmed black men, including the African immigrant Amadou Diallo, hit nine-teen times by undercover officers who emptied their pistols at him as he stood outside his Bronx building. In reaction, a wave of civil protest washed over the city, with regular demonstrations outside City Hall.

What had happened to me was daily life for most of the men around the Supreme Team. Nearly every one of Milton's boxers had confronted the criminal justice system: Dave Marrero, Julian, Efrain, Victor, Zeus. The one fighter who did not speak of arrest was Will, an immigrant (and the only college student on the Supreme Team). My black and Spanish gymmates were regularly stopped and frisked by the cops.* For Victor, in the South Bronx, it was a weekly occurrence and a source of little anger.

They're usually cool with you, he said, if you're cool with them.

But it must be annoying to get stopped all the time walking around in your own neighborhood, Milton said.

You get used to it, Vic said.

---

*According to the NYPD's own statistics, in forty-five thousand stop and frisk searches reported in 1998, 90 percent of the suspects were black and Latino (*Village Voice*, December 5, 2000).

But you don't go reaching into your pocket real quick, I said.

No. Victor laughed. You don't do that.

I'm on the bus again with Giuseppe, rattling through a cemetery in Queens. He straightens up in the driver's seat.

Houdini was buried here! he exclaims.

No kidding, I say.

Yeah, he continues. And every Halloween, there's about two hundred people lined up outside, because Houdini said, "One day, I'm gonna pop out of my grave on Halloween, but I'm not gonna tell you when." Can you imagine that? Houdini said it. I mean, I didn't hear him say it; this is what people tell me. And you know, Halloween, and there's hundreds of people lined up outside the gate. Like they're waiting for Houdini to come out of his grave. Can you imagine that? Of course, being that I'm born-again, I really don't believe any of that.

You're a born-again? I ask. I knew there had to be some reason why Joe was so nice.

When I was fifteen years old, I became a born-again Christian, Giuseppe says. I try my best to stop cursing and doing things that I'm not supposed to be doing. You know? Sometimes I wonder if I'm going to make it to heaven, man. 'Cause it's hard. In the Bible it says, "Very few will enter the kingdom of heaven," man. You know? I mean, think about it. There's gotta be a God, man, you know what I'm sayin'? There has to be. I mean, look at people that die. They're dying, they're on their deathbed. Who do they cry out to? God, man. When you're in trouble, even yourself, I mean, you think about it.

Joe says he looks on me as someone who could be saved.

You were brought up Catholic, he says, so you must believe that Jesus Christ is the son of God.

I'm not convinced, I say.

Maybe God is telling me to say this, Joe says. Don't take it personally, but you know, maybe God put me here in your life at this time.

I agree that anything is possible.

———

Although Laura had departed, Milton still used her image to illustrate our style. He would show the tape of her winning the Gloves to Supreme Team rookies: Laura in battle garb, schooling a black woman in the Garden.

Watch this, Milton would say. A three-punch combination. Look at that uppercut. In the other girl's corner, those idiots are telling her to come in low, and she's walking right into the five. We're killing her with hooks. Here's a standing eight. I can't believe we didn't knock her out.

Laura's dominance was complete: If the other woman tried to slug inside, Laura battered her; if she stayed away, Laura dangled her on the end of her jab like a pom-pom. Old Gil Clancy, the announcer, narrated the fight in world-weary tones: "Kielczewski just hit her with a great hook. She'll hit her again."

"People tell you it's a slap," Julian would say, pointing at the screen, "but when we hit you with it, it don't feel like no slap."

Hey, Bob, you got a box cutter or something? Vic asked, needing to sever a thread from his wraps.

Yeah, I think so, I said, and took out a blue-handled cutter from my gym bag.

Milton seemed surprised. Bob, you carry a knife, why?

I used to work as a carpenter, and we had to have them, I said.

I hadn't done carpentry in a while, but I hadn't stopped carrying the cutter. I'd had one drawn on me the winter before. In Midtown, at 8:30 A.M. A rainy morning, and a fat black woman had jammed her umbrella into my neck, going by. "You should be moving faster," she said. So I'd smacked her umbrella with my (closed) umbrella. We began swearing at each other on the sidewalk. "I'm not fucking around," she said, rummaging in her purse—lipstick, compact, wallet—finally drawing out the box cutter. Another pause to click it open, and she waved it in my face. We circled each other as astonished commuters streamed past. I was waiting for her to move forward, at which point I planned to block her lunge with my umbrella and drop my left in her face. A cop arrived, however, to send us on our way. The event left an impression on me.

Bob wants to give somebody a souvenir, Vic said, with his gentle smile.

I want to pick up a scar like Victor's, I said, only I don't want to die for it.

Milton got scars from being shot and stabbed, Victor said.

You need a scar on your face, Milton said. That's the best place to have a scar. I got this one from a razor.

He pointed to the dark scar that ran from under his eye across his cheek.

That's from a razor? Vic said.

Yeah, that's from a razor. And this one, he said, rolling up his sleeve, is where I got stabbed.

I noticed the blade mark beneath the dark hair on Milton's arm.

He shoved the sleeve farther up and pointed to a circular impression. And this is where a bullet went through.

He pulled his shirt up his hairy torso and showed us another knife scar. I imagined Milton at twenty-five, how hot and loud and troublesome he must have been (and I wondered how he'd lost the upper canines from either side of his smile).

Julian had left his house. He and his partner (his babymoms, as he called her) of five years were not getting along, and as a result, Julian was left in limbo. Every time I had called him at home, I could hear his kids playing in the background, but now his partner was threatening to take the children and leave the state.

I try to be there as much as I can for them, Julian told me, so they can know who I am, so they can remember Daddy, you know what I mean? Because I know their mother is going to try to take them away. If things start getting worse than what they are now, she's gonna leave, and the next thing you know, she's going to be saying, "Yo, your daddy wasn't here to do this. Your daddy wasn't here to do that." We don't have the best of situations right now. We just trying, you know, to work things out. We been together for what? Six years already, you know? From kids. Fifteen years old. She don't understand I'm boxing for a future. I try to explain to her, like, the amateur boxing, we don't get paid, but we fight a lot. Word? That's just like college basketball. You prove yourself in college, so when you go to the NBA, you know what I mean, you already a marquee player, you gonna make money. So if you a good amateur, you know, in the boxing game, you gonna make money as a pro. I'm telling her that what I'm doing here is marking my territory, so I can make money, so I could provide better for my family. You know? "Oh, you doin' this because you . . ." You know what I mean? I was like, "All right, whatever." I know what I got to do. I know what I'm good at.

Afraid of being apprehended on the day of my fight, I took the train to the criminal court building the week before. A case of the flu distorted everything I saw. The grimed building hulked over the street. Police buses with their grilled windows pulled up and disgorged cuffed prisoners in orange jumpsuits. I went through the metal detectors, waited in the lines, saw my old file for the fare-jumping arrest, mug photo of me at thirty looking tan and goofy. I sat on a bench for nine hours, dull with fever, waiting to be called. As my time drew near, a Legal Aid lawyer went over my file with me.

This warrant is three years old! he exclaimed. What the hell are you doing here?

The cops have started coming to my house, I said.

He shook his head and sighed.

The judge might want to assign you some community service or something, he said. Are you okay with that?

I thought about scraping disks of gum from subway cars.

Can't I just pay a fine or something?

I'll see what I can do, he said.

When I did stand before the judge, she too laughed over the ancient warrant and sent me on my way. No fine, no community service, which might lead you to ask, "What the hell were the cops doing at your door at five A.M.?"

Going to the courthouse was a magical act: I was trying to propitiate forces I only dimly understood. The case was the same for much of the black and Spanish youth in New York City. Warrants for loitering, possession of small amounts of marijuana, trespassing, disturbing the peace, fare evasion . . . It doesn't matter what the charge is; what matters is that it's something. The object seemed to be: get something on someone so they will have leverage against him. Most kids would plead guilty on a first offense rather than face a trial and lengthy stay on Rikers (say, for having a joint). Then a party would be busted, and the kid would be there, arrested for loitering, and the police would run his name, and *voilà*, a repeat offender. And once you get your toe stuck in the criminal justice system, it's very hard to pull away.

I started turning on my lights again at night and stopped pulling my Supreme Team hat over my brow when I got on the subway. I'm still not completely sure they won't come back as I'm not completely sure why they showed up in the first place.

K N O C K E D

Thoughts of my coming fight recalled my last fight, four years before. I had lost, but not badly, a 3–2 decision in the Bed-Stuy boxing club. Just a week before the fight, however, something had happened that contributed to my leaving the sport.

John had come to Darryl sometime in the spring with a Golden Gloves dream. He was an outer borough type, Italian-American, had the harsh accent and a Roman nose. With a job selling medical equipment, John was more flush than most of the guys at 12th Street. He owned a new Japanese sedan and a Jet Ski that he buzzed around the Sound on during the summers. John had been sent to Darryl by one of the scam trainers you see circulating around gyms, guys with two-line ads in the back of the *Voice* that offer "professional boxing lessons," ads that draw white-collar marks who stick out their jabs like the pope offering his ring to kiss. The white-collar victims can be soaked for months, around and around in the ring, back and forth in the ring, for months, while the gym regulars snicker behind their hands. John had seen through this and, wanting the Gloves, had ended up with Darryl.

That spring I was coming back to the gym from a layoff. My poor form was obvious the first time I sparred with John. Obvious to Adam, Darryl's prize welterweight.

"What's wrong with you guys?" he asked. "You looked like a pair of monkeys out there."

A monkey I might have been, but I soon learned how to get the better of John, or Army, as he came to be known for his camouflage outfits. Besides being green, Army was very slow. Nothing pleases a boxer more than a slow opponent. I could generally move in, hit Army and move out again before he had a chance to react. Army took his lumps in those first months. Once, near the end of a round with me, he gave up from exhaustion. Just gave up: took himself to a corner and dropped his arms. On the gym floor behind him, Darryl waved for me to move in and keep punching, but I couldn't bring myself to hit the defenseless Army. It was just supposed to be sparring. We were supposed to be on the same team. I stood and waited for the bell to ring. Not long afterward, Adam improved Army's physiognomy by fracturing his nose.

Army persisted in the face of these setbacks, however, and although he didn't get any faster, he did get better. His defense improved, and once, as I cockily moved in to hit him, he caught me with a right in the belly that almost blew a hole through me. There was power in Army's right hand, a shadow of something dangerous in his awkward movement. Army could hurt you with that right hand if you stood in front of him for too long.

The summer was almost over, and I was training for my second fight with Darryl. I had agreed to do it from some burst of enthusiasm early in the summer, feeling tough that day, or a dreamer again with a brilliant boxing future in front of him. By the time the fight was only a few weeks away, however, I hated the idea of it. A note in my journal from those weeks proclaims that it would be my last fight ever. I was tired of making my way down to Julio's dingy subbasement with its rancid pools of water and the roaches crawling on the shower room walls. My body was worn down with the nagging injuries that come from regular training. I had a sprained thumb and bruises on my arms and chest. My lower back always ached. Boxing had never seemed like such a waste of time. I should have been writing, not getting my head knocked around. Just a few blocks away from the gym at Richard Foreman's theater in St. Marks Church, my first show was about to go up. When I came in to watch the actors, my director couldn't understand why my nose was always swollen and my face scuffed from the glove leather. Worst of all, I still didn't feel I had learned how to box. I had good days, and I could take advantage of novices like Army, but that didn't make me a fighter. Darryl's answer to my every concern was that I needed to train harder and spar more.

About two weeks before my fight, I walked into the gym to see Army sparring with one of Darryl's part-timers, Rafael, a slightly over-weight, genial Puerto Rican with a baby face. Rafael was pawing Army with soft jabs when Army hauled back his right arm and hoisted it toward Rafael's chin. The deliberate movement resembled a blacksmith raising a hammer over an anvil and letting it fall. Rafael dropped like several sacks of laundry sewn together and lay crumpled on the canvas. I had never seen anything like it during a sparring session. Darryl raised the wobbly kid back to his feet and sent him back into action with typical Darryl encouragement.

C'mon, Darryl said, you have to get right back in. That's what makes you tough.

Across the floor, I marveled with the other regulars.

Do you see that? said Gavin, a tattooed bulldog of a kickboxer who played guitar in a thrash band. That was a blast! That punch shut out the lights!

We laughed and shook our heads about the unfortunate victim. We whispered that his chin was made of porcelain. The knockout inevitably made Rafael less to us. For the next few days Army wore an abashed, somewhat witless grin whenever the subject of his punch was raised.

Boxing is a sport of endless doubt and labyrinthine self-deception. You armor your body: muscles plated atop deltoids, sturdy ridge of the latissimus dorsi, bulging neck, all so you can lock down in your crouch, gloves drawn up to cushion the jaw and face, elbows tight to the tender ribs. Fighters steel their minds as well but doubt is never far. Success only increases the possibility for doubt. Become the top fighter in your gym, and you have to worry about the city. Become a contender and the belt holders stand above you. Champions on their brief peak can never relax vigilance; someone hungry always waits to knock them down.

The KO banishes doubt, at least temporarily. The fight has ended in a result without appeal. With a supreme demonstration of his force, the winner has come close to murder. The loser has been crushed. No more would-haves or should-haves, no more blaming bad decisions, bad judges, hometown crowds . . . No one believes it can happen to him. Public emasculation, led trembling from the ring or taken out on a stretcher. Many boxers never recover from a KO. For those who try to fight again, the reconstruction of the ego begins with the sentence "It was just a lucky punch." I don't remember if I ever saw Rafael again at 12th Street.

Less than a week later I had the worst day of my boxing life. I was supposed to spar Army that day, but when I arrived at the gym, neither he nor Darryl was there. I sat on the couch for a while with my feet up and my sunglasses on. This was according to Darryl's advice. "If you're supposed to spar and your trainer's not there, don't do anything. Just sit down and wait. Go to sleep if you feel like it." When no one showed up for another ten minutes, I decided to take a holiday. I changed into my gym clothes and began to work out. I didn't want to spar. My hand hurt, I was fatigued, I thought I might be coming down with a cold . . . I just didn't want to. I was tired of boxing. Here was the chance to sneak out of my responsibilities for the day. I'd start to work the floor, and by the time they arrived, if they arrived, I would have the perfect excuse not to go in the ring. I still had plenty of time before the fight, almost a week. I would spar the next day, and the day after that. Anything. Run marathons, drink Lysol, anything.

All too soon, as I jumped rope, Army walked into the gym.

You should take it easy, he said. We're going to spar today.

Not me, I said, gleeful with my get-out-of-jail scheme. You guys are way late. I've been working out for an hour.

But Darryl's going to be here in a few minutes, he said.

I pretended not to hear. I jumped rope faster, every second taking me farther away from a bruising in the ring. Yet when Darryl did walk into the gym, I was helpless.

Get ready, Bob, he said. We're going to spar.

I don't really feel up to it, Darryl, I said.

You don't feel up to it? he said with disgust. You don't feel up to it? As if I'd admitted a sexual predilection for young boys. You have a fight on Friday. Are you going to feel like it then?

I mumbled something about my injured hand and poor health, but I was already donning my wraps and Darryl wasn't listening.

In the first round I fought scared, tossing jabs in retreat and grabbing Army under the arms whenever he came too close. My behavior gave Army confidence. When he realized I wasn't fighting back, he pressed me harder. Since he was the bigger man, it was easy enough for him to shake off my clinches, and the pursuit would begin again.

When the bell rang to end the round, I returned to the corner and Darryl's scolding.

What the hell is wrong with you? he said. I want to see you fight out there.

I stood in sullen silence. I'd told him I didn't want to spar that day. This was the result he deserved.

The second round brought the same combination of holding and running on my part. As I backed up, a lucky jab from Army caught me in the throat. I say lucky because this is something that almost never happens in boxing. From the first day, fighters are trained to keep their heads down, and it is difficult to stick the large glove into the small area of the throat. Certainly it had never happened to me before. I fell back against the ropes gagging, and then I wasn't there anymore.

I returned slowly, in pieces, threads of sleep still dangling from my brain. I was waking up, from out of the maze of wandering thoughts and dream chains. It was an ill waking, though, from an uneasy sleep of nightmare or hangover when some not very pleasant things had happened the night before. I returned to find myself standing in my corner with my hands up. The bell must have rung to start the round because I sailed forward to fight again. Somewhere in the debris of my mind coiled an intense anger at the fact that someone had hurt me so badly. Yet I could barely see my opponent waiting on the other side of the ring.

As I took my first steps, I saw a tiny Julio rise far across the room and hobble forward to wave off the action. I wouldn't be fighting anymore that day. Somehow my gear came off, and I headed for the locker room, the gym surging at my back. The gym spoke words of comfort to me: in Julio's voice, "It happens to everybody"; in the punk rock bulldog's voice, "Just yesterday Big Joe hit me with a shot that had me out on my feet"; in Darryl's voice, "Don't worry about it, a lucky punch." I was beyond all comfort. I showered and dressed in a dismal fog. As I put on my shoes, Army sat beside me in a locker room that had emptied. We did not speak. I knew that as soon as I left, the gym would be talking about me in a different way. The bulldog had offered me support, but I knew he would be marveling at my collapse. Army would once again wear his abashed grin at the narratives of his further feats of strength. "Army's knocking down everybody these days. He's got a cannon for a right hand." As I was leaving, Joe, the gym assistant, a burly Puerto

Rican, tapped my shoulder (Joe was an old friend of Julio's. He'd just served out a long prison term [for armed robbery, I believe] and was having trouble finding a job. He couldn't have been making fifty dollars a day at the gym).

Don't worry so much about it, he said. That kid is a natural welterweight. You're a featherweight. He's much bigger than you.

Thanks, Joe, I said, and walked up the stairs.

I left the senior center for the sun on First Avenue. A breezy day in high summer, Mexican clerks outside a Korean deli washing heads of lettuce, young mothers pushing strollers, the river of traffic with taxis like frantic yellow beetles. I pushed through the bodies, the dark events in the gym clouding my eyes. Underground at the First Avenue subway station, I realized I had a small problem. I no longer remembered where I lived. I sat on a bench considering this as one train passed and then another. I had been very drunk any number of times, but I had always remembered where I lived, had even, barely able to walk, found my way home across enormous distances. Yet there I sat, broad waking and clueless. The knowledge had been pounded right out of my head. One thing I did remember was that I no longer lived where I had lived two months before. I remembered having moved from 169th Street in Washington Heights. Go there, and I would find changed locks and somebody else's bed. Where I had moved to, however, remained a mystery. At the time I didn't find my situation remarkable ("How strange that a man can forget where he lives") or terrifying ("I've forgotten where I live!"). My thoughts scrambled around a slick and obdurate surface without catching hold, the tip-of-the-tongue sensation when you forget a friend's phone number or the name of Duke Ellington's first tenor chair. Since instinct had led me to the train station, I decided to take the train and exit at whatever stop felt right. When the next train came, I got on and stood gray and dull among the commuters.

After finding my way home, I narrated the sad story of my fall to my flatmate and her friend Kenneth. Before I go any further, a few words about my apartment, my flatmate and her friend.

We lived in a third-floor apartment over a busy intersection in an ungentrified section of Williamsburg. Directly below us was a Spanish/Chinese restaurant that filled our rooms with its warm reek seven days a week from eight A.M. to midnight. On the other three corners stood three open-all-night businesses: a Spanish fried chicken place, a Mexican bakery and a bodega. The three businesses and the wide streets kept the intersection booming until dawn, big cars with tinted windows and Jeeps blaring merengue double-parked in a line before the stores. Adding to the confusion, a number of retail heroin houses operated nearby (one fronted by a taxi service with a scale in the back room), so that any late-night return home demanded a vigilant lookout for junkie beggars, crackheads and drunks.

My flatmate was a talented, disturbed woman who became a little more lost every day. Her sign was confusion. Rose was an artist who made little art, her aborted projects scattered through the general wreckage of her life. She had crammed the rooms of the apartment with debris that she planned to clean, sell, organize. There were rowing machines, Rollerblades, stacked canvases, photo albums, fine ruined furniture she intended to restore. Her unwashed clothing stood in frayed mounds. Hair from her animals (three cats and a big, sloppy dog) lay clumped in the hallways and stirred in the floor-through breeze (the dog and one of the cats, an old tom, were annoyed by my male threat in the apartment and would urinate in my bed whenever I made the mistake of leaving my door unlocked). Although Rose possessed excellent office skills, she had trouble holding even the most casual job. She would arrive on time for the first few days of work but would rise so late by the second Tuesday that she would be ashamed to go in. Rose feared sleep and would only drop off past midnight in a recliner, the television buzzing loudly, three lamps shining suns on her face.

Heroin added to her confusion. She had a small habit that came and went. With a few friends, Rose circled the drug at varying orbits, closer—hotter, faster; farther—cooler, slower, some of the group finally dropping into the crush of addiction. They could not leave the drug completely and lived in lies, promises made and broken to themselves and everyone else.

Kenneth would score somewhere on the Lower East Side and then come over to use. A grad student with a fellowship at an Ivy League school, he was an intellectual of the bright, twitchy type. He would show up at the apartment talking fast, hands rubbing up and down his thighs in nervous enthusiasm. Then he would excuse himself and disappear behind the bathroom door. A short time later he would emerge a different man: mumbling, cadaver gray, clutching the walls as his knees betrayed him.

On that day Kenneth and Rose were comfortably high when I returned to the apartment with my woeful tale. Rose offered me a line of dope for my pain. Although I don't particularly like heroin, its somnolence and low-grade euphoria, I accepted. I didn't care what I did. There was no future, no consequence that mattered (in the same way, I sometimes feel so good in that there is no future beside the good feeling). After a few minutes of conversation, the drug touched me, thickening the air. Then it ran me over. I stumbled into my room, and the bed reached out for me. I lay there overwhelmed, wondering if I felt good or bad.

Rose poked her head into the room a while later.

Don't die, Bob, she advised.

I chose not to answer. It was much better to do nothing at all, to lie and let the molecules in my body vibrate in their dark singularities. I wasn't going to die, but I had overdosed in a minor sort of way; calibration of drug purity and quantity calculated poorly for the novice user. In a few minutes I passed into the next stage of the drug's disquiet, a wave of nausea. I managed to get up and go to the bathroom, where I emptied my stomach into the toilet. Fifteen minutes later I repeated the procedure. And fifteen minutes after that. And fifteen minutes after that.

Later on we decided to take the dog for a midnight walk. Williamsburg late, a quiet of building sides, alleyways, blue shadows. Every hundred yards as we walked, I would have to puke into whatever receptacle offered itself. That routine continued for the next ten sleepless hours, although after all the juice was squeezed from my gut, I was reduced to long bouts of dry retching.

The next afternoon when I returned to the gym, Joe saluted me.

He's back, Joe said. That's what a warrior does.

But I didn't feel like a warrior. My confidence had been shaken, and my little binge had cost me five pounds and strength just a few days before a fight that I would lose, too exhausted to continue punching at the end of the last round. The following day a disappointed Darryl handed my book to me, and I felt finished with boxing.

BLACK (AND BLUE)

From my first days in the gym, it was Milton's oft-repeated contention that he was going to "turn me black"—to endow me with a boxing style that would be recognizably African-American. Were Milton able to do this, we all agreed, it would be a very good thing indeed. That Milton called me Elvis thereby made perfect sense, yet another white guy benefiting from a black style (or as Vernon put it, "Bob's like Eminem and Milton's his Dr. Dre").

But what, exactly, did a "black" boxing style signify? For Milton, "black" connoted style, speed, slickness, grace; a style earmarked by fakes, jukes, backpedals, sidesteps and an ability to hit without getting hit; a style in which *looking* good played a role in *doing* good. The black style could also be understood in terms of everything it was not. Everything "white," that is. "White" to Milton meant slow, stiff, mechanical, plodding, easy to hit, and when hit, easily cut (that thin white skin). The only good thing he could find to say about white fighters was that they could absorb extravagant amounts of punishment. "White guys refuse to go down," he would say. "So you got to frustrate them. They go crazy when they find out they can't hit you and then they'll start walking into shit."

The question remains as to what led Milton to believe that blackness, in boxing, was his to bestow. After all, Milton was Puerto Rican, not African-American. But then, if we were speaking strictly, neither was Will (Guyanese), Victor (Puerto Rican), or Vernon (Barbadian). In the gym, this confusion about what "black" was led to conversations like:

Julian: It's weird. Born and Sean don't talk like black guys.

Bob: Sean's black? [Sean wasn't much darker than me.]

J: Yeah. His dad is from Jamaica, and his mom is French or some shit.

So, while in Puerto Rico Milton might be referred to as *trigueño*, he could easily be considered black (in the Second World War, Puerto Ricans were surprised when they were banned from serving in the navy and kept in segregated camps). Milton's race did come into question among some black Americans. When angered, one of the boxers would shout at him, "Milton, you fucking albino." Yet when Milton said, "That's what the cops have been doing to us for years," he wasn't talking about other Puerto Ricans. African-American culture had played an enormous role in Milton's life, and the fact that he often identified himself as black said something about his opinion on the matter.

One day in the studio, I slipped the Curtis Mayfield *Superfly* CD into the player. Magic followed the first notes: Milton left the director's chair and began to jig around the room, while Vernon enunciated approval from a prone position at the lip of the ring.

All right, Bob! he said. You got good taste in music for a white boy! All right!

I blinked, rubbed my eyes, stared as Milton swaggered and said, "This one's for Bob," and gave falsetto accompaniment to Mayfield. Milton grabbed the CD jewel box from my hand and pointed to the sleeve photos from the film. For every scene he knew the dialogue and recited it at length, in appropriate voice for each character. The two men put "Freddie's Dead" on repeat and reminisced about Harlem in the late seventies.

Man, this movie was huge up on the streets, Vernon said. *Huge.* I'm gonna go out and buy the album tonight.

Everybody wanted to be Superfly, Milton said, but I wanted to be the Mack. I had the hair and the clothes, everything.

Have you ever been around that culture, Bob? Vernon asked.

I admitted that I had not.

We got to take Bob up to Harlem, Milton said, show him . . .

He began to name players with exotic names, members of a street scene that certainly no longer existed. Milton made a call on his cell phone.

I want you to go down to the video store, he said in the mouthpiece, and pick up two movies called *The Mack* and *Superfly*. Yeah, we'll watch it tonight. Great.

The next day Milton told me they had not been able to find the movies in their local video stores.

Vernon asked the guy where the films were, Milton said, and he pointed out the Black Exploitation section over on the bottom shelf. Then Vernon said—what did you say, Vern?

I looked at the videos there, and I said, "Man, a hundred fifty years after slavery, year 2000, and niggers are still on the bottom shelf."

The two men burst out laughing.

O n occasion Puerto Rican trumped black in Milton's cultural hierarchy. As I trained one day, Milton spoke with a Puerto Rican couple who had dropped in to visit him. He was indulging in one of his favorite rants against whites.

Yeah, they all want to act black, but I bet Bill Clinton wouldn't be too happy if his daughter showed up at the White House with some black guy from college. "I hope that fellow is just here for my autograph, Chelsea."

The couple noticed my eavesdropping and turned nervously for my reaction.

Oh, don't worry about Bob, Milton said. He's a brother; he's just the wrong color.

Milton then digressed on aging and the vagaries of life. He had recently had a chance meeting with the great beauty of his early manhood, the belle of the South Bronx neighborhood he roamed as a teenager.

It's strange, Milton said, to see someone you knew, after so much time and . . . It's not the same at all. She'd had a kid and everything. I mean, she looked good but . . . It wasn't the same.

Milton seemed wistful. He described an "old school" dance he'd attended with a friend the week before.

You're forty, he said to the male gamete of the couple. Someone would look at you and think you're twenty-five. Me, I'm forty-four. But you see some of these people our age . . . they look rough, like they just got out of prison after ten years. I mean, their faces are all beat up, their teeth are missing, they look like they been dragged behind a car. Of course, it depends on what crowd you're with. These were people I knew back in the day.

He looked over at Julian shadowboxing in the ring and lowered his voice.

This was a black crowd, he whispered. If it was Latin, it would have been different. When Latin people go out, they look sharp. Sure, they might be a little overweight, losing their hair, but . . . they look sharp. They got nice clothes. They don't let themselves go. But the blacks. Some of them with their teeth knocked out. They just look beat up.

Within the Supreme Team, race did matter, and while I may have been black inside the ring on a great day, I remained on the other side of the color line. A misunderstanding made this baldly apparent in the early days of the Golden Gloves tournament.

Travis joined Supreme at roughly the same time as I did; another middleweight, he had very dark skin (so dark it flickered with blue highlights) and a triangular face. Although he had little boxing experience, he quickly acquired the important defensive elements of the style. "Watch Travis, Bob," Milton would say as Travis sparred. "You see how he's got the defense going? Moving his shoulders, using the two hand to block both sides? That's what I'm talking about." I would stop and watch, envious of the praise, hoping to improve my own defense in the coming days. Travis's prognosis earned him ring time with Julian, Will and Victor, a dubious honor. I watched him absorb terrible beatings, particularly from Julian ("You've got to keep your hands moving," Milton would intone as Julian clubbed Travis around the ring. "This isn't Victor. He's gonna throw more than one punch"). Yet overmatched as he was, Travis blamed only himself for his shortcomings, turned his frustration on himself and clenched it in stiff silence.

After more than three months in the gym with Travis, I still felt a frost in his presence. Like people everywhere, boxers tend to socialize with their ethnic peers. Boxers also further subdivide themselves into weight classes; it makes sense that you would talk more with your sparring partners: You have the bond of shared violence. With Travis, though, I felt that it was something more, a blanket distrust toward . . . I suspected white people. He would pointedly shake only the hands of the black and Spanish fighters as he entered and left the gym, even if I stood among them. My greetings to him dropped into silence. A conversation he had with Julian tipped my suspicions.

The two men were talking philosophy, religion, science in loud voices on a December day. Julian seemed to have a broadly Christian outlook. He announced that "Christ was recognized as a prophet in four major religions." Travis asserted that the Christ we knew about was the wrong Christ, a Christ who had come to us through the white man's Bible. The real Christ could be better understood through the teachings of a modern-day prophet who had synthesized the world's major religions, the Reverend Elijah Muhammad. I understood immediately: Travis's beliefs came from the doctrines of the Nation of Islam. Elijah Muhammad had taught, among other things, that whites were subhuman devils, the creation of an insane scientist who wished to destroy an original peaceful black civilization (while a black American doesn't require the NOI to be hostile toward whites, it certainly helps).

Julian had done most of his reading in prison; Travis was equally self-taught and prey to the more exotic black nationalist doctrines. Their conversation spanned an impressive range of topics, including the debate between faith and reason.

Julian: When you're dead in the ground, how do you know something happens to your soul?

Travis: I don't believe in soul; I believe in spirit.

J: Soul, spirit, how do you know that anything happens to it? No one ever came back to tell what happened.

T: I believe . . .

And on it went. Travis declared that Negroid features on Olmec statues in Mesoamerica could be explained by continental drift from a primeval supercontinent. Julian proceeded to give a convincing demonstration of Hume's fundamental negative contention about causality ("But how do you know what caused that? And then how do you know what caused that? Science is just theories. You can't prove that anything made anything else happen. It's just in your head that things are connected"). I was impressed by the scope of both men's knowledge and depressed by how random it was.*

Travis had the autodidact's paranoia and bent for conspiracy theories. He had bought heavily into Y2K fears (remember Y2K?). If we were to believe the pronouncements of Travis, the end would come with the millennium: Toll midnight for January 1, 2000, and jets would drop from the heavens, skyscraper lights would flicker and dim as misprogrammed computers set their clocks to 1900. There would be rioting, looting, blood in the streets. Putting money where his mouth was, Travis bought a portable stove and a drum of fuel. He informed us that he planned to relocate to a cabin northeast of Atlanta and bunker down in the woods as the cities burned (Milton's take on Y2K was somewhat more casual. "Hey," he would say, "have you stocked up yet on your Y2K jelly?"). Up until the day before the New Year we expected Travis to go, but there he was in the gym in the first week of January, face as expressionless as always.

Milton lay in wait on the padded bench.

So, Travis, I thought you were headed down to Atlanta?

I wasn't going to get up and go like that, Travis said. I had too much to protect here in the city.

Milton wasn't about to let him off so easily.

So what about all that stuff that was supposed to happen with Y2K? The planes crashing and shit like that?

Travis had come prepared. He reached into his bag and flourished a sheet of paper.

I copied this off a Web site, he said. They listed all the problems that arose from Y2K.

Milton grabbed the sheet of paper.

"Food shortages in Britain?" he said. "A train derailment due to a failed microcomputer?" "Delays in Seattle." Delays in Seattle? What the hell is that supposed to mean?

Travis scowled.

---

*"In New York City particularly, poor or black and Latino students are far more likely than white or middle-class students to have low-quality, inexperienced teachers" (*New York Times*, October 5, 2000).

It's right there on the paper, he said. Go to the Web site and look it up for yourself.

"Delays in Seattle," Milton repeated, laughing. Now that's something that's going to keep me up tonight.

On the night of Will and Julian's Gloves prelim, I took the subway to the site with Travis and a few of my friends (experience had taught us not to rely on Milton's driving). Travis knew the way and had us slip from subway to bus somewhere in the middle of Brooklyn. En route he asked me if I had any background in computers. When I said "a little," he told me that he had just bought one and was considering taking an expensive class for certification in the repair of Windows systems. Anything, he said, that would let him quit his job driving a white minibus for the city. I asked him if he had ever considered word processing work. When he said no, I told him that he could clock decent money with only a little experience (word processing being more integrated than many other job sectors in the city).

As we left the bus and walked to the school where the fights would be held (a fortlike structure as welcoming as Alcatraz), I enjoyed an afterglow from our conversation; life in the gym would be more comfortable if Travis and I could be civil. I could tell Travis the interview routines in a few minutes and even loan him a book or two.

As we approached the school, Travis hung back.

I'm going to buy something to eat, he said, then slide in with Milton for free.

Like Travis, I also hoped to slide in for free. My friends were shooting a documentary about boxing, and after a great deal of suspicion on the part of the *Daily News*, they had received permission to film at the Golden Gloves. Inside, a series of lunchroom tables barricaded the entrance to the gym, the guardian crone behind one table with a claw out for her fifteen-dollar fee.

We're here to do some filming, I said. We have permission from the *News*.

Oh, you do? she said. Are you on the list?

She pawed myopically at the sheets of paper in front of her, then seemed to make a decision.

Okay. How many of you are there? she asked.

I looked behind me at my friends and the equipment they trundled. Travis had rejoined us, standing a few steps farther back.

I hesitated.

Four, I said, numbering the film crew and myself.

Four? said the woman. Well, won't your friend be offended if you leave him out?

As a matter of fact, I am offended, Travis said, very offended.

I looked back to see if he was joking. A scowl creased his face, and he shifted from foot to foot. He was not joking.

Well, I, uh, you see . . . I tried to stammer an explanation.

The guardian crone grew suspicious of our disorder.

I have to talk to someone about this, she said.

She disappeared inside to return moments later with a florid *News* official.

Yes? the man said. Can I help you?

I explained that we had contacted his office by fax and telephone about filming at the Gloves. I told him my name and offered my hand. He looked at it as if I were presenting him with roadkill.

Oh, yes, I suppose it's all right, he said, but you all have to pay to come in.

Travis had vanished.

I sat and watched my friends struggle to shoot. Although the crew had worked both professional and amateur boxing events without friction, they were hounded from point to point by the *Daily News* staff. Then the *News* supervisor blustered that they had to leave the building (the director of photography, a Russian, said he had been treated better by the KGB).

As I helplessly witnessed this, one of Milton's clients approached me.

I just got off my cell with Milton, she said. He started yelling at me about Travis and why did we hate black people and why hadn't we gotten Travis into the show. I told him that I wasn't even with you guys.

I dreaded Milton's arrival, but after I told him what had happened, he dropped the subject. Travis was a different story. He refused to look at me that night or over the next few days in the gym. I wrote him a short note explaining my troubles with the *News* people and why I didn't want to risk bringing extra people into the show. When I tried to give him the note, he pushed my hand away.

Just forget it, Travis said angrily, just forget it.

The note fell to the floor unread.

We did not speak again as Travis thumped his way through to the Gloves semifinals (ironically, thinking he wasn't ready, Milton had tried to convince him not to enter the Gloves). Naturally, Milton enjoyed our conflict and teased me about Travis.

If you're not careful, Bob, he warned me, I'm going to put you in to spar with Travis.

After losing his semifinal bout, Travis disappeared.

I've played out that night at the school a thousand times, turned it in the light, shifted it from side to side. Had I betrayed Travis as a teammate, the one black face among the white ones of my filmmaker friends? Had I suffered a spasm of knee-jerk racism? In the moment I had felt that I couldn't risk "putting one over" on the *Daily News*, but it had made no difference. The door crone had counted Travis as one of our group and pointed out my exclusion of him, my separation visible to a stranger. For Travis, I assume it was a confirmation of the views expounded in the writings of the Honorable Elijah Muhammad.

Boxing presents a world where whites are a feeble minority. Urban African-American culture dominates: The music is hip-hop; the fashions and dialects are street. Those few skilled white fighters have generally been around this culture most of their lives and mimic its speech and styles (when Milton said, "Bob, leave my white guys alone," it was the highest praise, kindling warmth in this wannabe's chest). In New York the gym is one of the only places where the races mix by choice, ethnicities linked by hip-hop, combat and sweat in dissonant harmony. You can almost believe that the only thing that matters is how rough and real you are in the ring, that boxing is blind to color. There's truth in this: Beat everyone's ass, and it doesn't matter what color you are, "That kid can fight" the first words out of the ringside gallery. In boxing, equality grows from the end of a fist.

Gyms are a rare place in American society where nonwhite men are in positions of authority (I never had a nonwhite male instructor until I started boxing). They are also a place where the blackout on discussions of race is sometimes lifted. Move around in the arts world in New York, and you might think racial tension didn't exist in America—because almost everyone is white. The gyms are no utopias, of course, and their openness on racial issues is a dismal commentary on the state of race relations everywhere else.

Leave the gym and the world reverts to a less remarkable reality. The white executive cabs to his doorman building, and Victor rides the subway to the South Bronx. Black and brown rule boxing because they're the only Americans desperate enough to conceive of it as a career, a small, barred window of opportunity. While a high percentage of black and Spanish men (especially over the age of forty) have boxed at some time in their lives, the vast majority of recreational boxers are white. The gym racial division is usually reflected in age as well: young blacks and Latinos hoping for a shot, older whites worried about cholesterol.

Of course, the hierarchies of the outside world do pass through the gym doors. Boxing history is a history of bias and exclusion against black fighters. In the early nineteenth century, a certain victory by the black fighter Tom Molineaux over the reigning British champion was disrupted by a riot (Molineaux's thumb was broken by a rioter). The flamboyant Jack Johnson, the first black heavyweight champion, was dogged by racial slurs and threats. After Johnson, it was decades before another black fighter was given a heavyweight title shot (and this exclusion applied to fighters in the other weight classes as well). The more recent search for a "Great White Hope" allowed a talented but limited white fighter like Gerry Cooney to command *Sports Illustrated* covers and million-dollar endorsements while only a contender. Outside the ring, most of the money people—managers, promoters, agents, etc.— are white, and sleazy enough as a group to have generated their own stereotype: the smooth-talking, stout hustler driving a Lincoln Town Car and wearing sunglasses indoors.

In the amateur ranks, where quality white fighters do exist, racial bias is alive and well. Popular boxing wisdom maintains that white amateurs will be awarded decisions in close fights or in not-so-close ones. In the 1996 National Golden Gloves finals, two white fighters were awarded terrible decisions over black fighters, although both white fighters had been severely pounded and one of them was nearly unconscious when his hand was lifted in the air (Al Bernstein, the excellent boxing analyst, shared my dismay over the decisions). This traditional discrimination may be changing, however, as aging white officials are replaced by younger blacks and Latinos.

How come they don't like us, Bob?" Busdriver asked me one day. "How come they don't like us?," coming from Joe Penna, who liked everyone, who persisted in being friendly in the face of rebuff, insult, slight; who had served in the military, the one arena of American life that could be said to be truly integrated; who had married a dark-skinned Puerto Rican and then a dark-skinned Dominican woman and all of whose four children would certainly be taken for "black" at some point in future schoolyards and on street corners: "How come they don't like us?" In response to the hostility he faced in the gym at times or from customers as he drove back and forth across Brooklyn, the all-too-present chill of separation between "them" and "us," between "black" and "white." I remember my fear walking in Bedford-Stuyvesant at the age of twenty-three when I approached a dozen black guys on the street; the relief I felt as I drew close and heard them speaking Creole French because I supposed I was less likely to be harassed by a group of Haitians than by American blacks.

Yet given the history of discrimination in this country; given the bias over everything from jobs to loans to police harassment; given Yusuf Hawkins, Amadou Diallo, Abner Louima, Patrick Dorismund and Rodney King, the crowded prisons, the wasted neighborhoods, the question would be more justly put: How come we don't like them?

THE FIGHT

The day before the fight I went with the dancer to her gym. Revolution itself did not have a scale. "We do not want our clients running to the scale every five minutes," huffed the Fitness Diva. "Weight is not an accurate measure of fitness." True enough, but it was a measure I needed. On my cheap home scale, my weight bounced between 126 some mornings and 131 some nights. The equally cheap Supreme Team scale gave me a lower number, but we all agreed it was reading light. I very much wanted to be certain, so the dancer offered help. At her gym, in a carpeted room filled with grunting bodybuilders, I stepped my gaunt form onto a medical scale. After I adjusted the balance, it read 132 pounds.

Quick, come here, I gasped.

What's the matter? the dancer asked.

I pointed at the number.

That can't be right, I said, already thinking about what I would have to suffer to lose five pounds in a day.

I don't know. Have you been eating a lot this week?

I haven't been eating *anything*, I wailed. I wanted to cry.

As I agonized over the numbers, one of the house trainers passed us and called, Oh, don't bother. That thing hasn't worked in years.

The dancer and I hauled two forty-pound dumbbells onto the scale base and saw that this was true. The scale read heavy. I felt relieved but I was back to where I'd started. In a city of eight million plus, there had to be a way to get an accurate read on a scale. Unfortunately, I didn't know what it was.

In the first round of the Golden Gloves, fighters are given a weight allowance of two or three pounds. I had heard different numbers from different people. Two pounds, no, three, no, two, no, three, two, three . . . That pound now seemed very important. Busdriver had told me, "You know if you come in a little bit over at the weigh-in, Milton will have you running around trying to sweat it off." I had an unpleasant vision of myself dashing back and forth in front of St. Catherine's Church as the spectators arrived, and decided to limit my liquid intake for the next twenty-four hours. Milton had suggested running no more than a mile that night, but I ran the usual four and went to bed on a mouthful of water.

Then it was February 29, leap year day. My last fight had been seven months before the previous leap year—fifty-six months, a boxing lifetime. At thirty-four I was the oldest person in my division. The U.S. Boxing people called me the old man. "Hey, Milton," they asked at events, "is that old man with you?" I had put in six months of hard training for six minutes of fighting. I thought about what losing would mean. It wouldn't be all bad. If I lost, I could rest. No more beatings. Cocktails. No more sitting at home, gnawing my fingers. If I won, it would mean up to two months more of pain, with the bonus of an exuberant Milton dragging me around for beatings from every lightweight in the metropolitan area. Still, I wanted to win. I saw myself fighting in the final at Madison Square Garden. I imagined the souvenir Golden Gloves in my hand, tacky and splendid.

I arrived at the gym near five. Julian, Milton and Hanson were already there.

You ready to go, Bob? Milton asked.

I said that I was, except for one thing. How about these shorts? I said. Can I wear them?

I pulled a pair of blue and gold satin Everlast shorts from my bag. I had bought them for my first New York fight, almost six years earlier.

Blue and gold, Milton said, that's the Gloves colors. If you wear those, you *have* to make the finals.

Try 'em on, Julian said.

I shucked my jeans and quickly pulled the shorts up, looking for Julian's approval. He shook his head. Where did you get those, Bob? Out of a museum?

What's wrong with them?

They short, he said, too short.

Panic seized me. What if I stepped through the ropes and people started laughing?

Maybe you can wear Vic's shorts, Milton said. Over there, on the wall.

I reached into the mesh bag and extracted the shorts. Satin, black and enormous, encrusted with various Supreme Team patches. They looked like the flag of a pirate ship. I dragged them up my legs. My calves poking from the bottom were pallid splinters, little white lambs. Julian nodded.

They all right, he said. They all right.

They're not too long? I said, watching how they billowed over my knees.

Naw, Bob, they're supposed to be long. Remember, if they ain't long, they wrong.

We headed uptown in traffic, Milton bullying and lunging with the van, our bodies snapped back with his accelerator push and then whipped forward with an urgent brake. "I've never had an accident," he boasted, but I didn't believe him.

At the Midtown Tunnel mouth, Milton stared into an eggplant-colored sports car moored beside us. The car was filled with Japanese hipsters wearing ghetto fashions, cornrows, baggies, even dark foundation to Afro-sheen their skin.

Bob, Milton said, how come everybody wants to be black?

I told him that I didn't know.

I bet they don't want to get their ass kicked and go to jail.

Milton's energy was high. I took this for a good omen.

You should have your own cable access show, Milt, I said, Brother Milton speaks.

I'd be worse than Farrakhan, he said, laughing. I'd tell the truth. They want to be black, but not *too* black. Not black enough for the cops to *think* you're black. The *no . . . good . . . bastards*!

Milton was referring to Amadou Diallo and the forty-one shots. That week a jury in Albany, to which an accommodating judge had transferred the trial, had given the four cops a get-out-of-jail-free card.

This whole system in the city sucks, Milton said, shaking his head. Everything in the city sucks. The *no . . . good . . . bastards*! What's my man's name who said that?

Khalid Muhammad? I said.

Yeah. At that Million Youth March he was saying, "Don't let those motherfuckers get away with *nothing*! If they attack you, you *grab* their *nightsticks* and you *attack them back*! The *no . . . good . . . bastards*!" He said, "You pick up anything in sight! Pick up the *railings*, and smash them across their *motherfucking* heads!"

With his talent for mimicry, Milton sounded exactly like Muhammad.

He didn't say that shit, Julian said, laughing.

Oh, yes, he did! said Milton. Yo! I was watching him one night; he was saying, "They shut the trains down!" And normally, if they have a white rally, there'd be no problem. As soon as a bunch of niggers get together, it's a goddamn problem. They shut the trains. They even tried to cut the air. Motherfuckers couldn't breathe. They had to go home early.

Everyone in the van laughed at Milton's rap, and the laughter kept me loose. Milton was in perfect form.

Those cops lied, he said, they didn't see crap. They probably ran there and stuck his wallet in his hand.

Julian didn't doubt it at all.

They tried to say it looked like a starter pistol, he said, some shit like that.

They . . . Milton sputtered. It looked like so many goddamn things, and yet, the reason why they started shooting was . . . My man . . . My man who was shooting first tripped, and they thought he got shot. So they started going crazy. "Oh, we got a free one."

Our glacial drift through the tunnel finally brought us to the tollbooths.

Yo, Milton said, pointing at one of the attendants, look at that fat fuck over there. Lucky that motherfucking booth is big or he wouldn't be able to get in *or* out.

Julian offered me advice.

Try to come to the head at first, Bob, he said. If you hurt his head, go real hard to his body. At least, that's what I'd do.

We paid and rose on a ramp above Long Island City. Queens stretched out before us, an expanse of rectangles in muted white, brown, gray, rectangles to the horizon, eerie in the twilight, the winter sun a red button on a dingy gray panel, the buildings stretching as far as we could see.

Forty minutes later we were there at last. At last! Against the doubt and fear, "at last!" It was strange to have that vanload of friends, that journey, for me alone.

The single preliminary round for featherweight novice fighters would take place at St. Catherine's Church in Franklin Square, Long Island, a few miles outside Queens and one town away from Busdriver's home of Lynbrook. The church lay in a small business district surrounded by suburban sprawl, like a fat man's skeleton. Inside, Catherine offered a benediction from an aisle alcove. Across the aisle, a bearded male saint carried what appeared to be a framing square. The narthex walls bore holy water ewers surmounted by intaglios of stylized doves and a statue of the Virgin. An enormous crucifix with a straining Christ filled the wall above the chancel.

That night's card also included further preliminary rounds for 147- and 165-pound open fighters (who went through more rounds because there were more fighters in those divisions). In the church basement, the fighters waited to be processed. We were told to strip down to our Skivvies and then lined up for the scale. I looked at the undraped bodies around me, most darker, although I was far from the only white. Some of the boxers looked like boys: narrow shoulders, shadow muscles, smooth faces (I saw the angel-faced Puerto Rican kid I'd almost fought in Yonkers). Others looked like men: mustaches, cabled arms, prison ink. There would be terrible mismatches tonight.*

Certain of the open boxers had competed in area tournaments and shows for years; these old hands greeted one another and narrated their recent battles. In general, however, the boxers stood silent, apart from the boxing people: the judges, referees, officials and trainers. The majority of these had been around New York boxing for decades, in some cases for their entire lives. They chatted under the fluorescent lights, the event a social outing with a competitive edge, a Kennel Club meet or flower show.

I waited in line and watched the scale, an electronic contraption, with a red digital display. The boxers stepped on and off, toes creasing on the tile. The vision returned of me jogging up and down on the pavement, wearing three pairs of sweats and two borrowed sweaters. My

---

*In preliminary bouts the U.S. Boxing matchmakers generally try to pair boxers by age and experience.

warm feet met the cold metal plate, and my number came up: 126.3, reported by the official as 126 and transcribed in my book as the same. I had made it. Time for a water transfusion and the energy bar. Then it was off to the doctor, with his blood pressure cuff and penlight. A few questions, the cursory exam and then "Good luck." I wondered if they ever disqualified anyone. Doubted it.

Artificial limbs? Right this way.

Multiple personality disorder? Go get 'em, champ.

A commotion erupted behind me. I turned to see a swarthy man step quietly from the scale as his trainer argued with the official.

He's not one twenty-five, said the official. He's one twenty-seven and a half. And I want you to keep quiet.

The trainer looked sulky but said nothing. He had shouted, "One twenty-five!" as his fighter stepped on the scale, fooling no one. The number was recorded as 127½, and they admitted the fighter. The weight allowance *was* three pounds, not two, after all.

Jeans and T-shirt restored, I sat and munched my energy bar. I went to the bathroom. I peered into the auditorium. Doubt surged and ebbed in me, as it had before my other fights. I told myself I could draw some teenage killer who had been boxing since the age of five. A junior De La Hoya with a hundred stripes on his record. Yet, unlike in past fights, I could quell the fear by telling myself that I had been in with pros, with amateur champions, and that my opponent would be young and feeling the same doubt, but without my years to balance him. I knew I had a solid chin (I hadn't been off my feet once with Milton) and six months of serious training behind me.

I sidled over to the U.S. Boxing table and made out the list of fighters in my class, my name printed there at the top. Only twelve novice featherweights had registered and passed their physicals, twelve for the entire tournament, meaning that two wins would put me in the Garden. Fifteen years earlier there would have been twice that, and forty years earlier, twice that again. Bill Butterworth, the videographer of New York City amateur boxing, has told me that when he started shooting the Gloves in the mid-eighties, an average prelim had thirty bouts. Now a good night would bring half as many; every year the tournament took up fewer column inches in the *Daily News*, where once the call "Support Your Battling Paperboy!" bannered the back page.

I sipped a diet cola to elevate my caffeine level into its normal range, and an unfamiliar trainer glared at me.

Are you fighting tonight? he demanded.

Yes, I answered.

Well, you shouldn't be drinking soda.

But it's diet, I said in my defense.

I don't care.

I shrugged my shoulders. Another bad omen? I wondered about the taboo on cola and hoped it wouldn't make a difference in the fight.

Stella and Laura had arrived together and stood before me. I was glad they had come.

There's only twelve guys in my class, I said, so somebody's going to get a bye.

But you *want* to fight, said Stella, who always did. I wasn't so sure. I did and I didn't. The tournament was already two months old. I'd been waiting a long time. It would not do to sit there in hope of a bye. It would weaken me. I had to convince myself that I had traveled those many miles to shatter the bones of my enemies.

Oh, yeah, sure, I said.

I looked up to see Milton bearing toward me.

They got a match for you, he said. He pointed across the room at the swarthy man from the scale incident.

I took a breath; I had crossed over.

His book says three fights, but . . . Something's not right about this, Milton said enigmatically, and stalked away.

I shifted my gaze toward the opponent. A rugged fellow who could have been thirty. Stubble darker than Milton's, chest fur up to his Adam's apple. Face scarred, bridge of the nose crushed flat. He wore the gaudiest pair of boxing sandals I had ever seen, a neon yellow and green, coming almost to his knees. Across the room, I noticed Milton leaning over the officials' table, speaking forcefully to the pleasant-faced blond woman who arranged the matches. She seemed the person least likely to have that job. Milton had claimed he held her in his pocket, and every show he played her with his contentious charm. I sat chewing my lip. There would be no escape tonight.

I went to the bathroom. At the sink, I waited as an older black man, wearing the U.S. Boxing laundryman white, shoveled water at his mouth, then spewed it across the sink and floor with shuddering hacks. As I watched him hawk and spit, he stood back, gesturing for me to use the sink.

I can wait, thanks, I said.

No, I'm gonna be a while, he said. I just had surgery for cancer, and they took out my saliva glands, so I got to do this every couple of hours. I'm still learning how to swallow.

Scar tissue seamed and charred his throat, loose flesh dangling. I looked at the water dripping from the sink ledge and puddled on the floor.

That's okay, I said. I'll wait.

I left the bathroom and stared into the church. People filed into the nave and filled the seats, shrinking the room. As I watched, a red manifold curtain slid over the enormous crucifix to shield the Son of Man from the brutal proceedings to follow.

Back in the annex, Milton's agitation continued. He muttered urgently into his cell phone and strode about the room. There was a sense that he was always about to perform some sleight of hand that would cost you your wallet.

Now he bore toward me, still discoursing into his cell.

This guy is a ringer, Milton said. He's got a hundred and fifty fights.

One hundred fifty fights? I said. That was a championship number, an Olympic number, the number of amateur fights a Hearns or Ali would have before turning pro. Maybe three other amateurs in New York State had that many amateur fights.

So am I going to fight him? I said, and wondered if I sounded shrill. I fingered the Golden Gloves shirt I'd been issued, blue with gold lettering.

That's what I'm trying to take care of right now, Milton said.

Milton left to join a conference that included the officials, the other fighter's trainer and the other fighter, whose face was no longer calm.

What's the matter? Laura asked.

I don't know, I said. Milton told me that this guy had a hundred and fifty fights.

Laura didn't appear surprised.

I *knew* something was up with him when he came in. I noticed him right away. He was just too calm. And then those sandals. The sandals definitely gave it away. They're tournament shoes.

I looked again at his Day-Glo dogs. A man who wore those would have to be supremely confident.

As Milton returned, Laura departed, the Arctic between them. The cell phone still clutched Milton's ear.

What the hell is she doing here? he said. So I found out all about this guy. He's Turkish. Had a hundred and fifty fights. Took a bronze in the Euro Cup.

How do you know?

I been around this game for a long time, Milton said. When he strolled in, I knew he didn't have no three fights. Just by how he walked across the room. I could see he was comfortable. He was too relaxed. I said, "This guy has to have more . . . This guy has to have had more than three fights." Three fights? I'm like, "Nah, no way." Still, even after I found out about his record, I was going to let him fight us, but . . .

I considered the aplomb with which Milton regarded "us" fighting Mr. 150 but let it pass. Milton had learned the fighter's nation of origin from his trainer ("Oh, where is your guy from?"). When the trainer denied previous boxing experience ("three fights"), Milton had taken another approach.

So after I found out where he was from, I called the Turkish embassy. I figured, he came over here, right? So they must have some record of him somewhere.

You called the Turkish embassy?

Yeah.

And they told you about his career?

Well, they told me some, and then he started talking.

Why?

Well, when I started pushing with the questions, he got nervous and spilled his guts. He would have said anything not to get thrown out of the tournament. I'm telling you. This is going to be the talk of the Gloves this year, just you watch.

So, am I going to fight? I ask.

They're trying to make a match for you now.

So they *were* out to get us. Will's loss, Julian's disqualification . . . We didn't stand a chance. I didn't need any more proof and prayed for a bye. It would be fine to relax and watch the competition, live to fight another day. Yet the absurdity also relaxed me. I couldn't do worse than 150 fights.

Milton's return put an end to my hopes.

They got someone for you. He pointed. Mexican kid.

My eyes followed his finger to a solid-bodied man with a perfectly spherical head, the roundest head I had ever seen. A Mexican was a misfortune. Mexicans were inevitably tough, practically indestructible. Their national boxing style had developed in response to the small stature of the typical Mexican man. Almost any non-Mexican boxer would be taller, so Mexicans did not jab, just slipped and launched titanic hooks. The Mexicans followed you, taking three punches to give one, boring forward. A Mexican would not give way. After handing me my Gloves shirt, Milton vanished, and I was left to consider my fate.

So they finally made a match for you, Laura said, smiling. You're going to be great.

I took a breath and sighed it away. Laura pressed a bottle of cold water to my forehead.

It's going to be all right, she said. You know, Mike Tyson used to cry before his fights? I couldn't believe it when I heard. I mean, Mike Tyson.

In my case I thought tears unlikely, putting me one up on Tyson.

This feels good, she said, placing the water bottle against my neck. Relax.

Milton returned.

Laura, why don't you go somewhere else? he said, snatching the water bottle from her hand. Why don't you go upstairs?

Can I have my water bottle? she said. Milton presented it.

Don't tell me what to do, Laura said.

I rolled my eyes at them and leaned against a pillar in the middle of the room. They stood there, glaring at each other.

Hey, guys, I said, *I'm* the one who's supposed to be fighting.

Laura walked away.

Dumb broad, Milton groused. What was she doing holding the bottle on your neck? She's going to make you cold before your fight.

Having banished Laura, Milton disappeared again. I changed into my shorts and was left alone in the almost empty room, the weight of the fight stacked upon my chest sixteen stories high. The matches made, everyone had departed to watch the action, and Milton was somewhere among them. Absenteeism was Milton's usual MO at bouts.

If you wanted to find him, the one place *not* to look was anywhere near his fighters. There were too many people for him to talk to, too many angles to work. Over the years the team had become resigned to his behavior. "That shit can get on my nerves sometimes," Julian said once, "but let Milton go do whatever. The one thing I ask is, just wrap my hands before you take off, you know? Do whatever, but just wrap my hands first. Sometimes he don't even do *that*." My own hands remained unwrapped.

My opponent sat with his trainer and seconds (I recognized the trainer as the owner of the Yonkers gym where I'd almost fought Angel Face). They sat close, talking and staring over at me. The trainer was skinny and shifty-looking, with drooping mustaches and a narrow goatee, a type you see sauntering out of a pawnshop or strip club at four A.M.

To cast off the weight, I decided to loosen up. In the shadow of the big pillar, I swung my arms and circled my waist, then took a stance and started throwing punches. As I moved, I noticed that Goatee had risen from his chair and sidled around the pillar to compass an angle on my movements. I stopped. As I looked at him, he stared nonchalantly in the other direction, the portrait of a pimp on a thoughtless Sunday stroll. I moved farther behind the pillar. A few minutes later I noticed that he had drifted in the same direction. I stopped again. He stared into the distance.

Julian saved me.

Come here, Bob, he said. He held up his hands for me.

Jab, jab. That's good. One-two-three; one-two-three. All right. It's show time, baby. Let me see the four. Good. I *know* you're ready. You about to take this kid out. Come to the body, right away. Boom, boom. He won't be expecting it. Body shots. At least, that's what I'd do.

Julian was always so modest with advice, never commanding, merely saying that in a similar circumstance, he would choose a particular action. We didn't have much time to get warm, though.

Milton ran in. We're up next, he said.

One match away, and my hands still weren't wrapped. Milton wore his usual black warm-up suit and black jacket, looking sardonic, sinister and a little dissipated. As he wrapped, then taped my hands, he couldn't get over the Turkish incident.

That was some funny shit, he said, looping gauze around my hands.
Everyone's going to be talking about that. You watch.

Yo, he said to Julian, a hundred and fifty fights.

One hundred fifty fights? Julian answered. He stood behind me, his
thick fingers kneading my neck.

That's what the little motherfucker had.

So did he get thrown out?

No, they pushed him up to open. Let him beat Peña's ass.

Who we fighting? Julian asked.

Milton pointed out the Mexican with an elbow.

I'm telling you, that's gonna be the talk of the Gloves. That's one for
the books.

In street clothes Julian loomed bigger than he did in the gym. He
wore a pinstriped dress shirt untucked, which made him seem even
wider.

Then the gloves were on my hands, and a *Daily News* robe was
tugged over them. I didn't need the robe, but I appreciated it. Another
election and anointing. Then the official was there with his clipboard,
calling my name. He was a tall brown-skinned man with bony wrists
and a natty salt-and-pepper beard. He squeezed the gloves and looked
me over.

No earrings, nothing?

Nothing, I said (an earring could catch on headgear or glove and tear
through an earlobe).

Your trainer is wearing an earring.

My trainer wears a lot of things, I said, which meant nothing at all.

On my way to the ring I heard the pleasant-faced official complaining to the Turk's trainer. I just can't understand how you can do that
and feel good about yourself.

I understood. It was boxing. Anything you could do to gain an
advantage. I barely recalled the incident, having moved to a different
plane. The Turk was a very long time ago.

The Mexican stood just in front of me on the stairs at the annex
entrance to the hall, wearing his gold shirt with blue lettering. His
trainer, Goatee, pointed at him and shouted to a woman holding a video
camera. "The next Golden Gloves champ. Just you watch." Another of
the officials, an older, demitoothed Puerto Rican I saw at every show,

exhorted the Mexican in Spanish. Then he smiled and tousled Mexico's cropped hair. What were they, related? None of the U.S. Boxing people was patting *me* on the head.

At the equipment table in the corner near the stairway, Milton made a request.

Suede, he said to the equipment manager, meaning suede headgear.

Sweat? the man answered in a heavy accent.

Suede, Milton said.

Sweat? the man responded again.

No, Milton said. *Suede, suede, suede.*

He lifted a helmet by a dangling chin strap and waved it in the air. The man gestured toward the ring and shrugged. Suede was in use. I would wear vinyl.

Drawn forward, down the aisle, conspicuous, a fleeced lamb. I wondered if I looked tough. I *had* to look tough. I didn't *feel* tough. I started to hate whoever had put me in this situation. I started to hate . . . the Mexican. Drawn forward, down the aisle with my little entourage. "Go back," the officials said. Confusion. The Mexican's group, just ahead, snaring with mine. Signaled to proceed again. Up the stairs to the ring apron, sucked through the ropes. Don't go through the canvas, Bob. I would not be shamed before hundreds of people.

Across the ring, my opponent limbered up, making a half bend, followed by an oscillation of the shoulders.

Bernabe Guerrero: from Mexico by way of a Yonkers boxing club.

Twenty-four years old.

A construction worker who "burned with a passion for boxing."

He had real boxing polish, there in the shoulder shake, in the way he kissed his gloves and raised them high when his name was announced. Very pro. Guerrero was distorted with muscle, his arms layered and curved, skin with a metallic density. His wide jaw gave him a shark smile. He stood about three inches shorter than I did (and, I would soon discover, had a shorter reach). All my protein powder and skim milk had paid off.

In my corner, Julian instructed me in boxing etiquette. "Bob, walk out to the referee," he said, at the appropriate moment. "Bob, lift up your gloves now," when my name was called. I was glad to have Julian there, a tower at my back.

Blue, hey, Blue. Blue! wafted to my ears from the judges' table.

Bob, they want you, Julian said, and I looked down at them. I was blue.

Blue, how do you pronounce your last name? they asked. I told them. "Ann-uh-see. Ann-uh-see." The announcer still got it wrong.

At the bell I came out fast. I had resolved to start fast. In my other fights I had started slowly and gotten clobbered. Bernabe extended his glove for a courtesy touch. Suspicious, I tapped his glove and immediately threw a left, which missed. I followed with a few light jabs and some long hooks, avoiding any sort of commitment. Bernabe rushed at me behind a wild hook, which also missed. I sidestepped and hit him with a counterhook. The momentum of my hook, added to his rush, sent him stumbling into the ropes. The referee stepped between us and rubbed Guerrero's gloves against his chest, an action taken whenever a fighter's gloves touch the canvas to cleanse them of foreign matter that might have adhered to them, matter that could abrade the face of the other boxer. Guerrero wasn't hurt, but it was definitely my punch that had made him stumble. An argument could have been made for giving him a standing eight, but I didn't make it.

As the round progressed, Guerrero pushed forward and I backed away. Most of his punches fell short, but I felt the wind from his great rainbow hooks. I had two inches of reach on him, at least, and the advantage of fighting someone with shorter arms became obvious. Those of his straight punches that did connect were exhausted at the end of their trajectory and had little force. On my side, I countered well, especially as he tried to get out of range after punching (the boxer with shorter arms must constantly put himself at risk in order to attack). Twos and threes, I remembered Julian's advice, twos and threes.

As Guerrero and I faced each other, he reminded me of a solid, ferocious Puerto Rican kid I had sparred at Revolution, the same build and standing in the same posture, stance a little open, exposing torso and head. I remembered hitting the kid with an uppercut at that range and decided to try the same with Guerrero. The punch dropped spang on the point of his chin. Delighted, I did it again, with the same gratifying result. Then I released the uppercut as he bore straight in, and it thumped against his chest. I kept pushing the button and whacking Guerrero, like a child with a new toy. It was one of the most thoughtful things I had ever done in the ring.

Meanwhile, I couldn't believe that I wasn't getting hit more and, when I did get hit, that it didn't hurt. I'd passed more grueling tests a dozen times at the gym. Whenever Guerrero forced me toward the ropes, I sensed them at my back and shifted away. It was a subtle movement that I didn't even realize I was making, the unconscious conditioning of hundreds of rounds of sparring. Guerrero allowed me the space to escape into the open; our boxing remained polite and technical, something that I didn't expect and that suited my style.

The bell came as a surprise also. I couldn't believe the round had gone so swiftly. Guerrero had cooperated with me by staying on the outside and trying to box. I sat on a stool in my corner with Julian and Milton over me.

Well, you won that round, Milton said, but there's a few things you got to work on. Try to wait on him a little more, slip and then come back with a hook. You're killing him with those fives, but you got to follow it with a three.

Julian sprayed water over my scalp and told me to relax.

You're doing good, Bob, he said. Keep the pressure on.

At the bell I jumped up and ran out into the ring.

In the second round, Guerrero tried to press, weaving forward in a crouch with his gloves close to the sides of his head. I missed him once or twice as he weaved, and his sweeping hooks rebounded from my shoulders and arms. I made him pay, though, scoring with counters and forcing him back. The round settled into a pattern of back-and-forth exchanges. I pitched fives whenever I could, and he still didn't adjust for them, every five landing solid. As he rushed in, I bowled another, but my arm somehow tangled with his. His forward motion snapped my arm back at the elbow, and I suffered a jolt of intense pain. I forgot about it immediately—thank God for adrenaline—but I didn't throw another uppercut for the rest of the fight.

In our most grueling exchange, we parked directly in front of each other and slugged. Guerrero landed the better blows at first, but I kept hitting. He finally sagged back, and as he did, I jolted him with a left to the jaw. His knees buckled and he staggered three steps sideways. I didn't see the weakness, and the referee didn't step in with a standing eight. It was probably my best chance for a knockdown, but I didn't follow. An experienced fighter would have tested him to see if he was really hurt, but I didn't have the eyes for it (I noticed his stumble only later, watching the videotape). Winded from the exchange, I stood facing him for a few moments. Then he recovered and attacked, standing in front of me until I scored with two good body shots. The bell surprised me again and it was back to my corner.

Well, I thought you won that round too, Milton said, but you got to remember the combinations. Don't throw just one punch. Use the dunh, dunh-duhs. Keep sticking out the jab; the jab can score points. You're doing great. You're hitting him hard without even trying.

On the stool, I rent the air with gasps that didn't bring my body enough oxygen. I felt enfeebled, on life support. Julian sensed my exhaustion and gave instruction.

Bob, lift up your hands. Lift them up. Now take a deep breath. You're doing all right. Breathe. You got this kid. One more round.

I remembered the exhaustion I'd felt the last time I sparred Joey. His pressure had drained me. In my regular sparring, I hadn't maintained this intensity; the competition hadn't pushed me to it. By the end of the rest minute, my breathing had slowed, and I felt ready to continue. The referee walked over to order Milton from the ring.

Seconds out! he barked. (Through the early days of British pugilism, the seconds actually stood near the boxers as they fought.)

As I stepped forward, a chill slashed across my back. Milton had emptied the water bottle on me, and water drenched the canvas. The referee grimaced and shook his head. Milton pushing the boundaries, once again.

Round three went slowly and ill for me. Guerrero's pressure was rewarded. Now when I was backed into the ropes, I could not shift away. Guerrero slipped more smoothly, and my twos missed over his head. He still wasn't scoring clean, but I was no longer able to drive him off. Milton's pullback worked for me, drawing my head out of danger, the big hooks brushing my nose. Whereas, in the first two rounds, I had moved faster than clock time, in the third I dragged through a syrupy nightmare. I clinched for the first and only time in the fight, leaning on Guerrero's shoulders until the referee separated us. I'm really tired, I thought, then: He must be tired too. That reassured me (he didn't try to wrestle out of the clinch). Still, he kept throwing, and a hook finally landed flush on the side of my head. I rolled with it and heard the crowd's exclamation (feeling the crowd noise as a physical presence, the cheers and shouts jostling my body). After the blow, I slid along the ropes, and what seemed like an instant later (it was full seconds on the videotape) another hook burst on my chin. It was the hardest punch I had taken, and I bounced back against the ropes. The punch angered me and stirred me from a defensive inertia.

I'd better start throwing, I thought, or I could get a standing eight.

Later I was glad that the referee had the temperament not to interfere,* that he "let us fight," because if he could have given Guerrero an eight-count in round two, he could have given one to me after the second hook.

I started punching again and we remained in front of each other, banging until the round ended. The ovation was enormous, a swelling embrace as we trudged back to our corners.

Well, you lost that round, Milton said as he cut the tape from my gloves and pulled them off my hands, but if they gave you the first two, you got it.

I walked out jaunty and a little confused. The referee lifted our arms to the same grand applause. The boxing people approved of us.

When the announcement came, ". . . for the gold corner," my knees sagged. It was only a physical reaction. I was too stimulated to feel the pain of the loss then.

Bernabe and I shared the boxers' embrace, and I left the ring. The next blue fighter passed me on the way to his match.

Hey, we thought you won that fight, a young boxer said as I went down the stairs into the annex.

I sat on a chair in the annex and listened to my friends' consolations. "You fought a great fight . . . I thought you had it . . .," etc. Giuseppe entered with two of his sons, the boys playing fighter and crashing into our legs as they dashed about the room.

That was not a good decision, he said. I was sitting with Pat Sullivan, who is a referee for U.S. Boxing, right up at ringside, and you know what he said? He said, "That's strange, I thought your friend won the fight."

I removed my *Daily News* T-shirt and dropped it on the floor. Fighting for a T-shirt, indeed (someone swiped it and I never saw it again).

---

*Many amateur referees will err on the side of caution, calling standing eights after punches that do not daze or injure the recipients.

My arms were covered with abrasions from Guerrero's gloves. My face was unmarked. I don't cut easily for a white man. In my months with the Supreme Team, I had not suffered a single scratch, swelling or visible bruise on my face. Perhaps the Mediterranean blood made my skin a little thick.

Milton entered with an announcement.

They had it five-zero for him. This shit is fucked up. I looked at the cards, and not one judge gave you the first round. He didn't even lay a fucking glove on you in the first round.

My paranoia spun out of control. The officials were out to get us.

Guerrero and his crew sat behind us, loose with victory. He tapped me on the shoulder, then gave me another hug. We shook hands.

How many fights have you had?

Guerrero stared at me and smiled blankly.

¿Cuanto peleas tienes? Giuseppe asked.

Guerrero looked at Goatee.

Three, Goatee says. This makes three for us.

At the officials' table, Milton gripped Michael Rosario, the local president of U.S. Boxing, by the arm.

So even if we had a big third round, Milton said, there was no way we were going to get that fight. And there is no way that the first two rounds weren't even at least. In the first round, he didn't even lay a glove on our guy.

Goatee put his arm on Milton's shoulder in an attempt to moderate. Sometimes the judges like it when a guy is aggressive, even if he isn't scoring with every punch.

Milton ignored him.

Michael had not seen the fight but agreed to look into the scoring and to look at the scoring on all the cards for all of Milton's Gloves fights that year. Michael was a small, calm man, the son of a legendary trainer and a three-time Gloves champion himself. He had been through all this before.

I changed into my civvies and drifted into the church to watch the action.

That was a good fight, Goatee said, there at my side, excitement and relief on his face.

Yeah, thanks.

We were worried after that first round.

I wanted to say he shouldn't have been because he won it on every card, but I didn't.

We were worried, because the one thing that all of Milton's guys can do is box.

Thanks, it's too bad that Milton's guys have a harder time with the judges.

I sounded bitter, and I wanted to give him his props. No matter what happened, he didn't have anything to do with it, and his fighter had fought well. So I said, Still, your guy kept coming after me.

Well, that's what we shouted at him to do between rounds. We were trying to get him to time your uppercut and come over it with a right hand. Anyway, it was a great fight. Whenever you want to come up to Boxing Connection and spar with us, we'd love to have you.

I thanked him again.

Six months, six minutes and out. The drama I had experienced seemed tiny, one fight on a night of many fights. I had seen so many fights take place, to be followed by others, the figures almost anonymous in their headgear and sleeveless shirts.

A bearded white man stopped me as we walked from the building. Don't worry about it, Blue. You fought a hell of a fight.

The ride home was somber. The Supreme Team had lost again.

THE OLD LION

Hey, you the stranger said, I want to fight. Come on.

I don't know, I said, glancing over at Milton.

What's the matter? the stranger said. You won't spar black guys? Let's go.

Well, what do you weigh? I stalled.

The stranger approached and glared into my face. The wide sclera riming his eyes made them wild, and his stare focused a little past my head.

What do you weigh? he said, still staring at some point past me. He was a black man of average height, broad through the shoulders and chest.

I'm one twenty-five.

I'm one thirty, he said. Let's go.

I looked to Milton for help with this scary black man. Bored with the game, the man shoved past me and began to work the floor.

Do you know who that is? Milton whispered as we watched the man spank the double-end bag.

I shook my head.

That's Curtis Summit.

I shrugged. The name Curtis Summit meant nothing to me. I studied him again; he looked a hell of a lot bigger than 130 pounds.

———

That guy's not one thirty is he, Milt? I asked after Curtis left (after demanding sparring from me for the next day on his way out). I prayed that he wasn't.

No, Milton scoffed, he's a middleweight.

Is he a pro?

Yeah, he used to be a contender but now . . . I think he's a little punch-drunk. He says he's going to be training here, but I don't know. There's something a little off about him. And he's trying to make a comeback.

How old is he?

Thirty . . . eight?

And he's making a comeback?

Yeah. He thinks he has one last shot in him. I was going to put him in with Efrain, but . . . a hard right from one of these kids and . . .

I didn't credit Milton's sudden humanitarian impulse, but there certainly did seem to be something "off" about the old man.

Over the next few weeks I saw, and heard, much more of Curtis Summit.

Milton, you fucking albino, why are your guys hiding from me? I talk too much? I bet you won't do much talking with my left nut in your mouth. Your guys spend a lot of time hiding in the bathroom, Milton. What the hell are they doing in there? I'm going to knock them out, one in every round, stretch them out on the ground, one after the other. I'm gonna leave you with an empty gym, Milton.

He grinned a fixed white-toothed smile. I wondered about this man, who shoved me every time he passed by, who shoved everybody, Stella included, and gave his wild-eyed glare.

Man, I'm tired of listening to this gangsta shit, he said, flinging the DMX CD to the floor. He put on a tape of early eighties funk and Florida hip-hop, music that dated him.

Now that's more like it. He nodded approvingly. Hey, Einstein [to me]! You ever hear this good stuff. Probably not. You probably listen to that cracker-ass James Taylor shit.

I've heard this, Curtis, I said. I'm almost as old as you. *Almost.*

Suck a fat one, boy. You ain't going to live to get as old as me,

Einstein. If you get in the ring with me now, this'll be your last day in the world. Don't worry, I'll take care of your mama tonight. Hey, Stella. Stella! I'm gonna bring some Chicago girls in here to *kick your ass.*

I'm ready, Stella said. Bring 'em on.

Or up in Victor's face.

C'mon, kid, let's go.

I got to warm up first, Vic muttered.

How you gonna warm up, you gonna do some Jane Fonda aerobics? Let's go.

No way, nigga.

Nigga? Nigga? Curtis glared around the gym, then back at Vic. How come you got to call that in front of all these white folks? You got no call to talk to me like that in front of these crackers.

Vic shifted uncomfortably, not knowing if he was required to respond, fight, run, if this man was joking, punch-drunk, insane.

In one of his fights, Julian said, Curtis knocked the guy out, and then, when he was lying on the ground, Curtis got down too and started wiggling around.

Julian chortled.

That must have been a big fight for him to do that, Milton said.

That was Igor Pedrozza, Curtis shouted, Thirty-two fights, thirty knockouts. You beat somebody like *that*, then come to me. Then you're a boxer.

The intensity that we recoiled from.

When my time came to move with the old man, he took it as lightly as I did with some of Milton's girls, letting me throw until my arms flopped, complimenting me when I caught him solid, cuffing me to keep me at a distance. My fists glanced off granite as he smiled. Afterward he worked pads with Milton. Screaming at him after a few minutes, always volatile.

I want you to respect me, Milton. You got to show me respect in here.

I do respect you.

You got me moving only one way. You got to show me more respect.

It's only the first round. We'll get there.

Afterward in admiration, Milton said, That old man can still move, huh? When he was in with you, he was jumping around like a jackrabbit.

Curtis shoved me into the doorway as he left for the night.

Next time we spar, I'm going to knock you out. Cold and dead.

Then I'm not going to spar you, I said.

I want to come see you fight, kid, he said. You're scrappy.

The Supreme Team gathered around the television in the studio, a tape of Mark Breland fighting Aaron Davis for the title in 1990, long and lank Breland, chin suspect after his boxing decades (Davis knocked him down with an early jab. A *jab*). Breland pulled away in the late rounds on technique and the advantage of his elongated arms. By the ninth round, Davis's face was wrecked, bleeding, his eyes closed by swollen tissue. The doctor examined him between rounds, let the fight continue. We gathered closer, the moment coming. Breland missed with a jab, and Davis caught him dead with a wild right hand, lucky punch, as he could barely see, and Breland dropped. The falling body, orgasmic flash, we rewound, rewound, "Oh, shit!" On the canvas, Breland's eyes were closed.

You know, Milton said, Curtis fought Davis in the fight before this. He beat him, but he got robbed on the decision. I mean, he clearly beat him.

Would he have beat Breland? someone asked.

Oh, yeah, he would have beat Mark Breland. No question.

T*his guy thinks he can get in with the top champions*, Milton told the middleweights, with Trinidad and De La Hoya. He can't handle that kind of competition. I want you guys to knock him around and send him into retirement for good. You'll be doing him a favor.

I'm just here for a month or two, Curtis told me. This is just for me to start to get sharp again. This ain't serious. When I start getting into top form, I'm gonna go over to Gleason's and take a step up. See what's out there.

Milton pushed his cubs against the old lion. Over a month of daily workouts Curtis grew hard; the little belly he brought to the gym transferred to his chest and forged into an iron plate. Fast on the double-end bag, short punches, a brawler.

It's a head thing, Milton told his fighters. You can't let him intimidate you. That's what he did to Vic. He got into his head. He pushed him around. You got to stand up to him. Don't give him that advantage.

That motherfucker's so dirty! Will complained, voice cracking.

Will doesn't want to get back in with him. Milton smiled. The last time they sparred, Curtis hit him in the kidneys and behind the head.

That guy is corny! Will shouted. I can't believe his shit!

Will seemed truly aggrieved.

He's trying to impose his will on you, Milton said. That's his whole game. You can't let him.

At thirty-eight, Curtis was old enough to have fathered most of the fighters in the gym. Over time I began to appreciate that underneath the bluster, Curtis was a kind and gentle man (if "gentle" is an appropriate term for someone who tells you to suck on his left nut every five minutes). The relationships began to shift, for all of Milton's talk of knocking him into retirement. The younger fighters questioned him about his travels, career, the game he'd been in for almost two decades. He offered advice on everything from management to ring strategy.

In a fight, Curtis told Will, I'll be telling a guy, "When you go back to your corner, your people are gonna tell you what to do. But you ain't gonna do it. I ain't gonna let you do it." It's all mental in there.

He just doesn't give a shit, no matter who you are, Julian said. That's the thing I really respect about Curtis. He'll say shit to anyone.

And no more talk from Milton of beating the old man into retirement. That would take a little more than we could give.

The banter edged into play as we tried to see what would come out of Curtis next.

I want to film you sparring Will, I told him, get it on tape.

Me sparring this guy? Curtis made a disdainful gesture. That'll be a short film. I'll knock him out so fast it'll be a white screen.

You ain't knocking anybody out, old-timer, Will said.

Oh, yeah? I'll bet you twenty dollars I'll knock you out in three rounds.

He pulled a bill from his pocket.

We can put it right up on the corner of the ropes.

And then what will you do? Will asked.

Then I'm gonna piss in your face, that's what I'm gonna do. You'll be so out of it you won't even notice. You better have a bucket around.

And then what? asked Will, who seemed delighted by Curtis's display.

Then I'm gonna put another twenty up there and do it again. You out of all the guys in here because of how your man, the albino, been talking about you.

You know what I'm gonna do to you? Will said.

You ain't gonna do nothing! You couldn't hit me if I closed my eyes.

Curtis's cell phone message featured the announcer, Michael Buffer, intoning his famous phrase: "Let's get ready to rumble! Tonight's main event features WBC Intercontinental Champion Curtis 'Rude Dog' [sound of hound baying] Summit!"

I met Curtis at the health club where he taught a boxing class. The club was a few blocks away from Revolution and was everything Revolution aspired to: big, shiny new and packed with limber bodies (and the occasional crone trying to will herself twenty-five with makeup and corsets). Curtis met me in the lobby, invigorated by his class, wild eyes locked down behind his visor shades.

Nice setup you got here, Curtis, I said.

It's all right, he said. I owe this to Stephan, though. I was substituting for him on the night he was hurt in the ring.

You mean Stephan Johnson, the boxer who died?

Yeah, man. Stephan was my really good friend.

No kidding.

Curtis told me about Stephan.

We used to, like, go down to Virginia Beach. Virginia Beach, it's a place where you just want to go to have fun. But we was down there doing sparring sessions with Pernell Whitaker, Meldrick Taylor. I ended up not boxing, but he was doing all the boxing. And on the weekends we had free time to ourselves. And Stephan . . . he loved to hang out in clubs, he loved to have fun. He seemed like a good brother, 'cause I never had no brothers. So when I left, I didn't tell him I left New York. I just went back to Joliet, right outside of Chicago. When I decided to come back, he had the same number. And I called him and told him that I'm in town. So he returned my call. "Yo, Curtis," he said, "I just wanted to tell you, I missed you, man. I'm glad to see you back." And I would have never expected to hear him say that. So we got together, and I told him that I love boxing, but I'm looking to do something else. And he said, "Why don't you come hang out with me, man?" He said, "I teach boxing aerobics." And I'm like, "That faggot stuff?" See what I'm saying? This is how I'm looking at it, you know? So when I went there, I seen his class. I mean he had a nice group of people that followed him. He had maybe fifteen peoples in his class. And it was amazing how he would just take all this talent that he had and share it with a lot of people that wanted to come in and work out. So I was taking a look at it, but I still wasn't feeling the energy was right. When they go in the health club, people just want to work out and show off their bodies . . . You know, it's nothing like a boxing gym. When you go in a boxing gym, people are preparing themselves mentally and physically to go and fight. But when I saw him, showing them different moves and combinations, they was really into it. And they do mitts and pads and all that. So I went a couple of times. But what really impressed me about the job was one day when I went there with him and he picked up his paycheck.

I laughed.

You know? He said, "Man, look." He said, "Let me show you what I make." His check was what changed my mind into really coming into the game. I said, "Stephan, you making that type of money?" He said, "Curtis, you can do it." And ever since then, that was when I went on ahead and got involved in it, 'cause it shows that it pays good. To do what you love to do.

So Stephan was telling me about this fight he had coming up. He said, "Why don't you come to my class a couple of more times so I can let the supervisors know you? And so the people that do my class will recognize you?" I said okay. So Wednesday came around, he was getting ready to fight on Friday. I saw him at Gleason's Gym. And he was skipping rope, and I was talking to him, you know? While he's skipping rope, skipping rope. But he looked like he was swollen. He looked bigger than one hundred fifty-four pounds, like he weighed one seventy or something. Man, Stephan looked *big*. While I was talking to him, he wasn't paying me no mind. So I'm figuring that maybe he's in the zone and just letting me, you know, cool out. But I was talking to him *loud*, and he wasn't paying me no mind. So what was I supposed to do? Before I walked away, I said, "Man, I'll just see you when you get back. Just call me." So he fought that Friday. When Saturday came, I called him, I said, "You ain't made it in." You know, his machine came on. So Sunday I called him, he still didn't pick up, so I cussed him out. I said, "Man, why are you doing this?" I said, "I heard you got knocked out. So what you get knocked out? Give me a call when you get back." Then a friend of mines called me and told me that he was in the hospital. So I called his house and talked to his mom on the phone. I made plans to go down there the following Saturday to see him. When I called that Wednesday, Bonnie, his fiancée, answered the phone and said, "Miss Johnson is not here right now, but why don't you call back?" I said, "Well, listen, just tell her I'm coming down and I'll be down this weekend." She said, "Curtis, I don't think that would be a good idea 'cause she got some of her relatives coming down to see Stephan." I said, "Okay, so just tell her that I'll call her back." So it surprised me she called me back. And she was like, "Curtis, I asked some of my peoples to come on down and see Stephan, and I know you guys are good friends, but I cannot have you come down right now. Why don't you try next week?" I said, "Cool, I'll do that." So I was driving with a buddy of mine in Queens, I'm in his truck. He said, "You know your friend Stephan died?" I said, "He died?" I said, "I just talked to his mom." He said, "Naw." So we was riding, and he pulled over and started talking to a friend of his, and his friend had the newspaper, the news article about Stephan's death. So he brought it out and I read it. Oh, man, I cried, I was crushed. Like me and him used to talk, that's how we was, the last time, you know, we was on the train, talking, just having fun, talking about how we gonna make a comeback. He was making a comeback, and I'm trying to, you know, position myself back into the boxing world. Stephan was a good friend, man. I'm not saying it because he passed away, but, you know, literally, I been knowing him since 1990. I met him toward the end of '89. We became very good friends. His death crushed me, because I always said to him . . . Of all the fighters I've known in the world, he's the only one that I was really, really, really close to. You know, we boxed together and we just hung out. Stephan was a true fighter; he was a true warrior.

Curtis Summit was born and raised in Joliet, Illinois, the only boy among eight children. His father worked for the railroad; his mother for Caterpillar, the construction machine company. Not long after Curtis graduated from high school, he joined the army. He had never boxed a minute in his life, but stationed in Korea, he joined the boxing team on a whim. He was almost twenty-one. When Curtis won his first two fights by KO and his first eight fights, he realized that he had a talent for the sport.

I was just natural strong, Curtis says. I was really powerful. And I was winning. I was winning jackets; I was winning trophies; I was winning medals. I won a lot of things. Boxing.

When Curtis returned to the United States, he was stationed in Colorado Springs. With no training, he entered the Regional Golden Gloves and made it to the finals. Soon afterward he won the all-army Force-Com boxing tournament, earning him a berth at the 1984 Olympic Trials. Curtis had been boxing less than two years.

Now, I'm in the Olympic Trials. I'm in Colorado Springs, Olympic training center. Everybody was very supportive towards me, 'cause Mark Breland was favored to win the '84 Olympic Games anyway. But now he had to face up in the trials. He was in my weight class. And he was like six feet tall. Tall motherfucker. He was in my . . . I was in his weight division. I was in *his* weight division because he ruled that division. Keep in mind, we was in the box-offs. The box-offs, whoever win goes to the Olympics. And Pernell Whitaker was there too. Whitaker was one thirty at the time. He was real light then. And Evander Holyfield, one seventy-five, you know? Tyson was there. Everybody was there. A good class, man. *Real* good. So they were like, "Oh, you Curtis Summit? You know Pernell there?" Pernell said, "We heard a lot about you, man." I said, "Damn, I seen you fight on TV before." But he was real cool and nonchalant about himself, you know? He said, "You know, you got to fight a tough guy. Mark Breland's my man. I been knowing Mark. You beat him, you going to the Olympics." So, in the tournament, boom, boom, I'm beating guys, you know. Guys were like, "This kid is tough." Now, I had one more fight to get by, to get to Mark Breland to fight for the finals for the box-offs to go to the Olympics. The kid I fought . . . I completely forgot his name, but he's from Washington, D.C. Before we fought . . . I had a girlfriend, living in Colorado Springs. They had me stay at the Olympic training center 'cause they didn't want nobody to leave. But we made phone calls. So I'm talking to my girl, you know? She was from Fort Wayne, Indiana. And she lived in Colorado Springs. She said, "Listen." She said, "What time you all gotta go to bed?" I said, "We got to go to bed about nine." I said, "The only thing they do is come check our rooms. And once they check our rooms, shit. You know, you can go to sleep or stay up." She said, "When they check your room, why don't you see if you can sneak out?" I said, "What?" She said, "Yeah, 'cause I want to make love to you." And she's getting horny. So I said, "Damn!" I said, "But I got a big contest tomorrow." She said, "Come on, Curtis. Please." So she was like being real . . . persistent, on getting me to leave, you know? So finally, I *did*. So they came, they checked the room. Virgil Hill was my roommate. Virgil Hill, he was the light heavyweight champion. Do you remember when Rodell Jones, Jr., hit that guy with a body shot, knocked him out for the light heavyweight title? Yeah. Virgil Hill was my roommate. So I told him, I said, "My girl want me to come." He said, "Curtis, you're getting ready to fight in the finals of the tournament tomorrow. Are you sure you want to do that?" I said, "Yeah, man." But I was young, naïve. I wanted to *fuck*, man, I didn't give a shit. You know? I said, "I'm gonna win. I'm gonna beat him. I'm gonna beat this guy." So, I climbed over the fence. She was right there. She picked me up; we took off. The next morning I go running back onto the camp like I had left that morning and come running back. The security guard said, "Hey, man, I didn't see you leaving here earlier." I said, "Yeah, you probably didn't see what I did. I'm sorry." He said, "Okay, go ahead." I go back to the room. Virgil said, "Man, I didn't think you were going to stay out all night." So me and the girl were up fucking all night.

So the fight came around. She was there. Everybody was there. Everybody wanted to see me and this guy fight, because the winner between me and him was gonna fight Mark Breland. He beat me. You know? He beat me. He beat me on decision. He beat me 'cause I wasn't really physically, nor . . . mentally I felt I was ready, but physically I felt that I really wasn't there. 'Cause I got tired. My girl, man, she kept me up *all* through the night. So, even now, as I'm telling you, I'm thinking she might've did that shit on purpose. You know? I'm thinking she did it on purpose. Because I had took her to a few fights. And when I beat the guy, she would always say, "What do you need to do to lose?" At the time I didn't know how people were. That's what they call player haters now. Back then I think that's how she was towards me. Because I see that what I was doing, it was keeping me away from her. And she wasn't enjoying that. My career was like, in the army and in boxing. And she saw that I was attracted to boxing more than I was to her. When I was like, "Yo, I got to go fight, Florence, so I'm leaving town," she'd try to get me to stay. I said, "I'm not staying! I got to go for two or three days." And she used to be real mad; she used to fight with me. I'm like, "Damn! Why is she acting like that?" She was young too, you know? She was just a young girl. But I didn't know, and she used to act really crazy when I'd go to the fights. "Flo, why are you acting like that? You know that I box. Why you be acting like that?"

So after the fight, I called my mother. I was crying. She said, "I can't believe you didn't go and knock that other kid out!" Everybody was talking that, you know? They said, "How could you let that other guy beat you?" I was crying. I couldn't believe it. Anyway, he fought Mark Breland in the finals, and Mark beat him on a split decision. I know if I would not have did what I did, I probably would have beat him, and beat the shit out of Mark. But it didn't happen. I thought I learned from that. But no, I did not. That was my last amateur fight.

After the trials and all that, I just stayed in Colorado Springs. I went to work for some newspaper company. I was a printer. I really didn't have no one to really help me out as far as making a decision about turning pro. I wasn't training. I wasn't doing anything. And out of the clear blue sky I had got a letter in the mail. This guy was interested in me and wanted me to come out to his camp and train to turn pro. His name was Ben Getty. He was from North Carolina. Fayetteville, North Carolina. Now who the fuck is this guy? He said, "I seen you in the Olympic Trials. I congratulate you on your fine victories to where you made it." He said, "Listen, if you ever think about turning pro, give me a call, you hear? I got room and board for you, food, whatever you need." I never got back in contact with him, but about a month later he wrote me again. You know? What the fuck is this guy doing? Anyway, I called the guy; he said, "Listen." He said, "Curtis, you know, I been reading up on you, I been trying to do some checking up on you." So I ended up finally going to see him. And that's why I started my pro career in Fayetteville, North Carolina. I went over there. I won eleven fights in a row before I lost my first fight. I fought a kid from Connecticut, and I beat him, but they took the fight from me. Clearly, I beat him. A month later he fought Mark Breland on *ABC Wide World of Sports*, 'cause they was bringing Mark up after the Olympics, and Mark knocked him out. But they didn't want to fight me. They said whoever won between me and him was going to fight Mark Breland. I clearly beat him, but they avoided me. They avoided me. Big time. That fight was in Atlantic City.

So that decision upset me, for a minute. But you keep in mind that I was still growing in this game, and I was still young, not really knowing. Now I know a *lot*. I know a *lot*. I always tell motherfuckers, "Listen, you better watch your ass. 'Cause people will get you. They don't care." They more vicious now than they were back then. One day I fought Tyrone Trice. At that time I was like . . . thirteen and one. When I was going to fight Tyrone Trice in Detroit, Motor City, he was with Emmanuel Stewart. He was real hot back then. And he just fought Simon Brown. He fought Marlon Starling. Marlon Starling beat him. So Ben Getty said, "Listen. You gonna fight Tyrone Trice." And I said, "Cool. Let's do it."

During the process of that fight—we's in Detroit now, I had my family up—it started raining. The fight was set to be outside. So we waited, we waited, we waited. But to go back at the weigh-ins . . . I think the fight was going to be at a hundred and fifty pounds. Okay? Between 'forty-seven and 'fifty-four. But Tyrone came in at one eighty. *One hundred and eighty.* They was giving me thirty-five hundred to fight that guy. Now they said they were going to give me five hundred dollars more if I took this fight 'cause of him being that much overweight. Ben told me it was five hundred. But actually they was giving Ben fifteen hundred dollars for me to fight that guy. Because I wasn't going to fight. They wanted to do everything in their power to make sure that that fight was gonna take off. Rain or not. There was TV and everything. They wanted it to death. So Ben said he was going to give me five hundred dollars more. Actually he kept a thousand. In his pocket. And I didn't know it. But I know it now; that's why I'm telling you this. So I went ahead and agreed with the fight: "Fuck it, I'll do it." So they gave me . . . what? Four thousand. Straight.

For the fight, we had to come outside. They put plastic on our boots. Plastic. It came way up here. They gave us a plank to walk on to the boxing ring. I guess they had a big tarp over the ring. The ring was outside in the summertime. They took the plastics off. The canvas was still wet. So, during the fight, I was so upset about what was taking place, I went out there and I started launching at him. Winging at him. Here I am struggling to make one fifty, you know? He was *real* big. I was just mad. So I go out there and I lunge, throwing all wild, falling on the canvas that was already wet. I'm slipping, I'm falling, referee counted, "One . . . two." I said, "What the fuck are you doing? I just slipped, you know?" I looked at my corner and shit. Now I'm even more furious about what's going on. I'm swinging again. I mean, he's running, he's bouncing. I'm swinging. Boom. I go down again. The referee, "One . . . two." I'm cussing, "What the fuck are you all about?" Screaming. He just kept on ticking. "One . . . two . . ." Now I'm really furious. I'm going at him, swinging again. One time I swing, he just stepped back, he threw a little punch. Wasn't no punch to make me go down. I was slipping anyway. I went down. The referee called the fight to a halt. Man, people started throwing shit in the ring; they started cussing and everything. There was going to be a riot there 'cause they know it was bullshit. So whatever took place, the referee was a part of it. He had to have been. So they stopped the fight, you know? Wasn't nothing wrong with me, wasn't nothing wrong with the kid Tyrone. The only thing that was wrong, it was a bad night, and bad weather, and they was bad. So they gave him the fight.

Anyway, that was my last fight with Ben Getty. Because later on that night me and him talked. And he told me, clearly, he said, "I'm gonna tell you something. I'm not here to try to hurt you. I just took a gamble with you. I just wanted to let you know that I really do care about you, and you one of the best fighters that I ever had. But I took some extra money from the promoters for this fight to bring you here." He said, "If you would have won that fight, it would have been a lot that could have happened for us. But being that you didn't win it, a lot of things are going to go down." I said, "Why the fuck did you do that, man?" He said, "Well, I was taking a gamble with you. In life, you gotta take a gamble. Actually, they gave you the money, the extra money, to fight. That's good." He said, "It's up to you if you want to stay and fight for me." I said, "Well, I don't think I'm gonna stay with you." My family wanted to kill that motherfucker. My family was gonna beat his ass, 'cause they knew something was wrong. Anyway, we talked on the train going back from Detroit to North Carolina. When we got back, his wife came and got us. Now I saved his wife's father who was dying. I rushed him to the hospital; he was having a heart attack or something. I took him to the hospital. Anyway, when she came for us in the car, she asked Ben, she said, "Ben, why did you do that?" So, I just hear her saying that. Next thing I know, her and Ben got into a big argument. And Ben kept saying something about a thousand dollars. He said, "I only took an extra thousand dollars." So I didn't know what the fuck he was talking about, a thousand dollars, you know? The guy gave him fifteen hundred. And he kept a thousand and gave me five. But she said, "Out of all the fighters, why Curtis Summit?" She said, "Curtis is like family to us. Why did you treat him like that?" 'Cause I'm nice anyway, you know? I'm cool. I feel that I'm a nice guy. I can be mean as hell too, I don't give a fuck, but I can be funny. And I can be nice. So, when we got back to his home, Ben said, "Well, I know you heard what took place." I said, "What's up with that thousand dollars?" He said, "I kept a thousand extra." I said, "Go and get my money." He said, "Well, I don't have the money. He's supposed to be sending me some money." I said, "Well, I'm gonna leave." So I packed my belongings and I left and I went back to my place, my hometown, Joliet.

And Ben Getty, what he did, he did not only beat me, but he beat hisself. He beat me and many other peoples. He had a contract with Russell Phelps, who is one of the top promoters for Top Rank Boxing, right now. At the time Russell Phelps wasn't with Top Rank. Russell Phelps was just doing his own show in Philly. On Broadway at the Blue Horizon. He was running that. I guess him and Ben had a deal about young fighters that Ben was going to bring down to fight. Now, I'm just now finding this out some years back. But it was something that I think that he took a big gamble on, and in taking that gamble, he lost out. But Ben was looking out for nobody but for Ben. He was looking out for Ben to make things happen for Ben. Now by him taking that fight with me in Detroit, Motor City, against Tyrone Trice, one of the hottest prospects in the world at that time, was unbearable. Why would he want to take that gamble, and why did he take the chance? Did he feel comfortable with me? Or did he just want to take the money under the table? What happened? I believe two reasons. He felt comfortable with me, and he took the money under the table.

After leaving Ben, I was out of the boxing picture. Actually, I was doing a lot of sparring sessions. Sessions with Mark Breland and Idris Coreyne. But I really wasn't doing it. They was just having me there, just in case somebody fall out. They was paying me, you know, just to stay there. Because I was giving their fighters a good perspective. You know, you go into a good boxing gym, you see all the potentials. You got to figure out what's going to make you better. Even with champions. Champions want good sparring partners around. That's gonna mentally prepare them . . . and also enhance them to continue working out. But you know, I got tired doing certain things. So I went home.

Back in Joliet, I started looking at boxing magazines and calling people, and that's how I met a couple of 'em. Two old guys from Port Chester, New York. I saw their advertisement, their boxing business, in the boxing book. And I called them. Jimmy Santangelo and Mike Caparhino. They said, "Listen, we get you out here, we give you room and board," you know? This was going to be my last ship.

They moved me out here, and I had two bad fights with them. First fight I had, I fought Kevin Pompey, from upstate New York. When I fought Kevin Pompey, he was a hot tamale. I never heard of him, but everybody knew he was hot then. I hadn't fought in almost three years. And then I come right back in, I trained for, like, maybe two or three months, they put me in with a guy like that. In Albany, his hometown. So we went the distance. They gave him the decision. Then, three months later, I fought another guy from New York, another world-class contender. And he beat me. They gave him the decision. So I lost two back-to-back fights. These guys were putting me in some bad fights. I wasn't at all ready for that competition. Then they told me that they wanted me to fight this guy named Aaron Davis. So I really got in shape when I found out I was going to fight him.

Now my record was fifteen and four. So they said, "Listen, fight this guy named Aaron Davis. You beat Aaron Davis, and you can fight Mark

Breland for the world title." So they was handing me money. Not much. I said, "Let me give it a shot." I got in great, great shape for this. Notorious good shape. I felt that I really beat him. Even though they gave him the win. The president of *ABC Wide World of Sports* came to me and said, "We feel that you beat this guy. You beat Aaron Davis. If we get the contract discharged from Aaron Davis, will you fight Mark Breland?" I said, "Yeah, I'll fight Mark Breland." So they ended up calling me and told me they could not close the contract with Mark Breland/Aaron Davis because they were already signed to it. The fight was going to be on *ABC Wide World of Sports*. Right before that fight, they highlighted his last performance fight against me. They highlighted how I was beating him. I was at home; my mom, everybody saw the fight; they said, "Wow. It's for real." I said, "Yeah." So he ended up knocking Mark out with a lucky punch. He hit him with one lucky punch. Listen. Even before Davis fought Breland, I was in Tampa, Florida, training with Mark, you know. We was in Tampa, Florida, I'm boxing him. And I hit him with a left hook, and he went down. I was so happy. Here's a guy, he's a gold medal winner, he's very well respected in the boxing world. So when I hit him, he went down to two knees. I was really happy, but I didn't jump around the ring, "Yeah, yeah, yeah!" We was just a sparring session. So Mark's trainer, Joe Fariello, bless his soul, he was like, "Marrrkkk. Marrrkkk. Are you all right?" So Mark stood up, shook his legs out. Joe said, "Walk around the ring." So Mark walked around the ring. Joe said, "Curtis, come here." He said, "You think you can do that again?" I said, "Watch me." True story, you know? So, we waited about five minutes; he made Mark feel better. He said, "Okay, we gonna work on a round." The guy who was helping me out, he said, "Man, you can hit Mark with the same combination. You can hit him with the same punch." Anyway, he was trying to set me up with this right hand. I was in my guard, and he was jabbing *real* strong. And I noticed what he was trying to do 'cause I could feel the jab when it gets stronger. So, he'd try to hit my right arm real strong and open it up so his right hand could come in here. That was his game. He had a *big* right hand. And he had such a tremendous reach. And he had powerful legs. So he stepped in, and he hit my arm real hard, so I would open up and he could follow his right hand up, boom! But I caught it, and as soon as I felt his right hand, bam! It was like a flicking light. He

went down again. Joe said, "Marrrkkk. Marrrkkk. Are you all right?"
So he says, "Curtis, that's it. No more sparring."

Later on that night Mark had asked me to come to his room. I went
to his room, and Mark said, "Curtis." He said, "What did you hit me
with?" I said, "You don't remember?" He said, "I don't have a clue." I
said, "Well, I noticed you was trying to set me up. If you had caught
me, you would have probably knocked my spark out. So what I had to
do, I had to capitalize on what you was doing, to make what works for
me." Then, as I was explaining to him, his trainer busted in the door.
"Curtis, come on, Curtis, come on. Mark, don't try and be here talking.
No, no, no." Mark was training for a world title. He was going to fight
Marlon Starling. So Joe said, "Curtis, come to my bedroom," right? I
said okay, and I went in his room. He gave me some money. He said,
"Here's your money." I said, "What's this for?" He said, "This is for
sparring." He said, "We can't use you no more." I said, "Why?" He said,
"Curtis, Mark is getting ready to fight for a world championship title.
You're not giving him no confidence." He said, "Curtis, we're gonna
send you off tomorrow, you gotta go." He said, "I'm gonna have to send
you away because you're going around, you're knocking Mark out. You
can't do that, Curtis. This guy is getting ready to fight a world championship fight. What is it look like, we training this guy and you knocking him out?" He told me I'm not giving Mark no confidence. If I'm
not giving Mark no confidence, he don't need to box me. I ain't gonna
let Mark be hitting me. Hell, no. I'm not no Everlast.

So the next day, whisshh, they flew me out. So cute, smooth, you
know? But I was coming back, 'cause the guy that owned the place told
me he'd like for me to stay because of Honeykin. Lowell Honeykin was
gonna train and was looking for a sparring partner. So they flew me
back. I'm cool, you know? At that time he was paying me three hundred dollars a week. So now I'm boxing Lowell Honeykin. I'm just
whacking him away. Boom! Boom! He's from London. I'm just whacking him up. They stopped me from sparring with him. They brought
some guy in, he had to have been about sixty years old. You laugh, but
it's true. And the guy was no bigger than you. And here was Lowell
Honeykin, he was a welterweight, beating up this guy about sixty years
old. You know? So, that there showed me a lot. I can't understand, with
the talent and with the power and strength that I had, why I couldn't

get anyone behind me that was talented enough to get me a world championship fight. Even though I didn't have a household name, with their help, I could have become a household name.

Before the Pedrozza fight, I was down in the Duvas' camp, training with Meldrick Taylor so that he could prepare himself for Aaron Davis. I was hitting him, he was running around the ring, like Joe Frazier was against George Foreman. You know that fight? Knocked him down six times. So Lou Duva told me, he said, "Curtis." He said, "We're gonna keep you in the camp because you're fighting Igor Pedrozza. He's with us. We're trying to dishonor his contract because his wife's giving us a lot of problems." He said, "I'd like for you to knock this guy out." I said, "Lou, I don't care what you like. I'm going to do it because I'm gonna do it. I'm not doing it for you." This was before the Igor Pedrozza fight. I told you they stopped me from boxing Meldrick Taylor because I was knocking him around the ring. I'm hitting, he's running. So, you know, I started boxing Steve Little. Steve Little, he became champion of the world at one hundred sixty-five pounds, a middleweight. You know, I'm boxing these big old guys.

Well, I fought Igor Pedrozza, and I knocked him out. So now I was very frustrated, 'cause Lou Duva called me up the next day. Called me up the next day, asked me to have breakfast. At breakfast, he showed me the newspaper. He said, "Curtis, read this article." So I read the article; the article stated something like, "Even though Curtis Summit and Igor Pedrozza wasn't the main event fight of last night on HBO it should've been." They said the fight of the night was Curtis and Igor Pedrozza. Curtis Summit knocking out Pedrozza in the tenth round. I mean, they had pictures, highlights, all that, you know? So Duva said, "Listen, people been asking me how you would match up with Meldrick Taylor." Man, I've been beating the shit out of Meldrick Taylor in sparring sessions. Duva said, "But your people want seventy-five thousand dollars to let you out of your contract, and we don't think you're worth that." Well, how do you think I felt then?

After the Igor Pedrozza fight, I was the man nobody wanted to fight. And I didn't have good enough management to make those fights. I took these guys to the state athletic office in Manhattan; Randy Gordon was the commissioner at that time. I said nothing was happening. First they gave me bad fights; then I couldn't get a fight in the USA. So he said, "Curtis, are you complaining that the problem you have is that you're not getting any fights?" I said, "I'm not getting no fights. They put me in bullshit fights." So he said, "Don King is looking for somebody to fight Julio Cesar Chavez, and Chavez is moving up from one forty to one forty-seven." They said, "Would you be willing to fight him?" I said, "Call him." So they called the matchmaker for Don King, we had a loudspeaker on. Randy Gordon was my witness, he was right there. Al Brickman was Don King's matchmaker. Randy said, "This is Randy Gordon from the New York State Athletic Commission. Now listen, are you guys still looking for someone to fight Julio Cesar Chavez at one hundred forty-seven pounds?" And he said, "Yeah, we are." He said, "Well, we have a guy here by the name of Curtis Summit, and right now his managers, they can't get him fights. Would you be willing to fight him?" Al said, "Well, how much the guy weigh?" He said, "The guy weigh one hundred forty-seven pounds. And he got his record fifteen and four." Al said, "Okay, cool, we'll call you right back." Within ten minutes they called back. Al Brickman said, "Randy, is that that guy who knocked out Igor Pedrozza?" He was talking like this on the phone. Randy said, "Yeah, we're talking about this guy." He said, "Randy, don't *ever* call me unless you know that we got a for-sure win on our hands. No, we don't want that fight." He just hung up the phone. And I just looked at Randy. I said, "Wow." So my managers said, "See, we can't get him no fights." So I'm mad, I'm frustrated, I'm crying. My man, I'm crying.

You know, it was so much I went through. I came up with every legitimate reason so I could dishonor my contract with them. So, when they finally made a decision about what was going to happen between me and my manager? Man, they gonna tell me they . . . have not found enough evidence to think that I should leave them. I looked at Randy Gordon. After all I went through, I done tore his office up. I'm throwing books, I'm throwing furniture and I'm cussing him out. And you know, he tried to stand up with me. He tried to show his manhood because of his position. I mean, we was nose to nose. I said, "I'll beat your ass, man." I mean, I'm cussing at him like that. I said, "You know boxing as well as I do. How are you going to sit there and tell me that you think these guys are still capable of having a contract with me?" So this guy pulled me to the side. He said, "Curtis, listen." He said,

"What's gonna end up happening, you gonna go to jail here." He said, "You cannot be doing that to the commissioner. You cannot be going around threatening nobody." He said, "The best thing for you to do is just to try to go to Europe. Stay in Europe until your contract run out."

My problem with my management was, they wasn't protecting me. You know what I'm saying? When you're under contract with someone, they should try to protect you. I had no protection. They wasn't feeding me no financial establishment. They wasn't doing nothing. Only time I was making money with them was when they asked me to go somewhere and spar with somebody. And I couldn't even do that. But after I knocked out Igor Pedrozza, they wanted to walk around like *they* the man. And they never was. They didn't even train me for that fight. When I fought Igor Pedrozza, I was in Virginia Beach training down there with the Duvas. So the guys I had a contract with didn't have *nobody* down there. They wasn't calling me; they didn't ask if I needed anything, ask me how my training was going. They followed up on nothing. So when I get to the fight, and I beat Pedrozza so bad, they want to walk around like, "*Yeah*, that's my fighter. *Yeah*, I did that." Man, you didn't do jack. You better get on out of here. I ended up going back to my hometown of Joliet. 'Cause I almost went to jail here. I almost hurt my manager, Mike Caparhino, he's an old, old, old guy. In Joliet, I got a phone call asking me if I wanted to go to Europe and box with a guy named Jaybell Daly. So I said, "You know what? I don't care."

When I first got to Paris, they put me in this hotel. I wanted to leave the same night. 'Cause I didn't understand not one word they were saying. How do I eat? I don't know nothing. So they just took me to a hotel; they just set me there. Nobody showed me around or anything. I'm sitting there going mad as hell and shit. So the next day they called me. They said, "Curtis, you got somebody on the phone." It was this girl, you know, speaking English. So I said, "Oh, you speak English?" I said, "Listen, I'm hungry. They got McDonald's breakfast? Order me some food up here." She said, "Okay, okay." I'm *mad*. So they brought me some food up. I said, "Well, later on I'm gonna be hungry *again*." I said, "Tell me what the hell am I doing over here? What's going on?" She said, "Okay, don't worry. You gonna see this fight tonight, and we're gonna take you to this place called Ram [Rhiems]. Ram is outside of Paris." I said, "Why I'm going there?" She said, "You're gonna box this guy." I said, "Okay. They paying?" "Yeah, they paying." I said, "They got American food?" "Yeah, American food." You know? So I went to the fight. I ended up . . . I jumped in the car with this guy, we ride for like two hours. I don't know where the hell I'm going, it's at night. I'm looking . . . I'm not seeing nothing but big cows and shit. I'm looking at this brother, he ain't even speak no English. "What the fuck did you say?" And he takes me to his house, he's from . . . some country. Black guy. So I go into the house. I see bambinos running around. I see his wife; he's married, you know? They put me in a room. They had no English TV; they had Pac-Man games. I was just sitting in the room playing Pac-Man. It was so awful. I was in the lost Twilight Zone. I didn't know where I was at, who I could call for nine-one-one, what the shit have I got myself into? I'm sitting here in this dude's house; his wife don't speak no English; his kids run around farting all day.

So someone called for me, the only thing they could say was "Telephone, telephone, telephone." So the girl on the phone, she said, "How's everything?" I said, "Somebody better get me the fuck out of here. Where the hell have you got me at? The wife don't speak English; the husband don't speak English. What am I supposed to do here?" She said, "You're supposed to box with him. Tomorrow you're gonna go running with him." You know how we'd conversate? They had this little thing, whatever I say in English, it translates into French. You type it up, so whatever he say in French, you type in, and it translate into English. [Mimes typing.] "What's up? How's it going? Any honeys over here? *Where's the honeys?* Stupid motherfucker. S-T-U-P-I-D."

The only thing we had in common, man, is that we were fighters. The first time we sparred—this kid could punch, right?—first time we sparred, boom, he hit me, I went, "Ooh, shit." Right? So I'm whacking his ass. A news reporter was there. They had some article and shit. Natalie read it; she could speak English. She said, "What are you doing to that guy up there?" I said, "Sheeit, what are you talking about?" "Well, in the newspaper they say you beating him up." I said, "That's what it says?" I was like, "That's why he hasn't been talking to me and shit." 'Cause he used to always type letters with me. He ain't typing shit now with me, you know? But we became good friends. He showed me around the countryside, everything.

My first fight in Europe, I fought on TV. I fought a guy, he just fought a kid for a world title. But I knocked him out in the third round. So that night, after the fight, we all went to this big hotel room, and they had a big TV screen, and they showed my picture. They showed my fight, and everybody was coming by, taking pictures and shaking my hand. They asked me, "What's going on? Why are you in Europe?" So I explained to them I was under contract and I'm trying to stay until my contract ran out. They said, "Give us the phone number." Two days later, they called the United States and talked to the peoples here. They said, "Listen, we got Curtis Summit over here, and we understand he's under contract with you guys. He's going to stay here two years until his contract lay out. He's fighting. Unless you want to negotiate. Seventy-five hundred." They sent them a check for seven thousand five hundred dollars for my contract. Seven thousand five hundred! And if they had let me go six months earlier, I could have been with Lou Duva.

So, I ended up staying in Europe. I captured my first title. I won a WBC International title over there. I defended that twice. When I went out, they pointed at me, "Curtiiisss, Curtiiiss, Curtiiiisss." It was a hell of an experience. So, I stayed, like, two years over there. They treated me like one of their own, like one of their champions. But I was homesick, man. You know, I just couldn't call my buddy, "Hey, man, come and pick me up." I couldn't call nobody. I ain't know nobody. I ain't know how to dial a number. If I dial an operator, zero, what could I say? "Oui, oui, ah, beeg beeetch." I didn't know nothing. I was so lost in Paris, man. They was ashamed. They said, "How much French you learn how to speak?" I said, "You go to McDonald's, I think I know how to get some french fries." It was terrible. I used to set around at the table, every single night everybody speaking French. I'm just daydreaming, "What is America like? What's happening in America?" You know, but I survived it. I weathered the storm.

This is a funny story about the kind of thing that happened to me over there. One time I was gonna fight in Paris. So whenever I see an American, God, I be happy, because somebody speaking English that I can relate to. I saw a brother, man, so me and this brother was talking. Black guy, you know? I said, "Yo, what's up, man?" He said, "What's going on?" I said, "Where are you from?" He says, "Washington, D.C." I said, "Yeah? I got friends in Washington. Washington's cool." He said, "Where are you from?" I said, "Outside of Chicago." He said,

"Yeah? What you doing here?" I said, "I don't know, man, I'm gonna be fighting." He said, "Me too." I said, "Who are you fighting?" He said, "Man, I'm fighting some kid. Man, I'm just gonna tear his ass." Now, keep in mind, right, I'm just an American to him, like he's an American, you know? He thinks he's fighting a Frenchman guy. So he said, "Listen, you know, this guy's in Paris, he's not a really good fighter." He said, "You know, he's trying to make a comeback. I'm gonna surprise them. I'm gonna bust his ass; I'm gonna make the promoters and matchmakers lose they job and shit." So, I'm nodding, "Yeah, do it, yo, yeah." I said, "Who is this guy?" He said, "I don't know, some fucking guy named Curtis Summit." I said, "Curtis Summit don't sound like a Frenchman name." And he was telling me this, right? He had this adventure in his mind, what he was gonna do to this guy, which was me. I said, "Have you met this guy?" He said, "No, but I heard that he's trying to make a comeback, and I'm gonna bust—" I said, "Well, let me tell you something, man, that's me." And he said, "Aw, no, that's you." So he was just laughing and shit. So that night we're in the ring and I knocked him out. I knocked him out cold. So, when he got up, he said, "Man, I wish you a lot of luck, man. You're a nice guy. 'Cause you could have given me a hard time when I was talking all that shit."

I was in Italy. I went to London. I went to Russia. I went to the Ukraine. I went to Cannes. I went everywhere. I had to really settle myself mentally, to understand that boxing was my goal to be here, so I must accept everything that comes along with that. I mentally prepared myself for that very strongly. 'Cause I could've . . . I could've cried every night. Fuck that! And I was on TV over there, I was in newspapers. I mean, I would go places and I wouldn't have to pay. They just pay it, you know? I'd go in at the mall, I'd buy clothes. Anything. Leather. And I just . . . you know, take it and go. Sheeit. I was like a baby. I was pulling shit out! They told me I had to slow down, though. You know, I got all kind of leather over there and shit. I was picking up sweaters and shoes. Shit was free. In the mall too. It was funny, man, you know? So it was a hell of an experience for me.

Every time I fought, I fought tough guys, but I was winning. I was winning a lot of fights, making money, I got back in the world's ratings. I was going to fight Julio Cesar Vasquez for the championship, the WBA championship, in Argentina. Now when I won the WBC International title in London, I defended it in Guadeloupe about a month later. The kid I fought was from Argentina. He was being managed and promoted by the same guys that was managing and promoting Julio Cesar Vasquez. So that fight was going to determine who would fight Vasquez for the world championship. Now I go back to Paris, they set me down in the business room. They said, "Curtis, listen. We have decided to let you fight Julio Cesar Vasquez for the title." I said, "Okay, where's it going to be?" They said, "You're going to fight him in Argentina." I said, "Argentina? That's where he's from." They said yes. I said, "Well, how much you guys planning on paying for the world championship title?" They said, "'Ah, don't worry about that. You gonna have enough money, you be all right." They said, "But right now we are setting you up to go back to the USA, upstate New York, to go up to the mountains and train." I said, "Okay." So two days go by. I said, "Well, how much I'm fighting for?" They said, "Don't worry about it, you know, it's gonna be okay." So I'm asking this girl named Natalie, she was really helping me out a lot. She could speak English, and she was French. I said, "Now, you better let me know how much they're going to pay me for the world championship." I made fifteen thousand for my WBC International title. It's a bullshit title. Okay? Now, when I flew back, they gave me ten thousand dollars. I put five thousand dollars in one shoe, five thousand dollars in the other. So I'm flying back to New York with ten thousand in my shoes, you know, dawg? I get to the airport; a good friend of mines, Gary Carrieri, picked me up; we go to upstate New York. He was my sparring partner. So I'm paying my sparring partners three hundred dollars a week. I'm paying for the food and rent up there. So we was somewhere . . . I forget, Catskills, Villa Roma, something.

So when I get there, they call me. First day, they say, "How is it?" I said, "It's okay." I said, "How much are you guys going to pay me?" They said, "We'll let you know in two days." I said, "Well, two days, okay." 'Cause I wanted to know so I could start feeling content about my training, since I'm satisfied with the pay. Originally, I was supposed to have been getting paid to box Jaybell. They never paid me. They said, "Curtis, we just let you fight and we pay you." But you know that don't work. I was supposed to get paid twice: for boxing and getting paid a salary. So all the time I stayed over there, they never paid me.

Every time I fought, I fought for like five thousand, seven thousand. Which is just pocket money.

Another day go by, they call. They still have no answer on my money. So I was speaking to Natalie, I said, "Natalie, let me know how much. I want to know so I can train right." She go and call me the next day. She said, "Curtis." She said, "You not gonna like what I'm gonna tell you." I said, "Okay. Pretend I'm not liking you now." She said, "They want to give you ten thousand dollars to fight Julio Cesar Vasquez." "They want to give me ten thousand dollars to fight for the championship title of the world in Argentina?" I said. "No. Ain't no way in hell I'm gonna do that. I can make seven thousand dollars for ten rounds here." I said to them, "If you can't come up with a better offer, then I don't want to do it." Man, listen, they didn't want to change their minds. That was their way of saying no to me. They don't want me to fight. If they had wanted me to fight, they would have given me . . . twenty-five thousand dollars is actually the start-up, the minimum pay. Twenty-five thousand, you know, to fight in the championship, depending on who you are. So they came way below that. You know, if they would have said twenty-five Gs, cool, I would have went there and fought. The thing about Argentina, if I would have ended up knocking that kid out, who's to say I would have survived walking out of there? Nobody. And of course, I would have never won a close decision. But hypothetically speaking, man, if I would have beat the guy, I would have got killed over there probably. 'Cause they rough over there. Let me tell you something—when I used to sit in Paris, I used to watch the news that take place over there. They show the news from London to Argentina. Man, listen, those fools would be fighting over *soccer*. I mean, *killing* each other. Let me tell you something: They love their athletes over there. You may not be listening, but . . . They will kill you for they champions. They will kill you. Literally.

So I came back to the USA and I hooked up with this guy, okay? My first fight I had when I came back, I lost. It was on pay-per-view. Then, my second fight, I beat Emmet Linton. I beat Emmet Linton on ESPN for the USBA. Left-handed guy. He's ranked number two now. Eight months later I fought Aaron Harlins on USA. I beat him. I had this manager named Lou Nidle. Lou Nidle. He has his own, what's it called? His place where, you know, you fix cars. Repair shop, that's what he had. He sucked, you know? Then I came back. I left, came back, went with a couple of other guys. I had some bad losses and shit.

I asked Curtis what Stephan's death meant to him as an older fighter making a comeback.

I didn't really know about the problem Stephan had in Canada, Curtis said deliberately. I know that he got stopped in the fight, but I didn't know what translated behind that. I didn't know there was a real serious problem. Because in *my* last fight . . . I got stopped in my last fight. Actually, I got stopped because I got notorious tired. I tell you, I was taking medication for my elbow that didn't show up on tests when you take it. And during the course of the fight, like, maybe after the first three rounds of the fight, I was totally in control. But after that I just got tired. I couldn't move. My legs got weak. The medicine I was taking wasn't even prescribed for me. It was someone else's medicine. The guy, he weighed like two hundred and fifty pounds. So the heavy dose he was taking—he was having the same problem I was having with his elbow—I was taking that. But it was too much in the dose for me. Luckily, nothing really, you know, happened except that I got stopped.

I think about what happened to Stephan, but . . . I do not let it play with me mentally. Because in life a lot of people die for unnecessary causes. But he died for something he loved doing. I'm not saying that's how life should be. But he didn't get shot up, he didn't get run over. I'm like this, man: When I pass away, I'd rather let it happen in the ring. I would rather go out that way than having some knucklehead robbing me or get run over by a truck or get into a freak fall or something in the city of Manhattan. Of course, I think if they can project a fighter having problems, he should not be fighting. No one should be fighting if he got a problem.

You know, people say, "Why don't you just walk away?" Boxing is like sex, man. How can you walk away from sex in your life? How are you going to sit there and say that you don't want to make love to your wife no more? Or it's the same as saying, you walk away from your kids, you can't love your kids no more. Or walk away from someone you love. You know? You can't do that. But eventually it's gonna happen. As of

now, I'm thirty-eight years old. In the gym I'm feeling better than I
have ever done before. Two days ago I beat the shit out of this guy. Beat
his *ass* in the gym. So I'm hoping that that will not affect me getting
good work at Gleason's. 'Cause everybody hated me and cheered this
guy. I don't why they were cheering him. This guy weighed about one
hundred and eighty pounds. I was destroying him. But yet they was
cheering him, trying to get him to come on and feel better and box with
me. And the more they was cheering him on, the worse he was getting
his ass kicked. I beat the best out of the best in the world, man. I used to
beat Meldrick Taylor real bad. Mark Breland, forget about it, I beat the
shit out of his ass. I remember Lou Duva saying, "Curtis, none of these
guys don't want to box you."

You get used in boxing. You get used like a hooker on the street.
They use you until your last breath is gone. Gone. Completely. I mean,
they don't care. They care enough where they can highlight you for certain things. But once that highlighting is gone, they pretend that they
don't know you at all. But they stuff is still strong because they made
money off you and they can always get another fish out of the sea. You
have to be strong to continue on afterwards, you know. Like I said, boxing is a brutal, brutal sport. It's brutal, not in the ring but outside. Boxing is *beautiful*. But the people are knuckleheads. The friction that you
got to deal with is terrible. And I was blessed, man, to be here for my
man Stephan to show me another way of life beside boxing. And I been
enhancing myself with boxing aerobics. Like I said, I thought it was a
faggot thing. To me it looked homo, man. But once you really get
involved in it, you see the people are really serious about it. Hell, I just
want to get paid. 'Cause I feel that my talent is strong enough to carry
me as far as anyone else. If I do have another fight, I'm gonna put
Stephan's picture on my trunks. I've got his picture.

Curtis Summit's story is one of the many stories of everything wrong
with boxing. The first times we talked of his career, I took his bitterness
lightly. Not that I didn't think he was telling the truth, but I thought
that the truth he told was small *t* truth. So he fought Aaron Davis and
beat him but didn't get the decision? So he suffered from corrupt offici-

ating, poor management, his own bad decisions? As my brother used to wearily say of his clients at the public defender's office, "Even when they admit they're guilty, there's always a reason." My attitude toward Curtis changed only when I saw the videotape documenting his best fights. I saw the Aaron Davis match, a nationally televised fight that everyone expected Curtis to lose (he had been brought in as "tune-up" to prepare Davis for his coming title match with Mark Breland). Everyone, that is, except Curtis, who dominated, mugging to the crowd and laughing when Davis tried to flurry him against the ropes. Yet since Davis already had a contract to fight Mark Breland for the title "signed, sealed and delivered," as Curtis says, the judges ringside went blind and gave Davis a decision (the judges in professional boxing are employees of the sanctioning organizations WBO, WBF and IBF, which in turn are allied with major promoters like Don King and Bob Arum). The only honest mistake in that fight was that made by the matchmaker who underrated Curtis, evaluating him on his age and record (going into the fight, Curtis knew that he needed a knockout to win). I saw his KO of Igor Pedrozza, the top-ranked contender in his weight class, a victory that should have guaranteed him a title shot. I saw him beat Emmet Linton, still a top-ranked professional today, and I saw him in the rings of Germany, France and England.

Curtis's blessing and curse in boxing were in not peaking until he was thirty years old, unusual for a sport in which many professionals are finished by their mid-twenties. His late start and years off meant that his skills lagged behind those of the top fighters of his era. It also meant that any potential investor assumed he was looking at a fighter past his prime. Yet one reason why Curtis was able to flourish as long as he did (along with his disciplined training and enormous physical vitality) was his late start. Unlike rivals boxing from age nine, seven, four (unlike Stephan Johnson, who had boxed from childhood), Curtis was over twenty before he began absorbing punishment.

The fact that Curtis did not receive the title shot he deserved will come as a surprise only to those unfamiliar with boxing. Unlike other sports, professional boxing does not feature elimination tournaments or a just ratings system. At the moment three major boxing organizations award "world" championships in seventeen different weight classes. Each organization mandates that the champion fight a top-ranked challenger within a certain time frame. However, the rankings have more to do with a fighter's representation than his accomplishments. Curtis did not receive a title shot because he didn't have management powerful enough to make it for him (since titles generate income, titleholders naturally wish to hold them as long as they can. They will accept real challenges only if forced to).

A few spectacular knockouts aside, Curtis did not possess a single devastating punch, the expressway to celebrity in professional boxing. Against his highest-caliber opponents—Pedrozza, Linton, Davis—he faced men who had faster hands and more boxing polish. He defeated them through willpower; he beat them down psychologically as well as physically (one reason he made such an excellent example for the Supreme Team middleweights). Yet the force of his will may finally destroy his health. Curtis's body has already suffered from boxing; his crooked stare is due, I think, to damage to one eye, and his sinuses require constant draining. His brain seems fine. No question, Curtis should retire, even if there is a chance of his receiving a title shot (and there isn't). There's no shame in it, he's almost forty, but he cannot accept that he may permanently injure himself. He cannot accept the fact that he will be forever denied the title he deserved. The same willpower that made Curtis one of the top fighters of his generation is the force that may cripple or kill him.

· 2 0 ·

SPRING

In the days after my loss, I hated: I hated the judges; I hated the *Daily News*; I hated U.S. Boxing and the Golden Gloves. In a swirl of paranoia, I decided they formed a vertically integrated citywide conspiracy organized to defraud me of my rightful boxing destiny. How could I have lost a five to zero decision when my coach told me I was winning rounds, when I wasn't getting hit, when so many people said I had won? At the gym, my teammates offered condolences.

Bob, Julian said, if they was using the Olympic scoring, you would have won like twenty to five.

I can't believe Laura put that bottle on your neck, Milton said. She stole your heat. That's probably why you got tired in the third round. Dumb broad.

What difference does it make? I said. I didn't get any of the first rounds anyway. I would have had to knock him out in the third to win.

Milton's water bottle thesis wasn't particularly convincing, but he insisted on it over the next weeks: Laura "stole my heat," undermined me, sabotaged the team. I didn't think that Milton actually believed this. He was just playing out the anger between them.

You got to get a video of that fight and show it to Michael Rosario, Milton said, show him that first round. No way we lost that first round.

So why didn't any of the judges give it to me? I asked.

I don't know, Milton said. They were still watching the previous fight?

That Mexican kid should win the Gloves then, Julian said.

No. It's gonna be the Dominican. The Dominican who got the first round knockout. You watch.

Milton sighed. What kind of Golden Gloves is this with a Dominican and a Mexican in the final?

Milton couldn't have cared less about who would be in the final (since it wasn't going to be me). He was just trying out attitudes, half smile on his face.

The pain in my strained elbow woke me up in the night, and when I woke up, I found I was dreaming of revenge and redemption. I would go to another state and enter the Gloves there under an alias; I would travel to Yonkers and spar Guerrero, thrashing him daily; I would investigate the judges and expose their corrupt decisions. I reviewed the fight a thousand times, wondering what I could have done differently and why I had tired so quickly in the third. Once again I was discovering how unpleasant it was to lose.

"This has been a terrible year," Milton said, but he took my defeat easier than I did. A Gloves of disappointment for Milton. While he thought I had won the fight, he believed it close enough to have gone either way. If he told me that it was a close fight, I was inclined to agree with him. He was generally objective when it came to his fighters' performances. After Efrain's loss all he said was, "You waited too long"; after Vic's, "You let the judges see you were tired." All he said to me was, "I just wish we could have gotten you a few more fights before. You needed the experience. But you definitely won that first round."

Name notwithstanding, the Pink Teacup in the Village is a soul-food restaurant. Its pink walls are plaqued with signed photographs of African-American celebrities, and dark, handsome faces crowd the blond-wood tables, studying the menu of sweet potato, okra, fried chicken, ham hocks, collard greens, grits. It is an unlikely place to find Milton on a Saturday afternoon, yet he and Vernon have been hanging here for years. What surprises me the most, however, is that Milton sits across from the old school rap hero Kurtis Blow, and their conversation about life back in the day is being videotaped for a documentary by a pair of L.A. film people.

In those days we didn't call them rappers, Milton says. We called them MCs. When I would MC, I used to introduce the musical acts with a little routine, a little rap. Then the bands started playing in back of us, and that's how it got started. From MCing, I got into parties. We would have crazy parties; we'd open a club wherever we could find a space. Kurtis, do you remember that club we had underneath the Empire State Building?

This is the first time I've heard Milton speak at length about that time. Across the table, Kurtis Blow is quiet, almost dour, but he tells Milton he wants to hear the demo of the singer he's promoting, he says he wants to come to Revolution and watch the fighters. I talk to the L.A. types, tanned, glib and celebrity-oriented, their clothes a little too Cali casual for New York in March. The real find is the DJ who's assisting with the production, a black man with a round body and head, his blackjacked face redeemed by a gap-tooth smile. We're talking about children, and he says, "Man, I got nine kids already, and I'm not even thirty-five." When I look at him in shock, he smiles, "I'm just kidding, yo," and laughs. He tells me he's known Milton since boyhood.

Milton was my idol growing up, he says. He dated my older sister and hung out with my older brother. They would go out to all the clubs. At some point Milton started taking me along. I really looked up to him. He used to call me Froggie [I can understand why]. Milton is an amazing guy. He helped me get started in music, and all the success I've had—I'm with Wu-Tang now—a part of that comes from him. Milton really helps people. He's a real philanthropist.

And I'm thinking, Milton?

Until I consider the hours Milton invests in young boxers, boxers like the Mexican brothers, eight and ten, whose parents can't pay dues. In fact, if Milton didn't want to come off as such a hustler, he would seem positively generous.

We walk out of the restaurant into the blustery day, teetering between winter and spring. Kurtis and Milton embrace and agree to stay in touch. Then Kurtis, the L.A. types and Froggie jump into a limo and drive away.

So who was that guy? What did he say his name was? DJ . . . DJ . . .

I don't know what his rap name is, Milton says, but he used to be Richie.

Did you hear him say he had nine kids? I said. I just looked at him.

Yeah, I was about to say, "Richie, if you got nine kids, there's a lot of lonely women out there."

Giuseppe's fight went down the week after mine, out on the Island near his Lynbrook home. I met his wife, a short brown woman with limited English, pushing a stroller as his son and her son dashed about the room. Giuseppe had the misfortune to be matched with the previous year's novice winner, a boy whose brother just happened to be a former light heavyweight champion and just happened to be working his corner. It was an ugly fight: Joe, intimidated perhaps by the former champion, ducked and clinched. The other boy was tentative also. He had fast hands and threw wicked combinations but didn't want to close. He had been knocked out in the Eastern Trials and perhaps hadn't completely recovered, or maybe he just couldn't fight southpaws. I worked the corner with Milton; between rounds we demanded that Giuseppe attack.

He's afraid of you, Peña, Milton said. He's ready to go.

I can't reach him, Joe complained.

I had studied his opponent at the equipment table, a strained look on his boy's face, seeming near tears, his brother shouting beside him. I sensed that the boy would have rather been anywhere else, and I thought that the pressures of having a champion for an older brother might outweigh all the benefits. Giuseppe lost the decision, and in April, his opponent ended up winning his second Gloves.

Milton's away, and the boys are playing, sitting around, relaxed, inmates in charge of the asylum, talking about what boys talk about—that is to say, girls.

I had an Irish girl once.

But Puerto Rican girls are the best.

You ever been with a Puerto Rican girl, Bob? They be doing this when you're fucking them [demonstrates hip swivel]. Then they start, like, marching and shit. Shit feels good, yo.

Someone delivers a lengthy, clinical description of anal sex, and Victor's face wrinkles in boyish disbelief.

That shit happens? he says. That's disgusting.

The conversation shifts from women to fighting and then to Tupac Shakur, the rap artist who survived one of two shootings and whose dedication to the "thug life" made him a model for young men on the streets. Julian knew him slightly and analyzes his errors.

The thing with Tupac was, Julian says, when he saw his friends beefing with somebody, he'd just jump right in. You know, he didn't stop and try to settle it down, see what had happened. He was wild like that.

Bob, come over here, Vic says, and summons me across the room. He dips a hand into a sack and pulls up . . . a gun and clip. Blued steel, tool heft, a functioning machine, crafted, sleek, and I have that handgun hard-on touching it. Victor has moved up from ice pick.

What kind of gun is that, Vic?

It's a Glock nine.

Vic, I say, someday I'm gonna read about you in the paper.

Two days later Vic summons me again.

Check it out, Bob, he whispers, gesturing into his sack. A gun again, a different model this time. Milton has returned, and the gym is crowded. I shake my head.

It's not the first time I've seen guns in a gym. A few years earlier a tough white boxer brought in a disassembled AK-47 to Kingsway and told us that he'd used it to scare someone in his neighborhood who had threatened to kill him. Of course, it's not only city kids toting firearms. My freshman year of college the Arizona cracker who lived next door to me kept an Uzi under his bed and would walk around campus in a ninja suit. Still, Vic is a lot more likely to die a violent death than the cracker, whose parents had sent him to a thirty-thousand-dollar-a-year college to discover options in life more fulfilling than commando.

I asked Julian if he thought there was anything we could say to Vic.

The only thing you can do, Julian says, is try to say, "Yo, I been through it. Yo, chill. Relax." Know what I mean? 'Cause the ultimate goal is to try to live. You know? And that's what you gotta try to explain to a person like that. "Yo, you want to live or you want to die?" I still got a couple of guns, but I know what to do with it now. I know that I just can't come off in the street holding no gun. A guy like Vic, he's part of a gang. So, he want to have a gun to prove to himself that he's a man. Only thing you can tell him is that when you in trouble, you get in trouble by yourself.

It seems, I say, like he got one foot in both worlds, you know?

No, actually, he don't, Julian responds. He got both feet in—in a life that's gonna send him down. Right? But the only reason why you could make an argument that he have one foot there and one foot here is that he boxes.

Yeah, that's it.

That's the only thing. But when he's not boxing . . .

He's out on the street.

Right, he's out on the street, you know? And when he do box, he's not focused. So most of his attention is out on the street, you know? Victor is my man. I like Vic, but if he was focused about boxing, he got the potential to be a much better boxer than he is. You know what it probably take? Maybe it'd take him getting shot. Or maybe it take him seeing somebody get murdered in his face or something like that. I done seen all that, you know what I mean? I know how it feels to be standing next to somebody, and they—and they get their brains blown out right in front of your face. Maybe he needs to see that. And then he'll see that it's not—it's not worth it.

I think but do not say that if it comes so close, then it might be Vic that somebody luckier is standing next to.

Or your friends got guns, Julian says. "Oh, I got a gun too." You know? "We're gonna shoot this cat." It's not worth it. 'Cause . . . when you go to jail in the end, *you* going to jail, you know? And then you'll see who your real friends are.

I watched the videotape of my fight, from three different cameras, two ringside, the third on a tripod in the back of the hall. I watched the fight once, twice, a hundred times. I watched it so often I lost all perspective: Sometimes it seemed a certain victory for me; other times it seemed a wretched defeat. I showed the fight to others. I tolled a punch count: In both of the first two rounds I landed twice as many clean punches. Still, I could see how someone might favor Guerrero. Over the fight, he's moving forward, I'm moving backward; he's attacking, I'm counterpunching. That's the style Milton teaches, or rather, that's one outcome of the style. A boxer using Milton's style feels safe in retreat, so that he might become hesitant to expose himself to the dangers of an attack.

After all that, it remained a mystery why not one of the judges had awarded me either of the first two rounds. Even if I'd dominated the third round, I would have lost. To win, I would have had to knock Guerrero out. But that's boxing, and there isn't a fighter out there who doesn't think he was robbed at some point. The decision in my fight wasn't outrageous. It was something I would have learned from and gone forward. Except there was no further forward for me. I was months away from thirty-four years old.

From the sidelines, I followed the accounts of the Gloves in the *Daily News*. Guerrero received a bye in the next round, won his semifinal bout on a KO and went to the finals, where he met the tall Dominican, who decisioned him, as Milton had predicted. Guerrero was quoted in the *News* saying, "I burn with a passion for boxing." The idea that a Mexican with a "passion for boxing" had never fought before coming to the States is about as believable as an American's moving to India and deciding to become a baseball pro. Oh, well, at least I didn't have to fight the Turk.

At Revolution, the hammer came down on just another April Monday. I walked to the main desk to sign in and greeted Hassan. He nodded and said, Do you know about the new rules?

I shook my head. He gestured to a sign in a little plastic stand that read, BEGINNING ON SUNDAY, APRIL ————, ALL SUPREME TEAM BOXERS ARE REQUIRED TO PAY A $5 DAILY GYM USE FEE.

Five dollars a day! I exclaimed.

I was furious but not surprised. So this was how the Fitness Diva planned to drive us from Revolution.

We have to pay five dollars every time we come to the gym? That's insane.

Hassan raised his eyebrows, shrugged. He didn't make the rules.

Actually, it's quite reasonable, said the Fitness Diva's blond partner, looking up from the desk behind Hassan. We have to get something from having all these people using our facilities.

But Milton pays rent, I said, my voice rising, and we don't even have access to the weight room or—

That doesn't matter, he said snidely. You have every opportunity to . . .

I stopped listening, shouldered my bag and went upstairs.

I found Julian and Victor there along with some other boxing room regulars (Milton being away, once again).

Did you see what they're doing downstairs, that nonsense about paying? I said, eager to learn how they had responded, how the Supreme Team would react.

Yeah, Julian said, they started doing that shit yesterday.

A few weeks earlier the Fitness Diva had hired Julian to teach a boxing class, and now his head shot adorned the wall in the trainer lineup while a flyer for his class shone beside the water cooler (Julian possessed crossover appeal). Like the rest of the house trainers, he wasn't making money. I wondered if the Fitness Diva had hired Julian to keep boxing at Revolution in anticipation of this day.

Vic, did you pay? I asked.

Victor looked at me scornfully.

Hell, no, he said.

Warmth swamped my heart. Julian shook his head.

I saw Victor coming in, and I knew there was going to be trouble, but it was too late. By the time I got there, Vic was saying, "I ain't paying shit." And he walked upstairs.

Julian laughed.

A few minutes later, as I slung rope, I noticed Hassan and the Fitness Diva in the doorway. Hassan gestured to Vic and me, and then they walked down the hallway. Julian looked after them in disapproval.

I know what that's all about, he said. In the old days, there were two kinds of slaves. There was the house slave, who worked in the master's house, and loved the master and did whatever he said. And then there was the field slave, laboring in the sun, who hated the master and his house slave. Now what kind of slave do you think that kid is? "Yes, massa, I'll go upstairs and get your five dollars."

It seemed to me that Julian was getting a little carried away. Hassan was no Uncle Tom, and pointing us out to the Fitness Diva didn't feel like a Judas kiss, especially given that an owner had been sitting behind him (I also suspected that Milton wouldn't tolerate the new tariff and therefore it didn't matter what individual actions we took). Hassan was doing his job and had no more love for his bosses than we did. Yet how quickly friend became enemy.

Although the five-dollar fee was required of all clients at Revolution, it affected the core Supreme Team boxers the most. Since I went to the gym five days a week, it would bleed me of over a hundred dollars a month. In effect, the fee system punished those who trained hardest.

As soon as Milton returned, he told us not to pay. "Just ignore them and come straight up here," he said. We would be leaving at the end of the month.

The search for a new gym accelerated. Every day Milton broke a new report. We had the Park Avenue space . . . and then we didn't. One of the investors had dropped out. "This fucking Russian dropped the ball at the last minute." Then Milton found a place across the street; tiny but cheap, it would be just like the old gym. "We'll hang a banner up that says BOXING HERE and drive that bitch crazy." Milton laughed. Somehow, that didn't come together either. Milton's courtship of the Revolution staff compounded the tension. There were whispered plans, shouting matches. The boxers walked upstairs directly now, bypassing Hassan and the sign-in sheet. The Fitness Diva's glare burned our skin. Milton said that until the new space was settled, we would be relocating to Gleason's (Park Avenue was ready to go. He just needed one more investor; they were waiting on the Russian. "Bob, you don't know anyone with a spare ten grand?"). Short-term, a month at most. Gleason's sounded good to me. Gleason's: boxing mecca, where the champions trained. I would see Laura and Joey, the heretics who had left Milton in the great schism. I was ready for the grime and attitude of a real boxing gym.

On the last day of April, I took the train over from Brooklyn to help Milton move. A few of the other faithful had gathered (Stella, Hanson) with a crew of movers from Milton's far East Village. The room grew as it emptied. We broke down the ring, dragged out the heavy bags, the pegboard for gear, the speed bag mounts, the plywood and lumber, installed just eight months earlier. Returning for a final sweep of the premises, I took a look at the Fitness Diva's poster in the hall. In juvenile protest, someone had improved it with a black marker mustache, goatee and horns.

At 125 pounds, Stella won the Gloves and then the National Amateur Championship—five wins over five days of eliminations. It was an impressive accomplishment for a woman who walked around at 118 and would stuff her bra with rolls of quarters before she stepped on the scale at weigh-ins.

We'd be there eating breakfast, Milton laughed, and everyone else was trying to lose weight. They'd have a piece of fruit, a half slice of toast. And Stella would have her plate heaped with food. I'd say, "More pancakes, Stella? You want another Danish? Have some more eggs." And I'd tell them, "Yeah, we have to get her weight up for tonight."

Stella won the Nationals the same way she won the Gloves, confusing bigger, stronger women with her unfamiliar style. She would sidestep her onrushing opponent and then nail her with hooks. By the middle of the second round Stella would amass such a point advantage the other girl would have needed a knockout to win, and for a knockout, she would have had to hit Stella. "You're bigger than she is! You're stronger than she is!" her opponent's corner would shout between rounds, and it was true, but unimportant, as Stella was the better boxer.

On the bus, where I had come to pay him a visit, Giuseppe told me he was questioning his commitment to boxing. A few months younger than I, he was eligible for one more Gloves, but doubt troubled him.

I had this guy today tell me, Joe said, he's a driver and a real fired-up Christian. He's like, "Do you really pray to God that you want to fight? 'Cause I just don't see, especially if you know the Lord, that you're going to get in there and mix it up." So in the back of my head I'm saying, you know, "Look at Evander Holyfield. He always puts God first and says he's a Christian." I says, "No, I guess it's really me. You know. Look, I really have to sit down and pray about it. I really didn't really ask the Lord what I should do or lead me into directions." I'm getting a lot of people coming up to me lately. Maybe it's a sign. You know, "You should stop. You should stop. You're too old." But you know, it's hard to get out. It's like a drug. You're in the game. How do I get out, you know? I'm in. How do you get out of the sport, something you love?

I told him he could always coach. Be a trainer.

Yeah, he said, but it's not the same.

Gleason's: the concrete floors, the makeshift equipment and the fragrance of sweating flesh, the frightening bathrooms and the poorly socialized fighters who shove you as they pass by. On our third day there, a water main burst, flooding the locker rooms. For a week we splashed through grimy puddles and there was no hot water. It felt like coming home.

The Supreme Team, or what was left of it, didn't seem to enjoy the move as much as I. While Stella seemed content, Will, morose since his Gloves loss, never made it to Gleason's. He had college classes and playground hoops and didn't need boxing so much; my last image of Will was him excoriating Milton for training so lazily. Victor decided to train in the Bronx until we found a new space. Julian complained, "I can't concentrate in here." His conditioning was suspect, but his skills continued to sharpen. I watched him thrash a professional titleholder for two full rounds while the champion's corner exhorted its man, "This kid's an amateur, take him out!"

I've got to make some decisions, Julian said. A good team wants me to come work with them, but they said, "You got to leave this Milton guy." I don't know. I promised myself I wouldn't turn pro unless I had a good team behind me. Milton's the only trainer I ever had, you know, since I was eight years old. I want him to be part of it, but he's not helping. I'm training myself here. I watched what happened to Rudy and Joey and these other guys. That's not gonna happen to me.

Julian was still having problems with his domestic partner, and I couldn't even guess what he was doing for money.

Milton had fallen: from proprietor of his own venue (no matter how stamp-sized or sans shower), to tenant of Revolution, where he was at least *the* boxing man, and now to Gleason's, one trainer among many. "I fucking hate this place," he said. He served his exile with the other trainers at a dominos table, losing steadily. He seemed distracted and tired most of the time, but that wasn't unusual (one of his East Village friends told me that Milton worked most nights doing after-hours carpentry in offices). I remained loyal; even in exile, he would always be a king to me.

I had been training seriously for over eight months: three hours a day, four to five days a week for eight months. You could teach a chimp (a determined chimp) calculus on that schedule. I'd come to Milton as a brawler, a windmill painted red. The magic wand of Milton's style had transformed me into a slippery counterpuncher. The only note Milton ever gave me anymore was "Stand in a little more. Stay in front of them, and make them miss; then come back with something." To improve further, I would have to take risks, to push forward when I had grown comfortable moving away, to find a balance between my new caution and the foolishness of my old assaults.

I took pieces of what I saw. I liked the way Curtis would push right into his opponents, moving his head, blocking with shoulders and gloves, asking, "Is that the best you got?" Julian weaved forward, side to side, shifting his body weight from leg to leg and moving his head, knees bent; this allowed him to surprise with either hand while always being in a position to shift his center and slip. I imitated Julian's movement and put a little bounce in it, appropriate to my lighter weight. It was the first semioriginal thing I'd done, and I polished it in the mirror.

Watching the mid-sixties Ali/Patterson fight, I made a discovery. Patterson advanced in the classic Cus D'Amato manner (a style most recently typified by Tyson), trying to work inside on Ali. Ali wouldn't let him, however, punishing the smaller, older man and sliding out of his range untouched. Ali killed Patterson with fours, just killed him, the fours coming jab swift, and as I watched, I finally understood how it was done. When I stood up from the television, I could do it myself. Ali's motion had corrected my own. It was so easy I couldn't understand why it had taken me nine months to learn. In the third round of my fight, Guerrero had slipped under my left (always slipping to my right). With a good four, I could fake the left and have him slip into my rising right hand.

"We need to get you some fights," Milton said, and fights were coming. Busdriver wanted to fight also, and we looked toward a show the second week of May, then a show the following week at the Yonkers boxing club one Bernabe Guerrero represented. "You can go up there and beat that Mexican kid," Milton said, but I had already been dreaming of it for weeks. Beating him would almost make up for the Gloves.

Although I didn't punch like Ali or attack like Julian, the improvement showed. Sparring Giuseppe, I no longer waited until his legs went dead; now I lifted my gloves and moved toward him, leaning back and under his punches but always sliding forward, waiting to counter. Milton looked up from his dominos game.

You're figuring this shit out, Bob, he said. You're breaking at the waist, and you're pushing him back.

In my first weeks at Gleason's, Laura treated me coolly, brief words and brushback glances. I asked her if there was something wrong.

Oh, she said, I just don't want to create a problem for you with your trainer.

Don't worry about it, I said. Is that all?

Well, Laura said, I have to say I was a little hurt when you told me what Milton said about the water bottle costing you the fight.

Laura, I said, you don't think I believed that?

I thought you did, she said, yeah.

Laura, I said, if I lost my fight, I lost it because of me, not because you "stole my heat."

And our friendship recovered.

Both Busdriver and I looked to Laura for sparring, but when Busdriver mentioned the idea to Milton, his face twisted.

Oh, she can't get any work here, so she wants to go with my guys.

But, Milton, Joe said, we need the work too.

I can get you plenty of work, Milton said, sharply, finally, and there was no point in further appeal.

Laura attempted to close the distance with Milton. She greeted him when he stood ringside or made comments for his attention. As Milton turned away in silence, his face bore a strained expression, wounded and dark, almost a child's. Because Laura denigrated Milton's style ("His hooks leave you too open") and his training skills ("He can take you only so far"), I was surprised when she told me she had asked him if he would train her again. Milton hadn't responded.

One day, as I waited to spar Busdriver, Laura jumped into the ring and began to slap-box with me. I felt Milton's eyes on us and sensed that she was using this to touch him. In distress, Milton shouted for Busdriver to hurry and get his ass in the ring. Milton wanted to act as if Laura were dead, and her activity threatened this illusion. I remembered Laura's mournful statement "I don't think he's ever going to change." Of course, he wasn't going to change. It's hard enough for people to change who want to and just about impossible for a forty-five-year-old working-class operator who looks in the mirror and sees one handsome devil and thinks his way is the only way. Laura couldn't help herself, though. She was the improving type. She had paid Joey's dues at Gleason's, found him a manager and promoter and loaned him equipment. When Joey disappeared after his victory, Laura discovered that Milton was not Joey's only boxing problem.

By the week after my fight, I had gained eight pounds, and the weight remained on my body through the spring. Months of dieting had taught me how to shrink quickly, however, and two weeks before the Staten Island fight I clamped down: blender drinks and vitamins, cabbage and spinach salad. I didn't need to reach any particular weight but thought I would get the opponents I wanted at '27 or '28. Everyone would be heavier after the Gloves. If I watered myself heavily in the week before a fight, I could lose another pound or two on fight day just by restricting liquid intake. I pushed my sprints to a full quarter mile, running four over the course of my four miles. I would not tire again.

My preparations foundered against the indifference of Milton, the man who bragged that he was "the laziest trainer in New York." I needed sparring, hard sparring, but it was difficult to find. The winner of the Gloves at 119, a short, sturdy Filipino, said he would go, but

Milton didn't arrange it. He sat at the dominos table slamming tiles instead.

Come on, Milton, I complained from the ring, watch us spar.

I am watching, he said, not looking up.

With Laura outcast and Joey gone, I had no one to play with. Bus-driver's commute to Gleason's took hours, so he appeared only once or twice a week. Then the Staten Island show went under. "Canceled," Milton announced.

"Why?" He shrugged. Boxing.

I don't want to go up to Yonkers, I said, unless I get some quality sparring.

Don't worry, Milton said, you will.

I didn't.

Three days before the show Milton said he might not go. The date conflicted with a youth tournament at Gleason's (Milton wanted to drop the Mexican brothers in the show like piranhas in a goldfish bowl).

When will you decide? I asked.

Oh, probably that morning, he said. My desire drained away. Bus-driver said, "What do you need Milton for? Just go by yourself. Yeah, maybe you're not a hundred percent, but you're what . . . eighty percent? Listen, I wish I was ever eighty percent." I understood. You do what you can because you love boxing. I understood, but I wanted to win. If I went to Yonkers and lost to Guerrero again, I would have to listen to my own excuses for the next twenty years.

Laura and I made a secret pact to spar. Yet every time we planned to meet, I would stroll into Gleason's and see Milton hovering over the dominos table. When I learned that he was driving to Virginia for a boxing show, I called Laura. Sparring her mattered to me; I hadn't since December, and it would be one measure of my progress. At Gleason's, I found Milton trying to create enthusiasm for the Virginia ride.

Bob, he asked, are you coming?

I don't think so, Milt.

A thousand-mile journey for a possible match did not appeal to me. And perhaps my interest in fighting had begun to fade.

How about you, Lisa? he asked one of his white-collar clients.

No, Milton.

Come on, Lisa, he said, grinning. Don't you want the chance to spend sixteen hours alone in a van with me?

What about the boxers? I said.

We'll make them sit in the back. We'll feed them sleeping pills.

After Milton left, Laura and I entered the ring. I asked Julian to work my corner as a counterpoise to her new trainer. The sparring went as well as I could have hoped: Where Laura had always been the elusive one, I felt faster, and the speed I felt was not speed per se (I was getting older, not faster) but the shifting of tasks from thought to reflex, experience in action. Laura had altered her technique slightly, shortening her hooks and attempting to force the action inside. I threw a long uppercut, and she countered with a straight left, a cinder block falling four stories onto my face. Laura still punched as hard as anyone I'd faced.

Within minutes after finishing our fourth and final round, I shivered at seeing Milton in the room. I greeted him and hoped he wouldn't notice how tousled I was. I didn't know what he might do if he found out I had sparred Laura.

Hey, I thought you went to Virginia?

No, we're leaving later, he said.

A few days later Laura told me that she'd felt uncomfortable sparring me, at the fact of Julian in my corner. I'd felt the same. We'd been sparring partners, teammates, part of each other's daily boxing life, and for reasons that had nothing to do with our relationship, we no longer were.

The end of Milton at Gleason's came in this manner. A woman pro, in Laura's weight class, had come to Gleason's. While recovering from her fractured wrist, Laura had watched the woman train and spar with the usual doubts and fears: "She's good. How good is she? Is she better than me?" The two women agreed to spar as soon as Laura was ready, and by late May Laura was feeling her way back. On the day they had chosen, Laura's wrist ached, but she didn't want to say no. The woman sensed her hesitation, however, and told Laura they could wait until she felt ready. "I know how these guys try to push us."

Then she asked, By the way, do you have some kind of problem with that Puerto Rican trainer?

What Puerto Rican trainer? Laura asked, snapping to attention.

That tall dark one.

Why?

Well, he's been talking shit about you, saying you were scared to spar me, stuff like that.

The two were speaking in the women's locker room. Laura thanked the other woman and went out in search of Milton.

What is your problem? she asked in a rage.

What do you mean?

I'm sick of you talking about me behind my back.

You're crazy. I didn't say anything about you.

Then why did that girl tell me you did?

In the ascending furies, Milton kicked Laura or shoved her with his foot (so Laura claims; Milton of course says nothing). Outraged, she punched him in the face. He punched her back, and the two were separated. Laura ended up in the office, bleeding from the nose. The police arrived and told Laura that they would not arrest Milton unless she left the scene in an ambulance. This Laura was unwilling to do. The police agreed to escort Milton from the premises, and they did, to Milton's vocal protests. The end result of this was the banning of Milton from Gleason's. Once again, the trainer of the Supreme Team was without a home.

That isn't normal, said Julian, who kept his eyes open. There had to be something between them. They had to have a relationship or something.

Had I been younger, I would have looked to the Metros and the Gloves the next winter. Fifteen years younger, and I would have been dreaming of Gloves titles and turning pro. Thank God I wasn't. I wanted to keep my brain intact (I talked to Laura about my worries, and she said, "Well, that's part of the fun, doing this and getting out before something happens to you." Which meant, "Nothing can happen to me"). One day at Gleason's I took a hard shot on the jaw sparring and felt an electric shock down my left arm. My hand went numb, and for the next week I had no feeling in a few of my fingers. That was interesting. Although it just seemed like a nerve problem, I wondered if my brain was becoming increasingly sensitive to trauma.

It was hard to leave boxing: If you trained, you wanted to spar, and if you sparred, you wanted to fight. The most difficult thing was finding a way to let go. I took a job outside the city for the summer and promised myself I wouldn't enter a boxing gym for several months.

One night shortly before the Laura debacle, I had taken the train back from Gleason's with Milton and Hanson. Milton claimed things were improving for him at Gleason's; he was drawing clients and finding an audience for his boxing philosophy.

It's getting better here, he told us. Every day a little better.

He looked over at the watch prominently displayed on Hanson's wrist.

Nice watch, Hanson, Milton said, Seiko or fake-o?

We left Hanson on the F and went to the L. On the platform, we passed a pair of buskers thumping and shouting. After we had moved around a stairway, Milton said, Damn, those Mexican musicians are everywhere.

Those guys weren't Mexican, I said.

You want to bet? Milton said.

I had looked over the musicians and recognized the song. There was nothing Mexican about any of it. Still, this was Milton, and that made me uneasy. I guessed that he hadn't looked and was just playing the odds.

Okay, I said.

Five dollars?

I accepted the conditions, and Milton walked back around the stairway. He returned a few minutes later with a big smile swimming on his face. Without a word he handed me a five-dollar bill. I thought I might frame it.

The contest lifted Milton's spirits. As we flashed across town on the L, he narrated a recent coup in his bar-cleaning business.

At this bar the guy who came in to clean had been robbing the register at night, Milton said. Now, he would unplug the surveillance camera when he did it, but he didn't know they had put in a second camera. So he ended up getting fired, and I ended up getting the account. They pay me a hundred fifty dollars to clean the place, and I pay this other guy seventy-five to do it, and he thinks I'm doing him a favor. You should consider going into the cleaning business, Bob. Money for nothing.

The train stopped at Third Avenue. A pretty Polish girl with blond ringlets boarded. Next to her was an empty seat beside a lump-headed, red-faced acidulous man. Before she could sit, Milton acted.

You should sit next to him, Milton said, pointing at the seat beside me. He's cuter.

The three of us began to laugh, and I felt no concern for Milton's future.

B O X I N G

At a birthday party for a friend, I began to speak to her father, an academic who writes about sports, among other things. I thought he might be able to offer some insight on my love, boxing.

Boxing, he said contemptuously, I'm not interested in boxing. It's not a sport. As far as I'm concerned, it should be outlawed. Baseball, that's a sport. I write about baseball because baseball means something; baseball offers us metaphors. A bat, a ball, those are metaphors; the diamond, that's a metaphor. Two guys beating the shit out of each other, what's that?

His response silenced me. I knew of course that people who disdained boxing existed, but I assumed they were merely ignorant, that all it would take to convert them was one of the great fights— Hagler/Hearns or Ali/Frazier I or Louis/Conn—events with the same relationship to two guys beating the shit out of each other that a baby shaking a rattle has to the Ellington band circa 1940.

Still, upon reflection, I realized that one could watch boxing a long time without seeing greatness. When I remembered that the great majority of televised fights are completely uncompetitive, with an "opponent" or "donkey" dragged out to receive a beating for a paycheck and that the important title fights are available only on pay-per-view; when I considered the scandals and deaths, the dull fights and the exploitation, it was difficult to imagine not that boxing didn't have a bigger audience but that anyone could ever come to love it. As with theater, that which makes boxing sublime is difficult to find, and as many people who have never seen great theater hate theater, so, perhaps, with boxing.

Boxing can mesmerize: The great fights transcend their outcomes and remain objects of devotion fifteen, thirty, sixty years later. My first viewing of Hagler/Hearns remains in memory as epiphany, although I knew when I watched the fight exactly how it would end. Yet in the building ferocity of the first round, the knockout to come mattered no more than the foreknowledge that Oedipus will be blinded or Hamlet killed. A great fight can be compared with tragic theater, not with the-ater as the "theatrical"—entertainment—but with theater as catharsis, the purging of pity and terror.* Merely decent fights are rebroadcast and circulated; great fights become timeless. How many baseball fanat-ics watch tape of a great World Series game of fifty years ago? And not one finds himself watching game 145 of the Cubs' season in 1963. After the immediate event, baseball games tend to disappear as anything but statistics, so that act of re-viewing, say, Roger Clemens's twenty-strikeout game is pointless; we know he struck out twenty. Baseball is important as you watch it in real time (if you have an interest in the team), while the outcome is unknown. Afterward the only thing that matters is the numbers (although postexpansion run inflation, creatine and hitters' parks have destroyed the statistical continuity of baseball).

In an era when sport dominates American (male) attention, boxing has almost disappeared from mainstream American life. Sport has dis-placed religion (Sunday is no longer the Lord's day but the team's day), yet boxing, telegenic and full of personality (in contrast with football, where a field of players are only identifiable by number), has seen its presence dwindle, as both spectator and participant sport, for almost fifty years. Excised from the national consciousness, boxing reappears like a ghoul only with the latest scandal or death. Tell someone I box, and the reaction is always the same. "Oh, you box?" the person says doubtfully, as if I've admitted a fondness for something disreputable but fascinating, like a sex act illegal in Georgia or biting heads off chickens. He may wonder what terrible things were done to me in my

---

*The theatrical dressing of boxing—the gaudy shorts, the pompous entrances—is irrele-vant to the essence of the fight. As the French critic Roland Barthes wrote, "Boxing is a Jansenist sport."

childhood to explain it. Yet my childhood was no worse than most, and if having demons made people boxers, almost everyone would be biting down on a mouthpiece and lacing up gloves.

The last golden age of boxing in this country, boxing as national pastime, ran from the 1920s, when it was legalized, through the 1950s (the sport's subsequent popularity, say, that of Ali and his opponents, or of the great middleweights of the mid-seventies to mid-eighties, was the popularity of something other, of Ali sui generis, or of African-American and Latin American fighters different from their audience in more than degree). Boxing in this "golden age" was something a majority of American men had done, in either their neighborhoods or the army. Boxing suited the ethic of a frontier society, where the bar brawl and street fight were common. Most public, private and parochial high schools had boxing instruction, as did the universities; even the Ivy League schools had boxing teams, and a crooked nose was a sign of distinction.

So what killed boxing? In one of his boxing essays (originally published in *The New Yorker* and collected in *The Sweet Science* and *A Neutral Corner*), A. J. Liebling cites television as the cause of death. "Boxers are in the same predicament as the hand-loom weavers of Britain when Dr. Edmund Cartwright introduced the power loom. Two boxers on a national hookup with fifty major-city outlets can fill the place of a hundred boxers on top ten years ago, and for every two eliminated from the top, at least ten lose their work underneath."

While I agree with Liebling as far as he goes, I think that the reasons extend beyond television and have much to do with the postwar affluence of the United States. White flight and the suburbanization of Middle America led to a media eclipse of blue-collar culture as job loss in manufacturing and heavy industry led to its actual decline (a decline that disproportionately punished blacks, stigmatized newcomers to the inner cities). If television destroyed the market for club fighters and city gyms lost their (white) clienteles, nothing rose to replace these developmental pillars.* The gyms didn't follow the whites to the subdivided

---

*One symptom of this decline is the real difficulty amateurs have in getting fights, the only way they can develop. At the moment the United States can barely field a decent Olympic team. In New York, the fact that the Gloves tournament extends over four months even further restricts fighting opportunities.

countryside (with exceptions, boxing has always been an urban sport), and because of its tainted reputation, boxing didn't receive the institutional support of other major sports (baseball, football, basketball, even Greco-Roman wrestling, which would no longer exist without university encouragement). At present the army, for obvious reasons, is the only major institution to encourage the sport. In Britain, by comparison, as recently as ten years ago boxing was taught at most schools (although, to judge from twentieth-century British boxers, not taught very well). The martial arts movement of the 1970s, with its broad middle-class appeal (and acceptance of women), probably did the last bit to extinguish boxing.

The absence of boxing from mainstream American life created a widening gap between fighters and their prospective audience (whereas most American men have some idea of just how difficult it is to hit a curve ball). This restriction of boxing to the ghetto has caused a mythologizing of fighters. In her excellent book of essays *On Boxing*, the writer Joyce Carol Oates is an articulate and sympathetic spokesperson for a boxing audience to which boxing exists "at the perimeters of civilization" as something alien and almost inconceivable. Hence Oates's deification of the young Mike Tyson, someone who perfectly embodies her myth of the boxer, and her distaste for Liebling, who boxed until he got too fat for the sport.

Growing up, I had no contact with boxing. In the fifties, my parents, in a fairly tough Irish, Italian, French-Canadian neighborhood, came into regular contact with it. My mother's brother boxed in the army, and although my father didn't, he regularly attended professional fights at a venue near his house. None of my peers boxed, and my first introduction to the sport came from *Rocky*, which had my eleven-year-old friends and me running home from the movie theater, singing the theme. I never saw a live fight or entered a gym until that day in the San Francisco Tenderloin when I was twenty-six.

The high from fighting is an ancient human pleasure: incentive in the struggle for mates and going out to kill the scary monster with a pointed stick (with its protein payoff). The first sports heroes were certainly hunters and warriors, the Michael Jordans and Muhammad Alis of their day.

People box, at least at first, because they enjoy it; they enjoy the rigors of training and the thrill of fighting. The large-scale entry of women into the sport and their discipline in mastering it disprove the notion that boxing merely is an atavistic male rite or a ticket out of the ghetto. Boxing can be an absolute experience, with extremes of intensity difficult to find in daily life. Boxing can swallow you up, subsume you into it. A college professor told me that when I found reading Hegel to be better than sex, I would know I was destined to be a philosopher. While this never quite happened with philosophy, boxing contains the most gratifying experiences of my life that aren't illegal or X-rated. Speaking to Laura and a friend, I mentioned that I often compared boxing with my vocation: writing, with its discipline, isolation, effort. The friend, a former dancer, said boxing reminded her of dance. Laura said she found that odd because she always compared boxing with the precisions of her trade, accounting. We each took what mattered most to us and attached it to boxing, enormous, generative, essential, capable of absorbing any analogy and remaining selfsame. It becomes life for those who enter it early enough and impossible to leave.

Boxers are insatiable people, and boxing is a sport of lack and hunger, literally and figuratively (Duran ate his way from lightweight to super middleweight; Ali said, "I am tired of training. I want to eat all the apple cobbler and drink all the sweet cream"). In the ring, given matched talent, it is the hungrier fighter who wins, the one prepared to suffer to the point of physical destruction (think of Joe Frazier in the first and third Ali fights, when he was nearly beaten to death). This might begin to explain why boxing draws most of its champions from the ranks of the poor, for when poverty doesn't break the spirit, it instills hunger. To professionals, boxing is a job, a job they can enjoy, and certainly better than most of the ill-paid, horrible jobs the poor do to stay alive—factory work, farm labor, etc.—with prospects for wealth and glory that no factory job offers. If more boxers could get paid, there would be more boxers.

The most populous and skilled divisions in boxing range from as light as bantamweight all the way through middleweight. There is a reason why Julian's middleweight division is, as he says, "loaded with talent," a reason that has nothing to do with five-nine black men of 160 pounds having a particular affinity for pugilism. The reason is that men of that weight and height are generally too small to thrive in baseball, football or basketball. Above middleweight, the talent drop-off in boxing is considerable. There are few quality light heavyweights, cruiser weights and even heavyweights (although a mediocre heavyweight has the potential to earn a great deal more money than all but a celebrity, say, featherweight) not because there are few talented athletes in this country over six feet tall and 200 pounds but because any talented athlete of those dimensions is likely to be pushed toward another sport.

If Julian were in a different sport that generated the revenue boxing does, his talent and national stature would have guaranteed him a lucrative contract. In boxing . . . Who would play basketball if being one of the top twenty amateurs in the country meant you still had to work a day job and had only a 1 percent chance of winning a base pro contract? While the top ten boxers are among the highest-paid athletes in the world, the income drop-off below them is precipitous, and the champions in lesser divisions are lucky to earn thirty-five thousand dollars a fight, a small sum when compared with the minimum in baseball and football, where a rookie might earn ten times that to sit on the bench.

Professional boxing is a sport of the desperate because it's nearly impossible to make money at it. Sure, there are big purses for the pay-per-view fights, but the boxing organizations are so corrupt, so riddled by cronyism and secret dealings, that even a great boxer has no guarantee of ever being in a position to fight for a title. A developing boxer needs to face the right challenges at the right times, take fights that will build his confidence, gradually lift himself through the ranks. Make a single mistake, take an opponent today whom you could beat easily in six months, lose a close decision, and your career could be over. Given that judges and referees have close ties to boxing organizations that are financially linked to powerful promoters, it is almost impossible for an outsider to fight his way up.* In 1999, for example, the heavyweight title unification bout between Lennox Lewis and Evander Holyfield was judged a draw, even though Lewis dominated nearly every minute of every round and was seen doing so by millions of people watching the fight (at fifty dollars a set on pay-per-view). The criminals who run the sport were brazen enough to believe they could rig the decision before

---

*Thomas Hauser's book *The Black Lights* gives a disturbing portrait of the machinations and luck it takes for a fighter to become a champion.

millions of viewers and get away with it. And despite the outcry, the headlines, the solemn declarations and the investigations, get away with it they did.

Since money isn't at stake in amateur fights, one might think bias would be less of an issue there. That is not the case. In the recent Olympic Games, judges were monitored by video with the hope that this would discourage them from cheating. They were also offered double the amount of any bribe offered them if the bribe was reported and verified. To judge from some of the decisions in Sydney, the policy didn't work.

Cleaning up professional boxing would be easy enough. The proposals on what it would take to do so—independent referees, a national ratings organization, union representation for fighters, mandatory medical testing, etc.—have been made hundreds of times, but the political will to do so is lacking, because the people who have power in boxing have no wish to change the system (and why would they, since it made them powerful?). The government chooses not to interfere in "the free operation of the marketplace," which is just another way it continues to allow the rich to exploit the poor and leave the young, strong, talented, *hungry* poor to risk their lives in desperate ventures—drug dealing, petty theft, boxing—to achieve something. The commentators on Showtime, HBO and ESPN (including Teddy Atlas) are uniform in their calls for reform, and the limited number of markets for fights are leading to a power shift toward the networks, which require a consistent product (thus meaning that boxing will rely on corporate television for moral balance). The disgust that results from a contemplation of "the way things are" in boxing, a sport of "perpetual crisis," makes it the only sport that one can love with intense devotion while calling for its prohibition (as the writer Gerald Early does).

My reports on the death of boxing are of course exaggerated. Over three centuries, boxing has survived outlawing on several continents, AMA crusades and its worst enemy, itself. A perfect world might have no place for boxing, but I'm not about to throw my gloves away. The recent entry of women and white-collar workers into the sport demonstrates its essential attraction and may help raise its profile enough to protect its most vulnerable component: those delicate weapons, the fighters.

A friend once asked me, "Aren't you afraid to get into the ring with some of these young thugs?" I answered, "But that's where I'd feel safest." No matter how much of a thug somebody is, in the ring he has nothing that I don't have. Within the ropes there is more possibility of purity and equality than anywhere else I know. Unlike life, where everybody is your competition and the odds never seem to be in your favor, in boxing you have to worry only about people in your weight class. And even the man hitting you in the face will have his arm around your shoulders after the bell.

POSTSCRIPT

Stop the fight! someone yelled, and the cry was picked up.

Stop the fight! Stop the fight! chanted an audience that wanted no such thing. Strange that I could hear it so acutely although I was struggling for my life. But you feel the crowd, its mood, its back and forth, and know if you have won it over or lost it. You fear its judgment; you want its support and strength.

Stop the fight! I heard distinct voices, just as I could hear Laura shouting punch combinations from the front row ("Two-four-five! Follow with a hook!"). I had become a giant, filling the room, everything that happened vivid and precise. My opponent and I clashed again, force against force, a dark collision.

The referee heard also and pushed between us. He pointed me to a corner and I went to gasp against the ring-post pads. For the first time I noticed the blood covering me: in places like dark raindrops, in other places gathered in thick blotches and smeared in a film across my skin. It wasn't my blood.

After I left New York for the summer, I tried to stay away from boxing. From Providence I heard that Milton had found a new home at a swank downtown health club that was trying to build a boxing reputation. Within two weeks, however, he was on the street again. This time it was Julian's fault. As Julian sparred a house fighter, the house's corner began to disparage Julian's style and skills. Feeling disrespected, Julian proceeded to give the fighter a painful lesson: "That doesn't feel like a slap now, does it? You're dealing with the champ." Milton was told that since he couldn't control his fighters, he had to take them away. Next stop was the South Bronx gym where we had attended a Metro prelim a year before.

Also that summer, an X ray of Giuseppe's perpetually injured thumb revealed a fracture. He had planned to enter the Empire State Games. Meanwhile, in a freak nonboxing accident, Laura tore a ligament in one of her fingers and couldn't fight for over a month. In August, I made my way to a Rhode Island gym. After a few days of training, I sparred a featherweight with seventy amateur fights. I felt like I'd been lowered into the piranha tank but I was able to make him miss, and to score on occasion. The sport still pulled at me.

Back in New York in September, I wanted to enter the Metros as my last amateur tournament. I made a few trips to the South Bronx gym. Victor trained there but had left Milton. I saw Victor and Julian war in the ring and it saddened me: teammates no more. Tired of the commute and Milton's unreliability, Stella had also left and was training at Gleason's.

Two weeks after registering, I dropped out of the Metros. I was working long days and the training stressed me terribly. It was hard to leave; I thought it marked the end of my amateur eligibility, but I couldn't justify the effort to myself. Then in late December, I received a phone message.

Is this Bob Anasi? Milton asked. I have some news. The stupid idiots changed the rules back to how it was. You can fight novice again in the Gloves this year.

I went out and picked up a copy of the *Daily News*. It was true. They had reversed the decision of the previous year, and now novices could again fight in two Gloves before turning open (another change meant I met the age deadline by two months). I sent in the entry form and told myself I would begin training by the second week of January. Even if my fight date was a few weeks earlier than the previous year, I would still have a solid month to prepare. Giuseppe, the Gloves scholar, assured me that '25 novices were never called before the middle of February. "My first year I fought on February 10," he said. "But it's been later every year since then."

I called Milton the first week of January, and when he didn't answer the message I called him again. Nothing. I walked into a gym on 14th

Street where he trained clients and found his heavyweight, Nelson, working the desk.

Milton's gone, yo, Nelson said. He's down in Florida with Shannon Briggs.

He's training Shannon Briggs? I said in amazement. Briggs was a heavyweight contender who had fought George Foreman and Lennox Lewis.

Yeah, Shannon's supposed to fight Tyson. Milton got a call to go in the middle of the night and the next morning he was at the airport. I don't think he's ever coming back.

A few days later, I received my card in the mail from the *Daily News*. I would be fighting on January 17, nine days away.

That never happened before, Giuseppe told me. There must be a lot of 'twenty-fives this year.

Actually, I was lucky. The first preliminary round for '25s was being held in two days. I had done the right thing by registering late and there was always the chance that I'd get a bye.

With no time and no trainer, I did what I could. I went to Gleason's and found some hard sparring with a pair of Russian kids who had followed their trainer to the United States just to box. Two boys, sixteen, one dark, one light. They were very fast and fought in an awkward European style that I had never met before.

I thought about quitting every single day as the Russians carved me apart. I did quit once or twice but changed my mind again within an hour or two. The tournament stretched before me, into the distant sun of April. My doubts gave me a new appreciation for the tenacity that had kept Laura training at my age for years, full-time job and all. I never wanted to quit when I sparred but as soon as I got home and saw another day swallowed by boxing, I felt a frenzied desire to escape. The day before the fight, I told myself that, win or lose, I would retire immediately afterward.

The prelim took place at a Catholic school in south Brooklyn, at the far end of the B line. I weighed in at 128 pounds even. An ounce more, and I would have been skipping rope in the hallway (or, depending on the draw, the officials might have pushed me up to '32). Thinking of the disappointments of the previous year, I wrote down Gleason's and not Supreme Team for my club affiliation.

The first five fights were announced without my name being called and I thought I might be free. Finally, however, I was matched. Number nine, the last fight that night. Nelson had agreed to work my corner, and as we sat together in a classroom (the fighters sprawled on tables or cramp-legged behind desks), he handed me his cell. It was Milton.

Anasi, do you know who you're fighting?

No, I've never seen him before. He's supposed to be from Gleason's. Some black kid.

Who's his trainer?

I didn't know that, either. I asked Milton how Florida was and told him I hoped he'd be there for my next fight.

My opponent was a tall, skinny black kid wearing a Police Athletic League boxing shirt over his Gloves jersey (which might have been an attempt at intimidation, for the PAL turned out good fighters). I felt a little jittery but not particularly tense. At the bell we walked out and started to throw. From the previous year, I had learned not to go back, and so I slipped toward him and kept punching, letting the referee separate us if we came too close. My opponent was orthodox and fought with a hands-down style reminiscent of my own. The first round was fairly even but in the second round I pressed the action; he was content to let me initiate and then try to counter.

The book on fighting southpaws says to throw plenty of right hand leads. There is some logic to this, but it doesn't take into account the fact that southpaws spend their entire careers evading right hand leads. The black kid became predictable; after I jabbed, he would immediately counter with a right. A few of these and I began sliding under them, then coming back with my left. The kid was actually fairly skilled, but he wasn't going to beat me boxing on the outside. My greatest fear—that as rusty as I was, a fast pace would tire me—proved groundless. I had all the time I needed to rest.

The third round provided a moment of humor. When the kid came out of his corner, he began to trash-talk. "I'm mad now, boy. I'm gonna fuck your shit up." Et cetera. The referee stepped in and gave him a warning. For the rest of the round, the kid mainly stood with his back to the ropes waiting on me.

As we waited for the decision, I had no idea what to expect. I thought I had done well, but the year before I had felt the same. When they called my color as winner, I bounced to one knee and up. I didn't know so much happiness could be stuffed into a moment. I had won a 5–0 decision.

The next day, I received a call from the *Daily News*.

Robert Anasi, the man said, we sent you a card, but because it's so soon we wanted to call. You have another fight next Wednesday in the Bronx.

Next week! I said.

That's incredible, Joe told me. There must *really* be a lot of 'twenty-five novices.

I considered quitting again.

A part of the reason for the influx of '25 novices had to do with the rule change. The year before, some trainers had held their fighters back from the Gloves, thinking that they would have to fight open the following year. Of course, those '25s who hadn't made it to the final (like me) found they could fight novice again. Perhaps there were just a lot of new '25s, also.

The next week, I made the weight easily but received a bye (I wondered if not representing the Supreme Team had something to do with it). Since I had the flu, I felt fortunate to have slipped through. At the officials' table, I found out I wouldn't be fighting until the quarterfinals in March, over a month away.

From the security of my bye, I watched Professor in his first fight receive a thrashing of terminal ferocity. His opponent, a young colossus, hit him at will, the concussive thuds reverberating through the hall. The Professor stood with his gloves pressed to the sides of his head and tried to counter (I doubt he landed five scoring punches). In the second round, a deep cut opened on the bridge of his nose and blood painted his face. We winced at the slaughter and wondered how he could endure, but endure he did. After the final bell I went downstairs and congratulated him on his courage.

After the bye, I no longer thought about quitting. The quarterfinals: two wins to the Garden, three for the title. Having a clear end to the tournament made it easier to bear, and I was growing accustomed to the training. To prepare, I did what I hadn't done the year before: get good sparring. Besides the Russians at Gleason's, I sparred Laura and Bus-driver and an old pro and a Dominican kid who'd almost been deported for beating his high school teacher with a chair. I went everywhere someone would give me work and ended up sparring in four of the five boroughs. To spar in an unfamiliar gym without a team or trainer behind you is frightening: everyone shouts for the other man, no one offers advice or tends to you between rounds. But it was good preparation for the fight to come.

Not having a trainer handicapped me in certain ways; flaws had crept into my form after the long layoff. A pro mentioned that I was jabbing with my elbow up, exposing my ribs. When sparring, I would sometimes forget to keep moving right against orthodox opponents. I was in a better position than many boxers would have been, however, since with Milton as a trainer, I had grown used to training myself. As I was bound for the quarterfinals, any number of trainers were willing to work with me but they wanted, of course, to change my style.

I progressed in those six weeks. The Russian boys were so fast that I couldn't raise my left fast enough to catch their rights, so I began to carry it above my chin. Watching Julian made me realize that my stance was too loose, so I drew my elbows closer to my body. I finally discovered how to throw good body punches and I learned the principle of following a cross with a strong hook (the back shoulder has to stay down and the weight can't come too heavily on the front foot). Given another hundred years, I might have learned how to snap a good jab.

On the day of my match, I felt confident. I knew I was a better fighter than I had been the year before. For the first time, my hands effected three- and four-punch combinations (you had to take a little off the punches to get a good rhythm). I was also catching up to the Russians; it was deeply gratifying to pound individuals who had tormented me for weeks.

That year, Julian lost in the first round again, to the eventual tournament winner, a Russian from the team I'd been sparring. The fact that Julian had been in Miami with Milton led me to suspect his conditioning. (Julian bounced back quickly. He placed second in the National Box-Offs and, as of this writing, is on his way to Sydney to represent the United States in the Goodwill Games.) At 165 pounds, Vic made it all the way to the semifinals, where he lost a 3–2 decision. He planned to turn pro following the Gloves. Since there were only eight '25 opens, Busdriver went straight to the quarterfinals, where, for the second year in a row, he drew the previous year's novice winner (and that year's eventual open winner). Minor surgery kept Stella out of the tournament.

My quarterfinal match was also set in far south Brooklyn, land of muscle cars and pizza parlors. Although six weeks had passed since our last fights, all seven other members of my class had arrived. I recognized most of them. After two months of tournament, we were a distinct group; I had watched them fight and trained beside a few of them. A boxing official led us into a small room and we selected lots to see how we would match. I drew one of the two fighters I didn't know. He was from a new gym in Brooklyn. We shook hands and went to change and then we were waiting at the doors to the hall, our fight just a few steps away. I studied my opponent covertly. He was Nicaraguan, tall for a featherweight but also muscular: I could see the etched tops of his pectorals at the low collar of his shirt. His book said he was eighteen, with two fights.

His gym is new, said Giuseppe, who had come out to support me. So that guy's got no experience.

I wasn't sure. He had a slick way of swinging his forearms around, both swift and efficient, like the rotation of pistons over an engine.

In the first five seconds of our fight I was nearly overwhelmed. He came straight at me with a hard, accurate one-two that crashed through my guard. I bounced off the ropes trying to cover up and he went downstairs, blasting my ribs and liver. My body said, "Are you kidding?" and tried to collapse. A strange feeling; I actually felt my frame sag and crumple. I had never before been hit that hard by a featherweight, and only a handful of times by larger fighters. The only thing that supported me in the drooping mush of my body was my will. I wanted to fall down but wouldn't let myself. After a few seconds, Nature's pain relievers kicked in and I began to consider how I might survive.

Tall and fast and strong: It hardly seemed fair. His speed and reach made it impossible for me to box on the outside and his power made me leery of trying to outslug him. If he was going to try to walk through me, though, I would at least be able to hit him. And I had some power too. With Laura shouting advice, I began to develop a strategy. He wanted to throw straight, long punches, and if I stayed close to him and bent his arms, he didn't throw as hard or as often. If I became worried, I grabbed him and he didn't try to fight out of my clinch. In the last thirty seconds of the round, I landed a good two to the body and he backed up for the first time. "Keep going to the body!" Laura shouted.

At the bell, I walked back to my corner and the medics went to work. "Deep breaths, Bob. Breathe. Let it out. Another," said Laura's newest trainer, Ray, who along with Nelson was my second. I understood the importance of the breathing. Oxygen primes muscle cells so they can reignite in the next storm.

That kid knows his way around the ring, Ray said.

He's only supposed to have two fights, I answered.

Bob, this is me, Ray Velez, talking. That kid knows his way around the ring! You can beat him, though.

My corner had seen the results from my body attack and encouraged me to continue. "Stay close to him and keep banging low," they said. "He don't like it in the body." It had been a difficult round for me: I lost on every card, one judge putting me down by three points (almost unthinkable without a standing eight or foul). Yet I had learned from that thrashing, from the intensity, learned more than I had in the past year, perhaps, pushed out to the edge of what I could bear.

I came out strong in the next round (for some reason, whether sparring or fighting, I usually have a good second round). I stayed close to him, inside and under his punches. When I tired, I would grab his left arm with my right and continue to belabor his body with my left. The referee broke us over this and gave me a warning. Laura's voice came clear through the ebb and surge of the crowd sound. "Three-four-five!" "More than one punch!" I tried to follow her advice but when she shouted out four and five punch combinations I wanted to say, "Aren't you being a little ambitious?" In a brief respite when we moved for a second out of punching range, I looked up at my opponent to see that his face had disappeared; blood had erased his face with a slick mask and blood continued to pulse from his nostrils.

Stop the fight!

From the neutral corner I watched the boy and the doctor, the doctor stepping onto the ring apron to manipulate the boy's nose, the boy leaning forward to meet him. I didn't consider the possibility that they would stop the fight, although it would mean a TKO. The break had taken me out of time to a gray plain where I waited, guzzling air. In the distance, I heard the doctor ask the boy if he wanted to continue. The boy nodded. Of course he did. Even if it was a fracture, it didn't hurt and wasn't an immediate danger. The swelling could affect his breathing and swallowed blood may nauseate a fighter, but those things generally became problems only over a long fight. We were only fighting three rounds.

As the referee moved to the center of the ring, I saw time approaching again, a rush of color and sound. The doctor pointed the boy to my corner to have his face cleaned. Blood continued to jet from his nose over his lips and chin. Nelson took a towel and swabbed his face.

Hey, that's my towel! I cracked, smiling. I was having so much fun.

ACKNOWLEDGMENTS

Heartfelt thanks to my parents; to Michael Lesy and to Nadia for helping me locate my center; to North Point Press, especially Brian Blanchfield, Jeff Seroy, Rebecca Saletan, Andrea Joyce, Don McConnell and above all Paul Elie, for taking a chance; to Lisa Dicker and Chris Byrne; to my people at the L: Wendy, Josh, Frank and Sarah; to the editors of the *Village Voice Literary Supplement*; to Milton and the Supreme Team; and, finally, to the fighters, with my admiration and respect.